THE BREWERS ASSOCIATION'S GUIDE TO

STARTING YOUR OWN BREWERY

Edited by Ray Daniels

A Division of the
Brewers Association
Boulder, Colorado

Brewers Publications
A Division of the Brewers Association
PO Box 1679, Boulder, Colorado 80306-1679
www.beertown.org

Printed in the United States of America.

10 9 8 7 6 5 4 3 2

ISBN-13: 9780937381892
ISBN-10: 0-937-381-89-6

Library of Congress Cataloging-in-Publication Data

The Brewers Association's guide to starting your own brewery
/ edited by Ray Daniels.
p. cm.
Includes bibliographical references and index.
ISBN 0-937381-89-6
1. Beer industry--United States. 2. Breweries--United
States. I. Daniels, Ray, 1958- II. Brewers Association. III.
Title: Guide to starting your own brewery.
HD9397.U52B74 2006
663'.420681--dc22
2006036328

Publisher: Ray Daniels
Production & Design Management: Stephanie Johnson
Cover and Interior Design: Julie Lawrason
Cover photo: Michael Lichter/Michael Lichter Photography, LLC
Special thanks to BJ's Restaurant & Brewery in Boulder, CO and Donna Baldwin Talent
Photos in Chapter 18 provided by Kevin Finn

Table of Contents

SECTION 3: Marketing and Distribution Programs

SECTION 4: Planning and Funding Your Brewery

Craft Brewing and Your Brewery Start Up

Welcome to Craft Brewing!

By Ray Daniels

FOR MORE THAN 25 YEARS NOW, A REN-aissance in brewing has bloomed in the United States, bringing a wealth of new flavors to beer drinkers. The continuing success of this industry can be seen in a number of indicators, such as the following:

- More than 1500 craft breweries operate in the US and sales of craft beer increase every year just as they have for more than two decades now.
- Today beer lovers from all over the world see the American beer scene as the most vibrant and interesting in the world.
- Innovation continues with new beers being offered and new breweries being opened every year.

Within craft brewing, there continue to be opportunities for new businesses making and selling beer. This book introduces prospective craft brewers to the fundamentals of craft brewing as a business, starting with the dream and ending with daily operations. No matter where you are along that path, this book offers advice and resources you will find useful in creating a successful craft beer business.

In this introduction, you'll find information on the structure of the industry and a description of some of the business opportunities available today. At the end of this section, we'll review the contents of this book, briefly describing the four major sections and their contents.

CRAFT BREWERS

In the early years of craft brewing, nearly all of the operations were small and members of the industry were known simply as "microbreweries." Those operating a restaurant on the same premises as their brewery took on the name of brewpub. When success lifted some of the new brewers above the 15,000 barrel ceiling chosen to define "micro" new names were bandied about. Eventually the industry settled on the term "craft beer" to identify what they made and "craft brewer" as an all-encompassing term for industry participants.

These days "craft brewers" are generally still considered to be relatively small with the limit set at less than 2 million barrels per year of sales—the point at which the Federal government prohibits brewers from taking the "small brewers exemption" on beer excise taxes.

But while size alone says a lot, it doesn't capture all the traits of a craft brewer. Most would agree that a craft brewer uses traditional production techniques like all-malt formulations that result in robust and flavorful beers. Brewers that cut corners in the interests of economy and at the expense of flavor can count on criticism from fellow brewers and consumers alike.

One observer of the industry has commented that the best craft breweries are those where a homebrewer is in charge of deciding what the beer tastes like. While hardly true in most cases, the phrase captures the essential feel of craft brewing. At its core, craft brewers focus on quality and character while rarely acknowledging the economic realities they manage in order to survive and thrive. And with that comes another common trait of craft brewers: independence.

Most craft breweries were started by individuals with a dream and to this day most are still owned and operated by those dreamers. When they make decisions about the beers they make and how they market them, they don't answer to a demanding regional director or some pencil pusher in a far-off cubicle. Craft brewers aren't the type to consult a three-ring binder full of company policies in order to resolve the decisions they must make. Instead, they think about the beer and the people who will drink it—the people who have grown to love the brewery and its lagers or ales.

INDUSTRY STRUCTURE

Given that general background, let's look at the structure of the industry today. As in the early days, we still divide craft brewing into two segments: brewpubs and packaging breweries. Brewpubs operate both a brewery and a restaurant together on the same site, offering on-premises food service and fresh beer to the consumer. Packaging brewers produce beer mostly for sale through retail outlets that the brewery does not own: bars and restaurants, liquor stores, grocery stores and other outlets. The "packages" offered by these brewers include kegs for draft sales as well as bottled (and sometimes canned) beer in a variety of sizes and collections.

Among the packaging brewers, we still denote those who produce less than 15,000 barrels per year as "microbrewers." Larger packaging brewers are called regional craft brewers.

As of January 2008, the US craft beer industry consisted of the following:

990 Brewpubs
446 Microbreweries
65 Regional Craft Breweries

In addition to these traditional craft brewers, a couple of other notable businesses also participate in the craft beer industry. One produces beer, another sells it in a particular local market. The first is known as a contract brewer. Contract brewers create and manage a beer brand but arrange for production of most or all of their beer at a brewery owned by someone else. Contract brewers face huge challenges in the craft industry due to its strong emphasis on quality beer and a "small, local and authentic" identity. Nonetheless, several very successful participants in the craft segment have followed the contract brewing route.

Another emerging sector of the craft beer business is the specialty beer distributor. As you will read in later chapters of this book, brewers depend on distributors to warehouse and deliver their beer in every local market. Because craft beer differs from popular brands in so many ways, some distributors have begun to specialize in handling these unique beers. New distribution companies are also being formed to carry craft beers and in some markets this may represent an opportunity for the entrepreneur interested in craft beer.

THE BREWERS ASSOCIATION

This book comes to you from the national trade organization for craft brewers. The Brewers Association draws upon the heritage of two organizations that merged on January 1, 2005 to present a united voice for small brewers in the US. The two organizations that came together include the Brewers Association of America founded in 1942 and the Association of Brewers founded in 1978 by Charlie Papazian in Boulder, Colorado. Together they have a long history of helping small brewers start and thrive in the US brewing business.

The purpose of today's Brewers Association is to promote and protect American craft beer and American craft brewers and the community of brewing enthusiasts. In order to accomplish this, the organization offers a wide range of educational and informational services for brewers ranging from a daily email forum where members can ask questions and exchange information to an annual conference filled with educational seminars and a trade show where you can meet with suppliers, distributors and fellow brewers. In addition, we publish a magazine for professional brewers (*The New Brewer*) and a range of books about brewing and beer styles. To find out more about the Brewers Association and memberships for breweries-in-planning contact our offices at 888-822-6273 or see our website at www.beertown.org.

ABOUT THIS BOOK

The Brewers Association Guide to Starting Your Own Brewery builds on a previous and related title called *Brewery Planner*. First published in 1991 by the Association of Brewers, it served the needs of thousands of entrepreneurs who worked on starting breweries in the early to mid-1990s. Since that time, the environment greeting start-up breweries has changed considerably as suppliers, local governments, distributors, retailers and consumers all have far more experience and knowledge with craft beer.

As a result, this new book bears only a passing resemblance to the old *Brewery Planner* in both design and content. Gone is the chapter on building a brewery from old dairy equipment and another focused on introducing consumers to the concept of craft beer for the first time. Relevant articles were reviewed and re-written to reflect today's marketing conditions and practices. New chapters were added from those who have entered the business recently to help you understand what today's start-up breweries face. And new data has been incorporated to help you understand the operational parameters experienced by breweries in the 21st century. The resulting book provides a thorough introduction to the craft brewing business, giving the aspiring entrepreneur the framework needed to pursue their dream of starting their own brewery.

The four sections of this book cover different aspects of exploration and preparation for entering the industry. In the first section titled "Brewers Speak: Tales and Tips From Those Who Have Traveled the Road of the Brewery Start Up" we hear from successful entrepreneurs from both brewpubs and packaging breweries. They relate their stories with an emphasis on lessons they have learned so that you can avoid the same mistakes. At the same time, they help you to understand the challenges and rewards of craft brewing so that you can both dream and consider the realities of pursuing your dream.

The second section of this book entitled "Facility Planning & Operations" deals with the brewing process and the facilities needed to start a brewpub or packaging brewery. As you will soon learn, the art of brewing takes many years to master so we don't try to turn you into a brewer with a few chapters. Instead, we present the information needed to plan a brewing business and begin the process of hiring a competent brewmaster.

The third section focuses on marketing and distribution issues. At one time, craft breweries were so novel that just opening the doors brought interested buyers to your business. But things have changed. These days consumers see scores of craft brands in any given month so you'll need to focus considerable effort on getting their attention and setting your beers apart from those they already know and love. The section titled "Marketing and Distribution Programs" presents the basic tools used in marketing craft beer with tips for how to get the maximum bang for your buck.

In final section called "Planning and Funding Your Brewery," the rubber meets the road. By the time you reach this part of the book you have dreamed, learned and considered some of the practical ramifications of starting your own brewery. Now it is time to draw up a game plan and start to think about how you go about turning your dream into a reality. In this section we cover many aspects of financial planning for your brewery business from insurance and site selection to capital structures and fund raising. At the end of this section we offer two very valuable resources: a sample business plan and operational surveys from current brewers. The business plan can serve as a model for what you'll need to prepare before you can incorporate and actually start raising money. And the operational chapters provide essential insights into the revenues and expenses of current brewers so that you'll have a way to reality check your own research and calculations.

FINDING YOUR OWN COURSE

We believe that *The Brewers Association Guide to Starting Your Own Brewery* offers the perfect starting point for anyone thinking about entering the craft beer business. It contains a wealth of knowledge and experience from successful brewers with an orientation to all of the essential considerations for start-up brewers. Of course it is just a starting point. As you read the first section of the book, you'll hear successful entrepreneurs say time and again that you can never have enough information, never do enough research. This will be true for you just as it was for them. Each new brewery is different and thus will face unique challenges along the road to well-deserved success. With luck, the information contained here will whet your appetite and we'll soon see you at the Craft Brewers Conference, the Great American Beer Festival or asking questions on the daily Brewers Association Forum as you dig deep into the many resources available for brewery entrepreneurs. We look forward to having you as a part of the industry and wish you good luck on your journey into craft brewing.

Cheers,
Ray Daniels
Editor

Section I

The Life of a Brewer

THE CRAFT BREWING INDUSTRY OFFERS every aspiring entrepreneur something that few other industries can: a broad base of successful startups headed by people willing to share their experience. In this first section, you'll hear what leaders of both brewpubs and packaging breweries have to say about their own challenges in starting a business.

In this section, we hear directly from brewers who have succeeded in turning their dreams into successful businesses. From Greg Koch of California's Stone Brewing Co. to Chuck Skypeck of Memphis' Bosocos and and Sam Calagione of Deleware's Dogfish Head Craft Brewery, each tell the story of how they became involved with the beer industry and relate some of the lessons that they have learned over the years.

More brewer experience comes to us from Victory Brewery in Pennsylvania and the McMenamin's group of brewpubs based in Portland, Oregon in the middle of this section. Finally we finish with focused tips from industry veterans as John Hickenlooper of Wynkoop in Denver, Marcy Larson of Alaskan Brewing in Juneau and Scott Smith of CooperSmith's in Fort Collins, CO each pass along their top priorities for success.

At the conclusion of this section you'll have a good idea of both the joys and the challenges of starting a brewery. Armed with both visions of success and words of caution, you'll be ready for the next section where we begin to look at the practical details of building and operating a brewery.

Chapter One

Better a Beer Geek Than a Rock Star

Stone Brewing Thrives On Southern California Roots

By Jim Parker

The New Brewer *magazine, published by the Brewers Association, caught up with the fast moving leader of Stone Brewing to talk about the founding and growth of this successful Southern California craft brewery.*

GREG KOCH AND STEVE WAGNER FIRST crossed paths in the Southern California music industry, where both were working in 1989. But it was a chance meeting at a University of California-Davis brewing class in 1992 that led them to open Stone Brewing in San Marcos, Calif. in 1996. The duo found each other's skill sets and personalities to be a perfect combination. Wagner is the quieter of the two, the business mind and a former home-brewer. Koch is more outgoing, a self-admitted "beer geek" and a born promoter who at one time dreamed of being a rock star.

The brewery burst onto the national scene a year-and-a-half later with the introduction of Arrogant Bastard Ale. The aggressively hopped amber ale bore a label that told drinkers, "This is an aggressive beer. You probably won't like it." It went on to practically insult potential customers by saying, "It is quite doubtful you have the taste or sophistication to be able to appreciate an ale of this quality and depth."

Beer lovers weren't put off by the haughty label and fell in love with the bold beer inside, shooting Stone's sales from a mere 2,200 barrels its first full year of production to nearly 32,000 barrels by 2004. To accommodate that growth, Stone built a completely new production facility and retail facility that opened in 2006. Here, Koch talks about arrogance, serendipity and staying true to one's self in the pursuit of being amazing.

The New Brewer: As you look ahead to your 10th year, how does the reality compare to what you had forecast in your business plan?

Greg Koch: We only had a business plan because we were forced into it. And since the day it was written, I don't think I have read it. I do remember I was always bullish about our potential. Go figure.

As with any entrepreneur you have to have a level of unrealistic confidence. That is a requirement. Because if you rely on the facts, there are always a ton to suggest the myriad reasons you can't be or shouldn't be or won't be successful.

TNB: From the beginning, you have tried to "push the envelope" in terms of beers and marketing. Was that because you saw a niche there, or is that just who you are?

GK: The second one all the way, the first one not at all. In fact, I was certain that we would only be successful by being ourselves. I often give the analogy of the music industry, which Steve and I were in different facets of before we started Stone. If you think of the best bands out there, the ones that are truly great and have longevity to their careers, they are bands that not only were talented, but also were true to themselves. So if you have a band that's true to itself but they suck, well...fair enough and good for them. At least they can have some fun. If you have a band that's very talented but is just trying to produce the flavor of the month, the sound of the month, well that's not going to have any longevity, although they might have a little flash in the pan success.

I can relate to what we do. We had to be ourselves, to have our own personality. I have sometimes been complimented by people who have the misconception that Arrogant Bastard was a brilliant little piece of marketing. It is not. It is what I felt. It is what I wrote. I was being straightforward and honest, granted having fun along the way. I will freely admit that, but it wasn't calculated. The only thing at Stone that was ever calculated has been the finances, the cash flow, the business side that you have to calculate. Steve has been the master of that.

TNB: You entered the scene with a beer with a fun name "Arrogant Bastard" at a time when the market was being flooded with cutesy names like "Bad Frog." Did you ever worry that might backfire: the people who buy beers for the label would, in your words, not be worthy of the big beer inside and those who would appreciate the beer might not take the name seriously and never try it?

GK: You apparently put a lot more thought into it than I did. When we first released Arrogant Bastard Ale, which was nearly a year-and-a-half into it for our brewery, we thought we might sell a few hundred cases. So if you think you're going to sell a few hundred cases, you aren't so concerned with what you are going to put on the label. We thought that the beer itself was going to be so far beyond the palates of everybody except us and a few of our beer geek homebrewing friends. They were liking the big side of Stone Brewing, which was just starting to emerge at that point.

TNB: What was your first product?

GK: We don't make products.[1] Our first beer was Stone Pale Ale. Stone Smoked Porter was originally introduced as Winter Stone. We quickly realized that we really weren't interested in jumping on the seasonal bandwagon. That was our one and only seasonal beer. And it ended up not being seasonal and we took it away for about a month or so and brought it back permanently.

TNB: You have built your reputation in a large part on big, bold beers, but from what you've said, that wasn't part of a big "master plan," but rather in reaction to customer response. Once you got that positive reaction, did you then decide to keep pushing the envelope until beer drinkers cried "uncle"?

GK: No, again, we don't push it. In my view we have brewed beers that are consistent with our own tastes. We figured if we are going to make a great beer—and it truly is a great beer, it's not just our opinion and everyone else thinks it sucks—then we're going to be just fine. It may take a little longer sometimes for people to catch on.

TNB: And people have caught on. Have you been surprised or gratified by the number of people who have caught on?

GK: I am extremely gratified. But I am also gratified by the increasing number of terrific beers out there from an increasing number of terrific breweries. I like living in this world.

TNB: Your little corner of the world has built quite the brewing scene in the San Diego area.

GK: Yeah, it has been some good teamwork. It hasn't been conscious teamwork of "Let's get together and do this." But it has been appreciation and inspiration that we've passed around to each other. And as it often is with anything, if you have someone else being great, it inspires you to increase what you do. We have certainly been inspired not only by other brewers here in San Diego County but well beyond.

TNB: That inspiration and your growth caused you to build a new brewery. What can you tell us about the new brewery as far as how it compares to your original home?

GK: We started off with 7,100 square feet. Fortunately we were in a multi-tenant building that enabled us to take over adjacent suites as they became available over the years. So we grew in that facility to 26,500 square feet. The new building—including brewery and offices and such—is 50,000 square feet. So that portion of it is basically double the size of the facility. And then there is the 8,500-square foot restaurant attached. It's actually part of

[1] While speaking at the 2004 Craft Brewers Conference in San Diego, Koch told the audience, "You never hear a musician say, 'I think you'll like my newest product.' Likewise, craft brewers don't make products, you make pale ales, lagers, IPAs and stouts." Avoiding the "P" word became the catchphrase of the conference.

the same building. At the same time we moved from a 30-barrel brewery to a 120-barrel system.

TNB: Was there any trepidation in making that large of a jump?

GK: Zero. I don't care how much we grow. I need to repeat that: I don't care how much we grow. We do not have any numbers for growth. Our philosophy is we're going to continue to make what we think are great beers and it will find its own level. And if we do it ethically and with solid business practices, when it does find that level it will be a healthy spot for us. We won't worry about chasing after volume by discounting or by trying to create a more "drinkable" beer, really suggesting low character.

TNB: How did you make the decision to get into the restaurant business?

GK: I think that was the result of the same head injury that caused me to get into the brewing industry in the first place. I never got around to getting it fixed.

TNB: What can you tell us about the restaurant?

GK: It is called the Stone Brewing World Bistro and Gardens. The goal for the restaurant is the same as the goal for Stone. You know we've never had a mission statement. We've never been able to come up with one. Mission statements are for companies who don't know what they're doing. Because if you really know what you are doing and everyone is on board, what the hell is a mission statement for? But I did hear a year or so ago about Google's, which is "Do no evil." I thought that was kind of interesting. So I wondered aloud whether "Be amazing" could be our mission statement.

The goal for the restaurant is to be amazing and to not compromise on any level. And we are going to take that to even the soft drinks we serve. There will be no soft drinks served that are made from high fructose corn syrup. Why, because I am against high fructose corn syrup? Absolutely not. Do I believe for one second that the very best sodas on this planet are made with high fructose corn syrup? No, I do not think they are. Therefore, if I am going to be amazing with my soda selection, it will only be ones with candy sugar, cane sugar, whatever, and not stuff that comes in 55-gallon drums.

We try to take [that attitude] to everything we do in the restaurant, including the wine list—I'm sure you and I have been to many terrific breweries with a wine list that is an afterthought at best. We may not have as long a wine list as Chez FooFoo, but it is going to be a selection of wines that are truly amazing in each of their own rights. Our goal is to be as much organic as we possibly can be. I'm not making any promises on that because it is quite a challenge even in this day and age to be 100-percent organic. Also to celebrate world flavors, whether it is chipotle or Thai- or Indian-style curries or Argentinean chimichurri sauce.

TNB: And I assume it will be big food to match the beers.

GK: Yes, it probably will be, but I am going to make the very best Indian curry that we can and how it matches with the beer is how it matches with the beer. If it's an amazing Indian curry and it doesn't match with the beer, then tough, it's not going to match with the beer. And if people complain that the curry is too spicy or it's too authentic tasting, then we should let that person know that that isn't the dish they should order next time.

TNB: The restaurant is not your first step outside of the box of just brewing. You also have your own distributorship. How did that come about?

GK: That was a case of necessity being the mother of invention. We had no other choices when we started, so it was a natural progression. Also I have been, am and will continue to be a firm believer in the philosophy that the more that people are exposed to great beer, the more people will drink great beer, no matter where it comes from. If you make great beer, then I think people deserve to have it. And that is why it is completely consistent with our philosophy to represent other great beers here in Southern California via Stone Distributing.

TNB: How important is it for you to maintain a high public profile as the face of the company?

GK: I think it's very important to keep the personality of Stone Brewing out there. I don't want Stone Brewing to be Greg Koch or vice versa, although I think vice versa is the reality. I am Stone Brewing to some degree, but Stone Brewing is much more than me, by leaps and bounds. I'm just a part of it and I have a blast in my role. As I sometimes joke, the role between Steve and me is he is the guy who does it and I am the guy who talks about it.

TNB: Is it important for a brewery to have a high profile?

GK: I think it is important for a brewery to be themselves. Because when you try to be something you are not, that's when you're probably going to have the least chance of success. I think you are going to find the personality of the brewery will emerge, absolutely, especially a smaller entrepreneurial company. So, should a reserved, quieter company try to become loud because it has worked for Stone Brewing? No, I don't think so. If you do a great job of what you do it will eventually work. It's like the old phrase, "You should never try to teach a pig to sing." You should be true to yourself.

TNB: Stone Brewing is involved with many charities. Is your corporate giving part of that attempt to be true to yourself?

GK: It's consistent with our personal and business philosophy. Not all of the money, I've got to be honest, has come from us. We've simply been the conduit. For example our annual Stone Brewing anniversary open house and beer festival is able to raise a great deal of money for local charities. However, it's not like we've decided to dig into our pockets and pull out more than $50,000. We have come to the realization that we can be a conduit. I like charity fundraising when it is both fun and sustainable. Because if it is fun, the public will want to participate and so will the charity. And if it is sustainable, then you can do it today, you can do it next week and you can do it next month. So we say yes to almost every single charity request we can. If it is a real charity and a real event, then we are happy to donate and typically it is via beer and not money. Beer is sustainable. We can make some beer and we can donate it to them and help increase the quality and fundraising capability of their event. And if someone asks us tomorrow, we can do it for them too. And if someone asks the day after tomorrow we can say yes. Each time it's bite-sized and each time it doesn't take the wind out of our sails and each time it helps us to support our community.

TNB: What did you do in the music business before you got into the beer business?

GK: I was involved in some management and a little bit of production. At one point I wanted to be a rock star. But remember what I was saying earlier about being true to yourself and being talented? I realized that forcing my lack of talent, or trying to force my lack of talent, onto the world was not actually being true to myself.

TNB: But now, through Stone, you have become somewhat of a rock star of the brewing industry.

GK: Um. I hesitate to use that word, but I appreciate it. That's very flattering. Thank you.

TNB: I've seen the way "beer geeks" will recognize you on the floor at the Great American Beer Festival and crowd around you.

GK: Unless [Dogfish Head Brewing's] Sam Calagione is standing next to me [laughs]. Then it's, "Sir, if you're done getting your autograph from Sam, can you excuse me so I can get in line?" ◗

Chapter Two

From Beer Dreamer to Brewpub Operator

Mid-South Entrepreneur Succeeds in Starting Brewpubs

By Chuck Skypeck

MY FATHER ENJOYED BEER. HE WOULD allow my brother and I occasional sips before we were eighteen. There was no mystery about those shiny aluminum cans in the refrigerator. They were just a normal part of our everyday life. After turning eighteen (I came of age in an era when the age requirement to enjoy an alcoholic beverage was more reasonable) I tried wine and spirits but I have always returned to beer as my refreshment of choice.

Perhaps it was not surprising that I was attracted to an opportunity in the beer business. I was living in Memphis, Tennessee in 1985. I had a successful but unfulfilling career in business management. I am not sure how, but I became aware of artisan, or craft breweries, that were springing up on the east and west coasts. I was intrigued. Somehow a few bottles of this craft beer made its way into my possession. The beer probably wasn't of the highest quality, brewed by a nascent craft brewery and subjected to the rigors of a long journey before arriving in my glass. No matter. Tasting this very different beer was an epiphany. I made up my mind. Nothing would stop me. I would open a craft brewery in Tennessee.

In retrospect, I have always wondered about the wisdom of making a life-changing decision while under the influence of flavorful craft-brewed beer. But seven years later in 1992, I was part of a partnership that opened Boscos Pizza Kitchen & Brewery, Tennessee's Original Brewpub, in Germantown, Tennessee.

What transpired in those seven years between the dream and that dream becoming reality? Well, I had a lot to learn. Learning to make beer was a big part of that process. I took up homebrewing. Not only did this teach me the basics of brewing beer, but also it gave me something tangible to offer people that I spoke to about my idea of a craft brewery. "Never heard of craft beer? Try this." I started a business selling homebrewing supplies. Besides supplying income, this business helped develop contacts within the supply side of the industry, contacts that I still value today.

I visited other breweries to see how they operated. This experience was invaluable. Without exception, other start ups gladly shared their experience and expertise. I also looked at numbers. So little craft beer was sold in Tennessee at that time that it was apparent to me that the volume needed to sustain a packaging brewery was unattainable. I decided I would open a brewpub.

But what did I know about operating a restaurant? Quite simply, nothing. I was certain that the long-term success of a brewpub in my market would be determined by the successful operation of the restaurant side of the business. I needed partners who understood the restaurant business. And there were a few legal issues. At this time, brewpubs were still illegal in Tennessee.

> But what did I know about operating a restaurant? Quite simply, nothing. I was certain that the long-term success of a brewpub in my market would be determined by the successful operation of the restaurant side of the business.

So you might think this is the point in the story where I find competent restaurant partners and the rest is history. It's never that easy. All the restaurateurs I talked to either weren't interested or thought little of my idea of brewing beer on the premises. Eventually a commercial real estate broker I had been talking to about my idea of an on-premise brewery told me he wanted to introduce me to a gentleman who wanted to open a restaurant centered around a wood-fired oven. The broker thought our two ideas were compatible. This gentleman was a stockbroker who had never run a restaurant. He knew as much about the restaurant business as I knew about the brewing business that, in spite of all the research we had done, was not a lot. But we liked each other's ideas and we liked each other's attitudes. We started a partnership based on trust and a willingness to work hard to get the job done.

We managed to pool our resources and raise enough money (a whole different story) to start the business. With the help of both likely and unlikely allies, we resolved our legal issues. (Also another whole different story.) The Tennessee legislation passed a bill to legalize brewpubs. The governor, who owned a Budweiser distributorship, signed the legislation soon there after. On July 1, 1992, it became legal to operate a brewpub in Tennessee. We were ready to begin work in earnest. We opened Boscos, the first brewpub in Tennessee, on December 26, 1992.

All it took was persistence, determination, stubbornness, diligence, faith, trust and luck. You could add hard work but that part was only getting started.

The restaurant business is extremely detail oriented. For that matter, so is the brewing business. As I mentioned, the sum total of my new partner's and my experience in our new business was close to zero. Never mind execution of all those details, we had to identify which details in this new venture were important and which were not.

In retrospect, several decisions we made early on were instrumental in our long-term success. We identified the product that we wanted to bring to our market. Exactly what that product was, and is still, is somewhat less important than the fact that once we made our decision on what Boscos was and what Boscos meant, we focused on making that vision a day-to-day reality. That vision was a commitment to run a slightly upscale casual restaurant with impeccable service with an inviting and exciting atmosphere, a restaurant that, as a very unique feature at the time, happened to brew their own beer. We focused on execution of this concept. We didn't try to be all things to all people. We didn't waver from focusing on our concept, even when the times were tough and it seemed like it would be a good idea to try something different.

> Attracting an existing customer back to your business is much less expensive than spending advertising dollars meant to attract a new one.

We also made a strong commitment to offering a quality product and to finding ways to differentiate our products. Both the restaurant and the brewery business are extremely competitive. We doggedly pursued ways to stand out, to stand apart from our competition. The desired outcome of this pursuit is brand loyalty. My favorite type of customer is a return customer. Attracting an existing customer back to your business is much less expensive than spending advertising dollars meant to attract a new one. Entertaining return customers means that you are doing your job right, something is working. Increasing frequency of existing customers works the same way.

At the start, we hired experienced restaurant managers to help with the execution of the nuts and bolts. This was necessary to help us, the owners, decrease the length of our learning curve. Ultimately it was apparent that we could have called these hired professionals mercenaries. They did a great job but having your heart in the business makes a big difference. Eventually we let them go after we learned to manage our own business.

As we grew, so did the need to hire managers again. Almost without fail, our best managers are developed from hiring within our company. Not only do we know them well and trust them, but also they have learned what is important to us, loyalty to the company and sweating the details.

As our business has grown and the demands of doing business have changed, so have the roles my partner and I have played. A third partner, who was silent in the beginning, became active in the business. A fourth partner was added when we allowed an individual to buy into the business. We now have four sets of hearts and minds. All of our jobs are easier for it.

> The elements that lead to success, attention to detail, dedication to achieving goals, good communication, are common among all well run operations.

One partner essentially runs our office. With three restaurants' payrolls, an office payroll, accounts payable, innumerable tax forms and returns, insurance issues, license renewals, etc., his job is extremely detail oriented. He loves it. And I am glad because I could never sit still for that long. Another partner is our operations manager. He handles day-to-day operations in our restaurants and the direct supervision of our managers. Another detailed and tedious job as far as I am concerned. I am responsible for brewing operations and all of Boscos advertising and marketing. Although I sometimes find wearing two distinctly different hats a challenge, the job is never boring. My original partner is president of our company, a role he is very well suited for. His visions and ideas for the company keep us moving forward, always ahead of the curve.

All four partners excel in their roles. We have different skills and we have managed to turn our differences into our company's strength. We meet every Monday morning for a few hours, to catch each other up on projects and issues. While we sometimes disagree on ideas or solutions to problems, there is never any doubt about our agreement on the desired outcome: making our vision of Boscos a reality. That doesn't change from day to day.

In the most basic ways, the restaurant/brewery business is like every other business. The elements that lead to success, attention to detail, dedication to achieving goals, good communication, are common among all well run operations. The satisfaction of owning a successful business that incorporates one of my life's great passions, brewing beer, has been an incomparable experience. I have never been adequately able to describe the feeling I had the first day we opened for business. Looking down the packed bar to see it full of customers that were not only enjoying our food and atmosphere but also the beer I had brewed from the brewery business I created was a moment I will always remember. ◗

Chapter Three

Dogged Pursuit of a Dream

Armed with a bit of bartending experience and very little cash Sam Calagione launched one of America's most talked-about breweries.

By Sam Calagione

I GRADUATED FROM COLLEGE IN 1992 with a love of beer that revolved more around a desire for quantity than a desire for quality. I moved to Manhattan to take courses in writing at Columbia. To pay my bills I began working as a bartender and waiter at a place called Nacho Mama's Burritos. While the name doesn't exactly invoke an image of leafy beer gardens, frothy steins, and ompah-music, through the restaurant owner's passion for beer it became one of the first bars in the city to seek out the small, domestic brews that were popping up around the country. I vividly remember my first pints of Sierra Nevada Celebration, Chimay Red, and Pike's Place Pale Ale. I also learned that I had a pretty good palette and was growing as an efficient guide for customers interested in expanding their understanding and appreciation for all these new beers with funny names that were on our menu. I learned to predict our regulars' stylistic preferences and could make recommendations they came to trust.

The restaurant's owner and I took our love of beer to the next step and began homebrewing in our apartments within a year of opening the Burrito joint. There was one shop in the city at that time that sold ingredients and brewing books. We would make weekly pilgrimages to that store where I would buy ingredients for my next batch and every piece of literature about beer that I could get my hands on. Books by Charlie Papazian and Michael Jackson became bibles, roadmaps, and encyclopedias for the journey I now found myself on.

The more I read about the craft brewing renaissance that was underway, the more interested I became in being part of it. The independence and opportunity for self-expression and creativity that came with opening a small brewery were very attractive to me as I always had a bit of a problem responding positively to authority. Here was the chance to set my own course, follow my own muse, and make and learn from my own mistakes. My first batch of beer, a pale ale brewed with cherries added during fermentation, turned out really well and I stood up in front of my friends the night we first drank that beer and exclaimed that my new goal in life was to open my own brewery.

My second batch didn't turn out so well but by then I would have been a hypocrite if I backpedaled. Besides, I was hooked on the idea of opening my own place and wasn't going to be deterred by my lack of knowledge and experience. I vowed to work on improving myself in those areas immediately. I spent a lot of time in those pre-Google days at The New York public library doing Nexus/Lexus® searches on all things beer and all things artisanal like cheese, wine making, coffee roasting, and baking, that I saw as similar business trends in terms of the philosophical and ideological approach of fleshing out a niche market where quality stood for more than quantity.

I didn't have the money to attend one of the full-on brewing schools like Siebel or U.C. Davis that I was reading about. So I decided to go the old-world route and seek out a sort of apprenticeship. I packed up my bags and hugged my roommates goodbye and headed off to Maine for a short brewing course being offered at Shipyard brewery in Portland – about an hour south of my family's house at Dogfish Head (a jut of land off of Boothbay Harbor). I shoveled out the mash tun and learned everything I could about the ingredients, nomenclature, and brewing process by day and drove home to work on my business plan at night. My vision for a brewery that stood for something personal and distinct became clearer by the day.

> My first batch of beer, a pale ale brewed with cherries added during fermentation, turned out really well and I stood up in front of my friends the night we first drank that beer and exclaimed that my new goal in life was to open my own brewery.

I began to see why artisanal businesses were beginning to thrive in our country. In the forties and fifties it seemed like the American populace was more interested in fitting in, in keeping up with the Joneses. But as the eighties gave way to the nineties, the homogenous, mass-market culture that took shape in the fifties became a forgone conclusion. As it did, cookie-cutter culture weighed heavily on American individualism. So consumers performed their own versions of the Boston Tea Party jettisoning derivative, all-for-one-one-for-all products and seeking out choices that reflected their own unique identities.

As I flip-through the coffee and beer stained original version of my business plan today I see a lot of things that I did wrong. I didn't plan for adequate operating capitol to get me through the bumpy start-up phase that businesses inevitably encounter. I didn't flesh out the roles of key management positions within the company. I underestimated my start-up costs in general. I didn't accurately predict that the craft-brewing landscape would shift within a few years of opening to a cutthroat market where demand no longer exceeded supply.

Fortunately, I did a few things right. Key decisions helped buoy my fledgling enterprise through the various storms that all entrepreneurial businesses must weather to survive the start-up phase. One of these was to seek out the growing tide of consumers who were more interested in standing out than they were in fitting in. I designed the whole philosophy of my business around this phenomenon. This philosophy is contained in an Emerson quote, our extended-dance-remix mission-statement that is carved into a 30-ft wall inside our brewery:

Who so would be a man must be a non-conformist
He who would gather immortal palms.
must not be hindered by the name goodness
but must explore if it be goodness for himself.
For nothing at last is sacred
but the integrity of your own mind.

It's kind of a long mission statement. I could barely remember it myself. So I knew I needed to distill it down a little further and into less lofty language if I wanted to successfully articulate it to my co-workers and customers. So below it in the business-plan is our mission statement cheat-sheet: "Off-centered ales for off-centered people." It works because it says everything it needs to about what I want the company to be about and who I want it appeal to. By its very definition it's obvious that we are not in business to make beers like those that already exist. It's also obvious that we have no intention of trying to sell these beers to the majority of drinkers out there.

I finally got the doors of my brewpub open in the spring of 1995. I decided to open Dogfish Head in Rehoboth Beach Delaware – down the road from the town my wife Mariah grew up in. We had rented houses together there in the summers through high school and college and I fell in love with the coastal beauty and relaxed lifestyle. I also wanted to open my brewery in a state that didn't have one yet as I realized that would help get the company a lot of regional recognition and by 1995 there were only a few states left to choose from. I always knew I wanted to brew big, strong, exotic beers and I said so in the business plan. I knew I wanted to someday distribute them across the country and that the strength of the beers would assure a stable shelf life to keep them healthy in an extended marketplace. I wasn't smart enough then to realize what an asset the geographic location of my brewery would be in allowing me to pursue this goal. Our brewery is only two hours drive from Philly, D.C., and Baltimore, and three-and-a-half hours from NYC. So it provides an ideal central location for a manufacturing company to distribute from.

Key decisions helped buoy my fledgling enterprise through the various storms that all entrepreneurial businesses must weather to survive the start-up phase.

TRIALS AND TRIBULATIONS

The first few years were really rocky. I didn't have enough money for a big boy, turnkey commercial brewery. So I souped-up a half-barrel system designed for homebrewing with additional pumps, converted-keg fermenters and a heat exchanger. It was pathetic from a labor perspective – I would brew two-to-three times a day five or six days a week just to provide enough beer for the taps at our pub. But it was great from an experimental perspective as I would get bored brewing the same recipes time after time and wander back from the kitchen with coffee, or apricots, or raisins, to try something new; so many of our best selling styles today were born on that tiny system.

I also had real challenges in running the business in those years. I hardly ever had meetings or spent time conveying the vision of our company to co-workers. I assumed I was leading by example but I was mostly just doing my own thing. I lost my best friend, who was running the restaurant-side of the business as a result of my inability to communicate where I was trying to take the company. But I slowly learned from my mistakes and learned how to run a company that was efficient, and financially-sound but still a lot of fun.

As Dogfish Head evolved, we out grew our initial equipment pretty quickly. We jumped from a half barrel brewery to a five barrel brewery made out tanks we cobbled together from a cannery auction. Next we jumped to a thirty barrel brewery that was outfitted with equipment we got at a yogurt plant auction. In fact we never even made beer on purpose-built brewing equipment until our company was five years old. That year, we installed a 50 barrel brewhouse bought from a bank who held the assets of a regional micro-brewer that had gone under.

In hindsight this struggle with used, random equipment turned out to be a great asset as well. We never went into the debt that would have come with a made-to-order turnkey brewery, so we never had brutal monthly bank payments during the years when cash flow was almost non-existent. Also, by having to MacGyver our own jalopy breweries each time we upgraded, we became better brewers. We had to relearn and reinvent the production process with every system that we put on line. So by the time we were making beer on actual brewing equipment, we had our process pretty well dialed in.

Once we were brewing on the new (to us) 50 barrel system, things really started taking off. We survived the shakeout period of the late 90's without dumbing down our beers or resorting to discounting. In 1997, we had a real battle selling $13 six-packs of 11% abv beer brewed with maple syrup and juniper berries and aged on chardonnay oak. What stopped us wasn't big brewery beers. Rather, it a lack of consumer awareness and knowledge that was our biggest hurdle.

To counter this, we put a huge emphasis on education from the get-go. Getting our story into the hands of the consumer, retailer, and distributor, getting them to sample the beer in environments where they could actually listen to our story (beer dinners, festivals, beer & food pairing events) became the center of all of our marketing efforts. Now as then, we try to be as innovative and resourceful in marketing our beers as we are in making them.

We try to design events and tools (bocce courts, tournaments, contraptions, theme-beer dinners, dogfish films, dogfish beer-geek-hip-hop) that make our communication and education efforts as distinct and exciting as we think our beer is. At the end of the day though it's not marketing for the sake of marketing. When done right it all goes back to the merits of what we've got inside the bottle. We cannot afford to let the battle escape from our comfort zone (the quality and distinction of what's inside the bottle) and back to the big breweries comfort zone (the marketing and advertising that happens outside the bottle). In other words, I'm convinced that the staunch and loyal big-three beer consumer isn't drinking a beer so much as he or she is drinking in an image or being brainwashed through the osmosis of a half-billion dollar ad campaign on why choosing one watery light lager reflects his or her personality more accurately than drinking another watery light lager.

It's relatively easy for us to decide if a new project or product is worth pursuing because we just plug it into our trusty "Off-centered (blank) for off-centered people" formula to see if the "(blank)" is worth pursuing. If you can consolidate the vision of your company into a bite-sized, distinct, unique definition – it will be easy to translate it to your consumers and your co-workers. This is what led us into such seemingly tangensial directions as our own themed beer hotel room package, opening a distillery, the vintage bottled-beer menu at our pubs, beer soap and shampoo, etc. The off-centered approach to these divergent projects is what holds them together and reinforces Dogfish Head's brand identity.

> I didn't have enough money for a big boy, turnkey commercial brewery. So I souped-up a half-barrel system designed for home-brewing

As I review the above paragraphs on the trials and tribulations that we have faced through the years – images of strange equipment, label designs, and ingredients don't come immediately to my head. The first image I have is of the people who helped integrate these ideas into the momentum of Dogfish Head. The reason our beer is selling well is because it's really good beer. The reason that it is really good beer is because it's being produced by really good people. I use the term "produced" instead of "brewed" because every single one of my co-workers is directly involved in Dogfish Head beer production. From the bartender who describes the difference between our 60 Minute and 90 minute IPA, to our sous-chef who develops a rib sauce recipe using those beers, to the brewers who actually turn the valves, we are all producing this beer.

BUILDING A TEAM

Probably the best decision Mariah and I have or will ever make in directing the company is our commitment to surrounding ourselves with a group of co-workers who share our passion and whose skills and talents compliment our own. The moment our company went from the red to the black we began using the bulk of our profits to attract and reward the people who could and wanted to help Dogfish Head grow. Initially we couldn't afford to pay people like our Brewmaster Andy Tveekrem and our CFO Nick Benz what they were worth. But we did offer them a very aggressive profit-sharing program so that, to a large degree, they were in control of their own compensation. We knew they were smart and talented enough to tie their own ambition into the ambition of our company in a way that would benefit everyone. We have worked hard to budget in a way that allows this philosophy to permeate every level of our org chart. Every co-worker at the brewery has a bonus package. Every full-time co-worker at our brewery, distillery and pubs has health benefits – even our waitresses and packaging workers. There is no other way to constructively approach human resources than to take care of the people who take care of your company.

Do not try to build your brewery in the image of some other brewery. First, you probably won't succeed since the consumer will see through a disingenuous or derivative approach. Second, if you do succeed, what do you have to look back on? A company that succeeded because you and the people you work with created every aspect of that success? Or a company that succeeded because of the work that a bunch of other people created? Which scenario do you think would be more rewarding?

About five years ago I did an event with beer writer Michael Jackson at the New Belgium brewery in Colorado. I had always enjoyed their beers when I got a chance to taste them, but I didn't know much about their company. During that visit, I was blown away by how they ran their company. In particular, it was obvious the employees were proud to be part of something special and having a great time.

When I returned from Colorado, I talked about my experience with my co-workers and those who had visited the brewery noticed the same thing. At some point a few empty New Belgium bottles made it to the top of the control panel of our packaging line. None of us took them down and they stayed there for years. They symbolized our recognition of New Belgium's ability to grow without losing what made them unique and special.

It's been really rewarding to be a part of the exciting growth that the craft beer renaissance has experienced in the last few years. I don't think I would appreciate our recent successes as much if we hadn't made it through more challenging times together. I think of that every time I get to have a few beers with other brewers and brewery owners around the country that have been on journeys similar to our own. I hope that our industry continues to grow and I think it's important to plan for a sustainable pace of growth when you start your brewery. I don't think it matters much if you plan to grow by a few percent annually to at least allow you and your co-workers to stay pace with the increasing cost of living or you plan to sustain double-digit growth from your first day until the end of time. You need to grow to keep things interesting. To keep things interesting to the consumer you need to keep experimenting and releasing new beers. You should always ask two questions when you have a new idea – will this new product/project help our company grow? And, will it re-enforce the consistent, unique, valuable identity of our company? If the answers are yes to both questions then you owe it to your company to explore the new idea.

You will have great days and challenging days as you work to sustain and expand your brewery. Having learned from watching successful entrepreneurs and nursing my own bumps and bruises, I believe inspired leadership boils down to two things. First, construct and articulate a clear vision for your company and its distinct position in the marketplace. Second, surround yourself with people whose talents complement your own. If you do your job well, these people will believe in the vision of the company, make it their own and help you grow the vision into something more powerful and meaningful than you could ever do yourself.

So: produce great beer. Produce great beer that is distinctly your own. Take care of the people who choose to help you produce great beer. And have fun. ◗

Chapter Four

East Coast Victory Conquers All Fronts

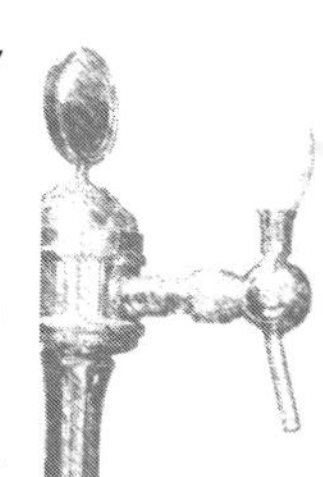

Long-time friends brew up success making all types of beer

By Lew Bryson

RON BARCHET AND BILL COVALESKI, a couple of friends who met in elementary school, are the brewer-partners who run Victory Brewing in Downingtown, Pa. The brewery has been noted for its mastery of lagers, its audaciously broad, geek-friendly portfolio, and ease of transition between innovation and traditional brewing. They talk about some of the key decisions they made when starting out as well as some issues attending their subsequent growth.

The New Brewer: The 25 bbl. brewhouse you started out with seemed to be an awfully big step to start out with. Why'd you go there right away?

Ron Barchet: Very simple. I saw that it had worked for Old Dominion. They had a 25 bbl. system, and it allowed them to grow to a certain point where they could consider buying a new brewhouse. 25 bbls. lets you generate enough profit to go to the next step. If you're starting at 40, or 50 bbls., and you can make that work, great, but that's really hard. I saw it work really well at Old Dominion: a 25 bbl. batch was a nice size. It allows you to make enough to get to 20,000 bbls., and if you get to 20,000 bbls., then you've got enough profit to make the next step.

Bill Covaleski: [In that] old brewhouse, there were a lot of things I used to lovingly refer to as 'highly functional bells and whistles.' The ability to decoction mash, to use whole flower hops; we essentially threw in all the options, because we wanted a brewhouse that wouldn't limit us on the flavors of the beers or the styles we could do. Then lo and behold, we got sort of famous for doing all these different styles of beer.

That brewhouse begat the new one. We almost had a problem because there were so many processes and things that we needed to do, that we couldn't get away from whole flower hops, we couldn't get away from decoction mashing. We didn't have this really narrow product line that would lend itself to a larger brewhouse with less functionality, more directed towards a single beer. So that sort of explains the jump to 50 also.

TNB: I know you've done well, but would you have done better faster if you had narrowed the range of your beers?

RB: No. When we do a new beer, we haven't had cannibalization. By offering a new brand, we're giving someone a chance to buy Victory, as opposed to a Stella, or a Rogue, or whatever.

TNB: So they're not buying Golden Monkey instead of HopDevil.

RB: Right.

BC: Or, they are; depending on the weather and the time of year.

RB: Or they're buying Storm King because they can get a Victory product instead of Rogue Shakespeare Stout, or Brooklyn Black Chocolate Stout. Why lose those sales?

BC: It's a pretty slippery slope, it's almost a collusion attitude: that brewery has that brand, so we'll only do this brand, and make it nice and easy for everyone. The consumer doesn't think along those lines, they want to have the latitude to flow in and out of the different breweries. A large product line has actually been beneficial to getting us to this point. It may become problematic down the road, as wholesalers who take us on say, 'Hey, wait a second, too many SKUs. I don't want a Moonglow and then a Hop Wallop.' Oh, what, you want a Storm King in between? 'No, hold on! Just give me one fall release.'

RB: And then they're making their sales with the fall release in their territory, and then they say 'Oh, this person wants this, and this person wants that! Can you get us that?' Inevitably, they want it too, when their customer wants one of the varietal pils, or one of the one-off beers we do.

BC: It's one of the few aspects of distribution where the consumer does get what they want, because distributors, even though they do want a small product portfolio, hate to say no to sales. So it works that way.

TNB: Were there changes to your business plan? Like the military says, no plan survives contact with the enemy. What surprises did you have when you started up?

RB: When we wrote the plan, there were no micros in Philadelphia. By the time we built the brewery, there were three: Yards, Independence, and Red Bell.

BC: Opening in 1996, that was the thick of it, that was the highpoint of openings.

TNB: You were probably on the far side of the curve a little.

BC: Exactly. The other thing that was a huge surprise, without the benefits of Microsoft Project, we thought we had everything lined up. But we learned that we would not actually be able to get the check from our SBA loan until we had our liquor license, and our PLCB liquor license required us to have all our equipment in place. So there was a really nervous period when we took our shareholder money and pretty much just lit a match under it. We had to get to Point B with equipment installed so that we could get that second check and not fall out of orbit. That was a big surprise.

RB: Another big surprise was that we had imagined a much smaller restaurant operation, maybe not physically, but volume-wise, business-wise. Our original plan had something like 7 people working in the brewpub and maybe $1500 a day. Well, it turned out that we had about 25 employees and on a good weekend night we were turning 5, 6, or 7 grand. The costs were much higher, but so were the revenues on the restaurant. That whole thing turned out to be a lot bigger than we anticipated. We could already sense that as we were doing the project. Bill and I would be working 12 hours and we'd want to go and get a beer or some food, and it was, like, where's there to go? Meanwhile, contractors are coming in here and saying, 'Man, this is great, you're opening a restaurant, there's nothing like this in Downingtown!'

BC: 'We can get pizzas and burgers? That'll be great!'

RB: Not just nothing like this, but not a lot of options, period. As we were building out, we got the sense that the restaurant was going to be a bigger item than we'd planned.

BC: It encouraged us to put a little more emphasis on it. Thank God, because the other big surprise is that our bottling line was six months delayed from its original date. So imagine having this great spreadsheet with all of your revenue streams, and everything's going on retail in your restaurant, and you've got all this wholesale component that's supposed to kick in, but it doesn't happen.

TNB: Good thing you had the restaurant, somewhere you could sell a lot of draft beer.

BC: We sold three kegs of St. Victorious Doppelbock to the Drafting Room, our first draft beer sale, and we didn't hear from them for three months. We sold it in February. The Weintraub brothers are good guys, they said, 'hey, we heard about your brewery, can we get some of your beer? St. Victorious sounds good, send some of those up.' And we didn't hear a thing for three months. I thought, oh, we're so screwed. The premier draft outlet in Chester County wants nothing to do with us. There was a waiting list of other breweries' kegs just waiting in line to get tapped.

TNB: Once you got over the initial hump and started to grow, what surprises were there in growth?

RB: That HopDevil was the lead. We expected Festbier to be the lead, or the Lager. Easygoing beers, not so hoppy.

BC: Festbier makes so much sense: amber, lager. That was a hot thing at the time.

TNB: You pushed the Festbier hard for a lot longer than I thought you should have.

RB: We still do! But we already knew: when we had the first staff training here, of the young women

– that was especially surprising – the young women we had for waitresses –

BC: The people who knew *nothing* about beer.

RB: – hot young women, we told them, hey, here's the beer you're going to be selling, try this out. I went through them all, and they all said *HopDevil*, they were all crazy about HopDevil.

Golden Monkey being our second-biggest beer was a shocker. It's been second for about two years now. Prima Pils and the Monkey are like this *(moves flat hands side-by-side in an up-down fashion)*, Prima's more in the summer, but over the whole year Monkey's on top.

BC: And Storm King hangs tough in that echelon as well, it's not far behind. One of the surprises with the actual growth was that it was easy to get initial wholesaler interest, but typically with crappy wholesalers who didn't know any better. We've done pretty well with our relationships. We've made some good decisions, we've also had the right attitude to stick it out and help people grow to become a better wholesaler for us. But there were some decisions along the way that we just had to get rid of. The other surprise is that when you have more beer, and you have more consumer interest, there are still some places where you just can't go, because there's no wholesaler that's either capable or interested.

RB: We couldn't get into Maryland for the longest time. Nobody'd take us. Nobody. We were getting really good reviews in the beer press, we were getting really good buzz. It was all positive. Finally, Old Dominion got so sick of it, they created their own wholesaler, and they took us. That's who we're with today.

BC: Access to market was an unpleasant surprise. We came from the beer geek mentality of, 'wow, I see all this stuff all over the shelves, it must be easy!' We didn't realize that that stuff had been on the shelves for 8 months.

TNB: I think your beer holds together a lot better [than other beers] after three months on the shelf.

RB: We spent a lot of money on that original bottling line when people were buying $10,000 lines that, you know, the beer had a shelf-life of three weeks. We went and spent $140,000 on a new bottling line that was as good as we could afford at that time. We didn't go all the way to Krones – it was SMB Technik.

BC: When he was getting quotes on bottling lines, I was getting sticker shock. And he said, when you're getting a Bang and Olufsen stereo system, you don't go to Radio Shack for your speakers, do you? We really did invest a lot into quality.

TNB: I think there was another thing, too. With the bottling line, you had that one screw-up with the Festbier, a third of a batch went out contaminated. What happened? You guys went out and pulled beer, people brought beer in and said, 'This sucks,' and you said, here, have another case.

RB: We actually went to the wholesaler and pulled it back, to the extent we could, there was stuff out there that had already been bought by the consumer.

BC: Some of the things that someone else might second-guess, that's part of the integrity. And people buy integrity, and will give it a second chance.

RB: It's important. If they'd had bad beer *and* we were obstinate about it, it could have been the end. We recognized that. It came at the exact time when we had to go back to the shareholders because we'd lost over $150,000 in the first year. It was not an easy decision – no, it was easy, because it was the only thing to do, but it was painful. It was a painful decision, because we had to give money back to the wholesalers, buy bad beer. And that's tough, if you're losing money already. But...the only thing to do.

BC: No brewery is completely safe-guarded against bad beer, so you always have to be vigilant about it. But the takeaway lesson is that if you acknowledge internally that you have bad beer, then you better acknowledge it externally as well.

TNB: Bill, you've talked about "throttling the beer." What do you mean by that?

BC: I throttle the beer flow.

RB: Up until now, well, we have had to throttle it back. But he's going to throttle it up as soon as we have the new brewhouse up. We could be selling more beer if we had it.

TNB: So you were juggling demand. Is that a bad position to be in?

BC: We've been in it so long, it's not really a bad thing. First the bottling was the bottleneck, and we hit a blessed period where we really had all the beer we needed. Then a brewer departs, or things like that. That's another benefit to automation: less dependent on particular people.

RB: Yesterday we were starting to work on plugging in recipes in the brewhouse. It's a program, it gets rinsed out this way, and decocted that way, and everything gets done the way I decide to do it. Whereas, I train people, yet I come back three months later and they're doing this different and that different. For the last four years I've felt like I'm losing control of the brewery, because people don't do what I tell them to. They have their own creativity they want to throw into it. That's great: get a brewpub!

BC: It's not a stable way for an organization to grow.

TNB: In a period when everyone else was pulling back to home territory and saying, 'Well, you can't just send beer out without someone there to sell it,' you guys flipped it on its head and sent beer to Chicago, to California. Why did you do it, and is it working?

BC: Our distribution is pretty much mandated by the consumer.

TNB: So where there's a pull, you go?

BC: Essentially, yes. We can only listen to so many e-mails and so many phone calls until we scratch our heads and say, gee, if we find a wholesaler out there who's willing and capable, then 'no' is a really bad answer! The other thing is, our business plan called for us to have more volume of business locally than we did initially, because of the guys that weren't on the radar screen when we formulated our business plan. Meanwhile, the phone's ringing with people going, 'People are telling me about your beer, and I'd like to handle it.' In hindsight, I think that was really critical for our success, because it created that Internet buzz. People in remote places started talking about it.

TNB: At one point, you changed wholesalers in one of your biggest markets, creating a brief firestorm. What brought on the change, what caused the controversy and are you satisfied?

BC: Our Philadelphia wholesaler was actually performing pretty well, but wouldn't get involved in any programs where we were doing co-op spending, nothing progressive, because he had this huge warehouse of brands that he sold for top dollar. We recognized that, especially with this new installation, we needed to move out from under that cloud. We couldn't just be part of that portfolio, just another brand. The ideal wholesaler was probably Penn Distributing, because they had a really narrow portfolio, a very deep sales force.

TNB: Penn's an A-B house, correct?

BC: Correct. And lo and behold, they started calling us. It dawned on us that we've got to solve this problem, and Penn's the best solution. So it was time to stop saying 'no' and start saying 'yes.' When we made a commitment to them, we approached it from a very professional standpoint by first talking to the old wholesaler and trying to get things ironed out, and overall that went pretty well. But everything comes down to dollars and cents. The old wholesaler accepted a figure and walked off with that. Then unfortunately some people in the retail arena cried foul, I think because they saw their control eroding somewhat. Victory pulled out of the slipstream and now was a force to be reckoned with. We weren't under the control of the guy who had all the good stuff. So it wasn't easier for the retailer of all the good stuff to control it.

There was an opportunity for a Philadelphia craft brewery to get wider exposure, in places where this retailer didn't own a place and that wholesaler didn't like to go to. We upset the apple cart. It was two guys trying to control Philadelphia, and a bunch of minor players. By moving our alliance to a wholesaler that was more progressive and covered a wider territory and did so with longer legs and more aggressively…that struck fear.

TNB: As you get bigger, things change. You may have to focus more sharply on one particular flagship brand; access to market becomes even more crucial; you have to deal with chain grocery stores. What changes do you want to make, contrasted to changes that are forced on you by getting bigger?

BC: Hmm, what is the next step for us? The problem with growing bigger is that when it was just two guys, and it was all our risk, and only our own mouths to feed, no one else was impacted if it went down. Now there's a lot more people involved that we have to take care of. Supporting what you've created becomes a big endeavor in itself. So you have to build stability, you have to not be reckless, and you have to build programs that are going to work for the long haul. Which would naturally lead you toward more conservatism, and you would naturally want to go toward less brands, and greater marketing emphasis of your flagship brands.

TNB: For you and your wholesalers.

BC: Exactly, to keep things simple. The path that other brewers have taken is a very logical path. I feel that our situation in Pennsylvania may be a little bit different. One of the things that encouraged us to do this step, and the previous one in packaging, was that every major metropolitan area in the United States has a dominant craft brewer. Philadelphia has a coal-miner's brewery from Pottsville! That model ain't working. At some point, there's a problem that some people are going to wake up and recognize. That gets back to another reason why we don't have a dominant craft brewer, the distribution system. Until we stepped out from under the thumb of Eddie Friedland, there was no one who gave a shit about a local craft brewery, who was willing to promote a local craft brewer.

We feel our opportunity's a little different from most other cities across the country because it's still ours to define, what the Philadelphia metro market is going to be. When I say 'ours,' I say 'ours' collectively: Yards, Flying Fish, we're all part of that. Right now we're the frontrunner, and we hope, through our distribution changes, to maintain that position and grow that lead.

RB: If you look at all the different breweries that have gotten ahead, there's no one model. We didn't start this by copying other people, we started this by creating our own model. Everyone has different models. I don't think you can take the approach of Harpoon and apply it to Philadelphia and expect to get to 80,000 barrels.

What I want to do here is cater to the beer geeks, but also to the people who are just learning about beer. There's no reason to say that Victory can't be both. We can make the varietal Pils for the geeks, we can make the lager for the people who are just starting to get a new flavor for beer, and we could do Belgian beers. The beauty of being a small brewery is that you can do all of these things, and there's no reason why you have to say 'I'm only going to market to the beer geeks.' Which essentially, if we'd stayed with Friedland, that was our destiny in Philly. I think Philly deserves access to good beer without going in a beer bar. I want Joe Blow to go into his Joe Blow tavern and have a Victory lager or Kölsch. ◗

Chapter Five

Brewpubs Galore in Oregon

A Conversation with the McMenamin Brothers

By Alan Moen

"MCMENAMINS" IS AN ALE-HOUSEHOLD word in the rich pub scene of the Pacific Northwest, and especially in Oregon. Even in a region that prides itself on being different from the rest of the country, the McMenamins empire of 50-plus taverns, brewpubs, restaurants, theatres, and hotels in Oregon and Washington is something of a world in itself. The company's flagship Edgefield estate, 15 miles east of Portland, includes a brewery, a winery, a distillery, and several pubs in addition to a restaurant, a theatre, a hotel, a glass-blowing shop and even a small golf course. Constantly expanding their locations, the McMenamins' clearly have established a formula for success.

With their multitude of projects, these energetic "brews brothers" Mike and Brian, weren't easy to track down. The New Brewer (TNB) was lucky enough to speak with both of them about their perspectives on the craft brewing business at their company headquarters in Portland.

TNB: How did you get started in your amazing business? Did you envision it becoming as big and as diverse as it is now?

MM: I was looking for something to do after college. I'd visited Europe and tasted a lot of great beers. I got used to the variety and thought, why can't we do that here? So I bought an old truck stop in Portland, Produce Row, and turned it into a pub in 1974. We put everything we could find on draft. Whatever we got, we sold. We wanted to be different, and to be fun. It's hard to think how it has all happened after that. We didn't have a plan, other than another pub or two in our heads. We were always evolving.

BM: I helped Mike open Produce Row — I was just 16 at the time. After I graduated from college in 1979, I decided to give it a run. We specialized in draft beer, carried every beer that was available. But there was no "grand plan." It had a life of its own.

TNB: How did you get into brewing your own beer?

MM: I had friends who were homebrewers, and I'd tried it myself, but I wasn't very successful. But I knew you could make that stuff. We had a pub in Hillsdale that became our first brewery in 1985, after Dick and Nancy Ponzi and the Widmers had changed the state laws to allow brewpubs. A lot of our customers were homebrewers, and a lot of imports were becoming available, which helped, too.

TNB: Many of your pubs are in historic buildings. Was historic preservation part of your original philosophy as well?

BM: It started by accident with the Mission Theatre in Portland, which had been an old church. Older buildings were cheaper then. Now, with all the building codes, they're actually more expensive.

MM: I thought, nobody wants this [Mission Theatre] building. I didn't realize then that old buildings cost you more in the end. But we loved the space, and a theatre seemed like a lot of fun. But it started up horrible. The location wasn't great. We tried film festivals, old Bogart movies. We didn't even have enough money to advertise. We had to shut down; we were at the last chapter. Then we decided to make it free, and everybody came after that.

But as far as historic preservation goes, I don't think that it really makes sense financially. There's so much more to it than that — the history of the place, the art. The community. Some of these places had the human condition oozing out of the walls.

BM: Like Edgefield [a former poor farm] — people never went there. We knew people wanted to see it. By that time, in 1990, our pubs and theatres were booming. We had lodging, we wanted to make wine, too, and have a place where we could throw all our concepts together.

We have to do it ourselves—we like to be there. I think our contractor would prefer it otherwise, but we like to be part of the details.

TNB: Has keeping the history of some locations gotten in the way of using them for pubs?

BM: Sometimes. Like in the Olympic Club [Centralia,WA]— we left the stains on the walls. We didn't paint the walls; we left that alone. But you've got to draw a line somewhere. Their bar stools are too close together there. We thought about changing that, but we don't want to go too far. It is what it is — the character is in the age on there. Our Rock Creek Tavern place burned down recently, so we purchased wood from an old barn to use to rebuild it. There will be recycled wood on all the spaces you can see. It will still be telling a story. We're not the owners of the building, just the caretakers.

TNB: With so many different businesses within your business, how do you manage them all? Isn't it difficult to wear so many hats?

BM: We're still a pub. It was a feel-good thing to expand. It was just part of the whole process. We saw the pubs as open-ended deals. But we're basically just a bunch of neighborhood joints.

For management, we hire from within, We haven't had much luck hiring from the outside.

MM: Pubs were a great base. We were expanding the idea of what a pub is. The evolution of the pub includes farming, overnight accommodations, etc. But it's a never-ending learning process. It's hard enough to do one thing well.

TNB: A lot is said about a McMenamins "identity" that carries through your different operations. Is there one, and if so, what have you done to create it?

MM: There's never been a conscious idea to create an identity, but just to make a pub that's comfortable to us. Simplicity is the answer. The less ornate, the more human it is, the more it allows the people to shine

BM: We have an ongoing interest in every part of the pub. Each has its own identity—we take what it gives us. We like to go antique shopping and get a bunch of crazy stuff—Dutch beer signs, things like that. We've got a great collection of old urinals now.

TNB: But what about the art in all the pubs, the ubiquitous painted and decorated brew kettles? Those seem to be a McMenamins trademark.

MM: We work with artists and the history of the building. It's all stuff we like personally. It's hard being inside the company to see the art as any kind of overall thing.

TNB: What about in the brewhouse itself? What's been your philosophy there?

BM: The brewer is an artist. It's hard to tell an artist what to do. We want them to be independent-minded. We have our staple beers like *Hammerhead* or *Terminator*, but we want them to be all different in different locations. We're not trying to homogenize.

MM: Grundies are the greatest things ever invented for brewing! Equipment shouldn't be more important than the beer. I've seen a lot of bad beer come from good equipment. People will follow different brewers. It's not a negative that the beer will taste different in each place.

BM: We still do modified Grundies for brewing. We believe in hands on, one guy at each location, a simple design. We want people to get their hands dirty.

TNB: What's your goal for your beer? What kind of beer are you trying to make?

MM: We want to make a Northwest beer. It's all here — the malt, the hops. We keep it simple. We only use whole hops, and we don't really filter or anything. You can have great stuff without trying too hard.

TNB: How do you market your beer in your own pubs?

BM: We do table tents, flyers. We advertise in papers about our events and seasonal beers. We also hold our own beer festivals, which are competitions between our own brewers, although we invite other local brewers to those, too. We want to be part of the community, and stick to the local flavor.

TNB: You've started bottling some of your beer recently. Doesn't this necessitate more uniformity and quality control?

BM: We're putting our *Hammerhead, Ruby* and *Terminator* in 22 oz. bottles now. We've had jars to go in the past, and never made enough to get beyond that. But if we bottle more, we might have to invest in a bigger operation.

MM: The bottling makes me nervous. We've resisted the pressure to go to one or two different breweries. Quality control does become more of an issue with bottling.

The beauty of the separate breweries is that there is so much more variety and experimentation. We have three to five seasonals everywhere at all times. It's one of the best jobs in the world!

TNB: You sell other beers besides your own in your pubs. Why is that?

MM: As we get bigger and bigger, we have to offer more. The competition thing has never been important to us. But we don't sell off premise, where it's not a lot of fun. I was involved in distribution for several years—it's a dog-eat -dog world out there.

BM: We were a pub first—we were brewers later. Eighty-five percent of our beer sales are our own beer. But I try to sample just about every beer out there, and a lot of our customers do, too.

TNB: What do you think is the future of the brewpub business? Have you seen any new trends in beer or food that are important to pay attention to?

BM: The small guys will get larger—merging will go on. But there will always be a place for the little guy.

Food is a bigger and bigger part of it now. Fifty-five to 60 percent of our business is food. And there's a wider clientele for beverages. We sell spirits now in all our pubs—it broadens our base. And carrying other beers besides our own is important. We may be carrying more in the future.

MM: I don't see any real trends. Wine has become bigger and bigger, and we do have spirits in all of our locations and we make both of those, too. And we have coffee now—we roast our own beans. Our food keeps diversifying.

As far as brewpubs go, I think every pub could have a brewery. The competition doesn't bother me—the more, the merrier. There are a million different avenues for beer out there.

TNB: What advice would you give to someone who wanted to open a brewpub these days?

MM: Assuming they're a brewer, have you ever worked in a pub? Most people know how to make beer, but not how to run a pub. Work in a pub for a year first before you decide. Experience is everything. I worked my way through college in a sandwich shop, so I got to know the service business. Don't eat up all your cash learning as you go.

And keep it simple. Don't make your menu too extensive. Limit how much you spend on the place. People are most important—people are really the whole thing. Without the right people, you won't make it.

BM: Environmental impact issues are huge now in starting any business. It's more expensive to get into brewing, but you don't have to be big. Why do you need a 20-barrel system? You can be small—it's OK. I'm surprised that more pubs don't brew their own beer.

TNB: You've been criticized by some in the craft brewing industry for not joining the various support organizations like the BAA or IBS. Why haven't you done that?

MM: We were involved early on in the Oregon Brewers Guild. I got into doing what I wanted to do. I did not want to be involved in someone else's deal. I just wanted to go out there and blast away! We work with people on a lot of different levels. But we're so involved in our own thing, we don't have time for these organizations. Meetings are not the answer.

BM: We pursue different goals. We're not marketing our beer outside our own premises. We've had our own lobbyist for government issues. I've never been big on brewers' conferences or things like the Great American Beer Festival. It doesn't do anything for us in Oregon.

TNB: You've said that people are the most important part of your business. What do you do to train and keep good employees?

MM: It's an ongoing learning process. We always have things like beer tastings for employees. People are happy when they're learning. We also offer opportunities in the company to move around, which keeps people energized. If you start cleaning toilets, you don't have to end up there. You can move up the rungs into management. In the hotel at Edgefield, there are 15 different departments people can work in. It keeps people plugged in.

We offer health benefits, bonuses, and profit sharing. There's no ownership by employees, but we do have a phantom stock plan for stock in the company that phases in over time. Longevity is where it's at. We have great folks that will be around for a long time.

TNB: Is the McMenamins empire going to endure?

MM: I hope so! It's been a lot of fun. Brian and I get mixed up occasionally, there's so much to do. But I have two kids coming on to learn the ropes. His kids are too young yet. ◗

Chapter Six

Creating A Culture of Success In Your Brewery

Building a Team that Shares Your Passion and Goals is the First Step to Success.

By John Hickenlooper

CERTAIN RESTAURANTS HAVE VERY distinctive personalities. I'm sure many of you have been to a Dick's Last Resort. Their personality is to be right in your face and to be funny to customers. That is very different from a Morton's of Chicago, where they are out there trying to woo you with silk and make you feel pampered. Those are both obvious examples of personality. The creation of personality involves a lot of factors ranging from what kind of people you hire to how you present your business in terms of decor and food and drink.

The culture of a business on the other hand, is a little more subtle. Culture encompasses the values, the beliefs, the norms of your business. (Norms, in this case, are what is expected of your staff, their standards of performance.)

One of the main reasons that culture is so important is that you want to have people who are happy to be at work. They have to enjoy working with each other and doing their job. If they don't it will effect you on many levels: the experience that your customers have, increased operating expenses for things like waste and pilferage, and even the amount of time you have to invest in hiring and training people because of high turnover.

There is no magic formula for creating a culture that makes people happy to be at work. But I think that there are basic rules about how you manage your business and what you expect from people that can help you get there. In addition, you have to recognize what it takes to maintain your culture.

One classic example of this is the Tattered Cover bookstore in Denver. At a time when independent bookstores are closing right and left, they continue to thrive. And part of the reason is their culture. Every new employee spends two weeks in training and the first day is spent entirely with the owner. What she imparts to new employees is a clear vision of the store's values and beliefs. That the more books that are in more people's hands, the better place the world is. She also provides very specific direction for interacting with customers so that each patron feels comfortable and appreciated in the store. This gets down to an incredible level of detail, but because of that, it is incredibly powerful and the store is nationally known for its customer service. I believe that approach and that level of detail can easily be transferred to the restaurant business.

A big part of what it takes to achieve this sort of culture, is setting high standards and making sure that you have a sense of urgency about meeting those standards. For instance, if something spills and a manager is standing there, they should take immediate action—even if they are talking to someone at the time. By doing that, they demonstrate to your staff what your standards are.

Another way of setting a positive example is in answering customer's questions. In our business, people are always asking questions. The first few times that people ask them, they are usually fun to answer. But eventually, the staff generally gets sick of answering the same questions over and over again. But every one of us is put in the same position on a regular basis and we can demonstrate how this should be handled by our own example – by being positive and energetic and by repeating phrases and stories that have proven effective in the past. Even after we have told them a thousand times.

A big part of what it takes to achieve this sort of culture, is setting high standards and making sure that you have a sense of urgency about meeting those standards.

One thing that makes this a little easier is to share your history and local culture with your staff. This can include the local history of your city, the history of your building, the history of your business. Those of you who have been in business for a few years probably have regular stories about how hard it was to raise money, the construction nightmares, the opening fiascos, etc. That is part of your culture. If you don't talk about it, your staff is not going to talk about it. You deprive them of that opportunity to engage the customers and therefore to make those customers a part of your culture and have some sense of ownership of your brewpub.

Those little bits of shared history, especially the ones that connect to your staff, broaden not just their ability to communicate with the customers, but their appreciation of you and through you, the business. This leads to happier employees

Ultimately, if your place is kind of fun and happy, and you are not afraid to do the dirty jobs yourself—to do everything you would ask them to do—it pays off. Specifically, your employees are going to be less likely to go out and take that extra buck an hour when the next new chain opens up down the street or across town. In the end, as much as I hate to admit it, your restaurant is a business based on making money, but its ability to control cost is not completely driven by the competitive environment. A lot of that has to do with your culture.

Not only might you end up spending a bit less on your employees but you will have great employee retention. Everybody knows it is expensive to train new employees. You will also generate referrals. Probably a couple of times a month we get a referral from one of our employees. They recommend a friend or even a relative and nine times out of ten, these turn out to be great employees. One of the secrets of this is that if your employee is willing to say that their brother or friend is going to be great, then you essentially have them helping you to manage that person. This means that someone else is taking ownership of that new employee and is going to push to make sure they do what they are supposed to do.

Another thing about a positive culture is the role it can play in helping you to control costs by doing it in a inclusive, positive way. Take for instance the problem of breakage with certain kitchen implements. No matter what happens they just keep getting broken again and again. But if you put a peg board up so that there is an easy, efficient way to hang things so they are not always getting tossed around, your employees appreciate the fact that you're taking that time, that effort. You are not criticizing them, you are not jumping down their throat, but you are trying to make their job easier while getting the desired results.

If your employee is willing to say that their brother or friend is going to be great, then you essentially have them helping you to manage that person.

Another benefit of a good positive culture is that it fosters something called intrapreneurship. Intrapreneurship has been a popular concept in much of the business world, but hasn't been used much in the restaurant or brewpub business. Basically it refers to creativity inside the company, by the employees. You are not hiring some consultant, you are not hiring some trainer, you are having one of your employees say, "Hey, here is a better way of doing this."

Interpreneurship doesn't just happen. You have to cultivate it. Part of that is the same old things of making sure you thank people, encourage participation in meetings, ask for suggestions and then take them seriously. Listen. Ask questions.

A final reason for creating a positive culture is your own happiness. You don't want to work someplace where people aren't happy and where people aren't trying to work toward the same goals as you.

Personally, I have to really work on these things myself. But we have gotten to the point now where, once someone has a good idea, we talk about it all the time. We try and praise that person even when they have been gone for several years. For instance, we used to have a Marketing Director named Matt McAleer. He had the idea of creating a Fat Tuesday party at the pub. He got one of the radio stations to co-promote it with us, we named a beer for the day and now we do three to four times a normal winter day's business on Fat Tuesday. I often refer to it as "Matt Maclair's Fat Tuesday," and try to tell the story of how he created it (despite my doubts). This is one way in which we encourage our employees to generate creative and effective ideas – by giving credit to those who have ideas.

A final reason for creating a positive culture is your own happiness. You don't want to work someplace where people aren't happy and where people aren't trying to work toward the same goals as you. You want them to be happy and cheerful and making jokes so that your life is happier and more cheerful. It is one thing to make money, but it is another thing to make money and make a lot of people happy.

CREATING A POSITIVE CULTURE

So let's talk about some of the things that go into creating a positive culture. I think the most obvious thing is to hire the right people. And a big part of that is to hire people who are going to be happy there. Look for positive attitudes wherever possible.

Another feature of a positive culture is fairness. When I speak at our all-restaurant meetings, I stress fairness. Of course fairness is a legal issue for any employer, but it is also one of those things that makes people feel good about where they work. To our staff, I repeatedly stress that if you ever feel discriminated against for any reason, talk to your manager. If that doesn't help the situation, talk to the general manager, and if he doesn't take care of it, call me. To help them with this, my phone number is right above the main phone at the host stand. And in twelve years, I have gotten just one phone call from someone that had a problem. And in that case, I was glad they called.

Of course when I talk about our commitment to fairness, I always mention that we are not perfect. We are going to make mistakes at times. But we, as a company, and as individuals, are going to try to treat each other as fairly as possible. That commitment goes a long way toward getting people to feel comfortable and having a sense of ownership.

Another aspect of positive culture is setting high expectations. Here we are discussing the Pygmalion Effect. This basically says that people will live up to the expectations that you have for them. The basic effect has been illustrated in school children, that classes taught by teachers who thought their students were "gifted" learned faster than similar students taught by teachers who thought their students were "average". The bottom line is that people perform based on what is expected of them. So the more that we believe our staff can achieve, the better they are going to do.

Having a positive culture makes it easier to hire good people. But sometimes you have to help people leave your company to help foster that positive culture. When one of our staff people leaves Denver and goes to another city, we try to pick up the phone and help them get a job. I'll refer them to another brewpub owner that I might know – or anyone in the business that I have contacts with. Same thing if you have an employee that aspires to do something else. All you have to do is find one great job for one of your employees and the rest of your staff really buys into that level of possibility, and appreciates your effort. These kinds of moves pay off in two ways. First the employees you have feel better about you as an employer. Second, the other brewpubs or restaurants or employers that you send people to will return the favor and send you people who are going to be good employees.

Training is critically important in any business—and too often overlooked. I think the key thing in training is to pay a lot of attention to what it feels like to be a new employee in a place that already has a strong culture. To help them get into that culture, you have to do things that they can participate in—ways that they can get to know other people at the company and become part of the organization. At the Tattered Cover Bookstore, which I mentioned previously, they maintain a wall with every single employee's picture and a job description of what they do. That's something that I think helps new employees become involved in the culture.

One thing that we have done is to throw a couple of parties each year for the staff. For the biggest one, we rent out one of the big parks and have softball, volleyball and of course food and drinks. At this point, we have several hundred people come to the event. One of the most important aspects of the event is that the managers and owners are the ones who are tending the bars and serving the food. In this setting, we are serving our employees and it demonstrates our customer culture to them.

We close for one day to do this, but it is such a big success that the staff talks about it for months beforehand and afterwards. Even though it is only a single day event, it has positive repercussions that carry on over a couple of months.

Another thing that we focus on is recognition and rewards. We have a monthly game looking at what percentage of each server's sales are in our beer—because of course that is the most profitable portion of our beverage sales. All we do is to keep track of who is selling the most Wynkoop beer as a percentage of their total beverage sales. At the end of the month, we recognize both the highest achiever and the one that has showed the most improvement. Prizes like a bottle of wine or gift certificates at other restaurants are awarded. It doesn't cost a lot of money, but it has a tremendous effect on the morale of the staff and the overall culture of the business.

In a similar vein, we try to monitor the complaints we get on various servers. We don't do this to be critical, but we want people to know that we do pay attention to this and we really have to in fairness to all employees. Then, if an employee improves in this area, they will be rewarded.

In general, this reflects our general approach to people management which revolves around positive reinforcement. As Scott Smith likes to say, we are trying to catch people doing something right.

Emphasizing the good that people do generally has a lot more impact if they aren't regularly subjected to criticism. I think that non-critical management is very important.

Let's face it, if someone puts you down, criticizes what you have done, there is no way that you don't feel in some way diminished. At least 99 percent of us feel that way. When you feel diminished, you are not going to work as hard. You are not going to be as creative. You are not going to be as happy. It is the quickest and surest way to plant a cancer in the middle of your culture. Going forward, even the smallest little cancers like that spread.

Our General Manager at Wynkoop, Mike Kostylo, is by his very nature non-critical. While a great practical joker, he does it in such a way that people don't feel laughed at or humbled. He is always looking for opportunities to praise people. His leadership in this goes a long way in setting a positive culture for the whole restaurant.

In conclusion, the one single thing that I want to leave you with is the importance of non-critical management. It is something that takes work, both from you and your managers, but with some effort, I believe you can create a management that avoids criticizing people ever. When you do this, you treat all of your employees with respect and in return they will respect you and your managers. When this happens, you have gone a long way to creating the kind of positive culture that makes your brewpub a more enjoyable place to work as well as a more enjoyable place for your customers to visit.

Chapter Seven

Ten Tips For Starting Your Craft Brewery

Industry Veteran Recalls the Labors of Startup

By Marcy Larson

WE OFTEN CALL ALASKA THE LAND OF THE individual and other endangered species. I've often thought that statement had a lot in common with the craft brewing movement and its distinctively flavorful beers. Beers with unique character, full of taste and something to say were very nearly snuffed before craft brewing came along. Now, I think the strength of the industry is in its personality. And I think successful brewing businesses must be based on the personality and individuality of its beers.

That said, you have to consider the following comments with the caveat that what works for one brewer may be a disaster for another. This is not a "how to" essay; merely a "what worked for us" list. Here are ten tips that helped us out.

1. RESEARCH, RESEARCH, RESEARCH

Information is the single greatest resource available to a new venture. We subscribed to every brewing and beer publication we could get our hands on. It's rather overwhelming to discover how much is written about one subject. We started collecting books, magazines, and articles concerning the beer business seven years before we started our brewery. It cost a small fortune, but it was the best investment we made. We still subscribe to many of the periodicals, and every now and again I go back and reread our collection of old issues. It can be very enlightening.

2. HISTORICAL RESEARCH

Another area of information that radically impacted our business was the historical section in our local library. Our Alaskan Amber Beer originated in the Alaska State archives. It was pure luck, but I was able to find detailed records on one of the breweries that flourished here prior to Prohibition. We discovered methods of brewing that made a lot of sense to our specific location. Until that point, we had been reading about breweries in the lower forty-eight and had formulated our plans according to what was working for them. Discovering the library archives opened our eyes, and gave our beers that much more local character. At the same time, we learned about other area ventures that didn't survive and tried to avoid their mistakes. It would have been all too easy to have wandered down the same path.

3. EDUCATION

Two days after our wedding, my husband, Geoff, flew off to Chicago to attend the Siebel Institute of Technology. We did honeymoon after he got back, but in the meantime I worked to pay for his education. And, what an education! He must have put on twenty pounds before he returned home. Seriously though, the folks at Siebel were really great. The instructors there provided our fledgling plans with a great base of knowledge. For us, they were not only good educators but also our first connection to the industry.

4. THE INDUSTRY

We were impressed with people in the brewing industry right from the start. We all want to make better beer. As a result, you can learn a lot from other brewers and suppliers if you are careful to not insult them. They worked hard for the insight and information they acquired. It is a slap in the face to expect them to hand it over to you. Some freely give and some are extremely reserved, but they have earned that right. If you can gain their respect, you will be able to tap into the real world of brewing.

5. APPRENTICESHIPS

Nothing beats working in a brewery prior to starting your own. If you can get paid to do it, all the better. But if you can't land a job in one, then see if you can find an apprenticeship. We did so and pestered the brewers and owners with a thousand questions as we inefficiently "worked" at the brewery. Even after homebrewing and completing professional brewing school we had a lot to learn. They were really nice to us and never lost patience, but I'm sure there was a collective sigh of relief when we finally left.

6. PAPER AND BALSA WOOD

Ideas don't become plans until they are on paper. And once there they can suddenly look really awful. While the business plan is a great tool, it is also something most brewers dread. A business plan can help you avoid a bunch of mistakes in the start-up and can also create a working reference for the next five years. In the roller-coaster ride of our first few years of operation, we found ourselves digging out the business plan every few months as we made countless decisions on a rapid-fire schedule. What was amazing to us was how much we had actually thought of prior to getting underway. The other great tool was our balsa wood model. Geoff built the brewery to scale in model form first and made sure he could add things for growth. It's much easier to push around balsa wood tanks than the real thing.

7. MARKET RESEARCH

A subtext of the business plan is the marketing plan. To put together our marketing plan, we looked at demographics, shipping routes, state gallonage figures, margins, distributors, and then we went out and talked to our future customers. We have an interesting marketplace because Alaska is so spread out. As a comparison, just one county in the Seattle area has three times the population of the entire state of Alaska! Our beer has to travel over five hundred miles just to get to the next biggest town. With this kind of market, we knew we had to look at packaging constraints right from the beginning.

8. RULES AND REGULATIONS

The laws controlling alcohol constantly change. Get current copies of regulations while planning and stay abreast of any updates. You have the Federal law, the state laws, and the local laws to contend with. We have found most administrators to be really reasonable if you are up front with them. They hate surprises. They also hate having to rush things through. So be sure to leave enough time to have all paper work and permits in order before sending out the invitations for your grand opening.

9. PERSONNEL

Don't make the mistake of thinking you can do everything yourself, or you will die young. We tended to schedule ourselves for twelve-hour days since we knew we could handle it. However, it is much better to plan for normal working schedules and let the overages happen than to plan on being superhuman. A new brewery offers the founders many hats to wear: choose the one(s) you want most and hire out the rest. I'm not sure how we got so lucky, but we have a dynamite crew that has stayed with us from the start. We consider our staff to be our strongest asset.

10. EQUIPMENT AND SUPPLIES

We make it a policy to get three quotes before placing our initial order for any item. It's surprising the variance you find if you look around. In planning your equipment needs, remember not to lock yourself in to any one size if at all possible. We've always tried to leave the door open for easy growth.

Early on an old-timer showed us a triangle with the corners labeled "time," "work" and "money." They are all connected, but you can only have two of them at the same time. For example: You can do it fast and right, but it'll cost you. Or you can do it cheap and right, but it'll take you forever. Or you can do it cheap and fast, but it won't be right. We found this useful in deciding what was important to save, and what we could look forward to giving up.

Most of what has been mentioned is plain common sense, but that's what worked for us. As I said before, I don't think there is a wrong way and a right way, there is just your way. After all, it's your beer! It should have your personality written all over it. So, say something and wake up another complacent consumer to good beer! Happy brewing! ◗

Chapter Eight

Ten Tips For Starting Your Brewpub

Guidelines for Mastering the Complex Brewery-Restaurant Equation

By Scott Smith

THIS ARTICLE OFFERS TIPS FOR STARTING your brewpub—but please realize that the subject is so large and this article so short that "tip" should be thought of as "tip of the iceberg." Each item presented here will take time, effort, and study on your part. All I can hope to do is start you in the right direction.

TIP 1: COMMITMENT

Make sure you know what you're getting into and that you are the right person for the job. A brewpub combines the restaurant business (yes, you must like people) and the brewery business (yes, you must be mechanically inclined, hard working, and process oriented). Both businesses require a distinct set of characteristics that either you or your partners must have. Before you commit to opening a brewpub, make sure you are in a position to quit your day job and go months without a paycheck while developing your concept, securing your financing, and building your facility.

TIP 2: CONCEPT

Is the brewpub a brewery with a restaurant, a restaurant with a brewery, or a unique combination of both? While most people prefer to treat it as the latter, there are successful brewpubs in each of these categories. Develop your concept according to your philosophy. Realize that craft beer is no longer a novelty in most parts of the country. To be successful, a brewpub must have quality food, beer, service and ambiance and must do a good job of controlling costs and managing finances. Resist the temptation to start out planning to open a chain of brewpubs. Open one, master the business and only then allow yourself to think about a second location.

TIP 3: SITE FEASIBILITY

When searching for your brewpub, answer these questions: Is the location appropriate? Does it have the necessary parking, exposure, foot traffic, and synergy with other businesses to generate the number of customers, and therefore sufficient revenue? Is it zoned correctly, ADA (Americans with Disabilities Act) accessible, and will the fire department and health department approve the facility? Are the utilities and ceiling height adequate? Is the roof in good shape and will it bear the weight of additional equipment? What will it cost to upgrade any deficiencies in the items listed above and is there room in your budget to do so? Answering these questions before you begin negotiations to lease or purchase the building will save time and may determine the success of your project.

TIP 4: KEY PLAYERS

There are four key areas of the brewpub that must be managed by different individuals:

1. The floor
2. The kitchen
3. The brewery
4. Administration and bookkeeping (payroll, payable accounts, cost of goods, and profit and loss statements)

Of the four key areas, only administration and bookkeeping can be subcontracted and handled off-site. But if you do that, make sure you get someone with restaurant accounting experience. The other key positions must be held by people working day-to-day in the operation. As a founder, presumably you will be filling one of these positions. Fill the others with the best people you can afford. When hiring, make sure these individuals have the same goals, philosophies, and work ethic as you. Do more than look at résumés and check references. Long serious talks over several beers are in order. When you have found the right person, pay them well, institute a bonus program, and allow them to earn equity in your company. Get them involved in your project as soon as your budget allows.

TIP 5: CONSULTANTS AND OTHER PROFESSIONALS

It takes a broad range of expertise from talented individuals to put a brewpub together. You and your partners may have some expertise; the rest will have to be hired. Some of those people are professionals you will retain for the life of your brewpub (CPA and attorney), others for the construction phase (architect, general contractor, and real estate broker), and others will only be involved in the start-up (restaurant, brewery, and marketing and graphic design consultants). Hire the best you can afford, but only after qualifying these individuals. Make sure they are locally successful, have appropriate experience, are politically connected, and most importantly, understand your concept and your budget. Money spent to buy the expertise lacking in your partnership will pay for itself many times over during the life of your brewpub.

TIP 6: DESIGN

Please remember three simple words when designing your brewpub: form follows function. While aesthetics are important, you must create a functioning manufacturing facility capable of producing great beer. Involve your brewer, kitchen manager, and floor manager in the design of their departments. Remember that many beautiful but impractical breweries and kitchens were designed by architects and interior designers. Listen to the people who will work in these facilities for input on how the flow of these areas will work and how they interact with the other areas. A plethora of ideas will be offered on how your brewpub should look. Remember it is your place, and you must remember your budget. If possible, allow room for expansion. This may mean taking an option on space above, below, or beside your facility. A well-run brewpub will most likely need additional space within three years of opening.

TIP 7: EQUIPMENT PURCHASING

Get recommendations from existing brewpubs. Meet suppliers at the Craft Brewers Conference and Trade Show. Get references, not only the ones they give you but find out who their last five customers are. Talk to those people and the brewers who operate those breweries. Find out what is and isn't included in the equipment package, and how much the extras will cost. Allow yourself enough time to make a well-informed, educated decision, and allow the brewery manufacturer enough time to fit you into their schedule. Avoid basing your choice of companies to buy from on who promises the fastest delivery. Kitchen equipment can be a mix of new and used equipment, but always buy new refrigeration and ice machines.

An unwritten rule of the restaurant business is that a good point-of-sale (POS) system will lower your controllable costs by 2 to 5 percent. A POS system is a computerized cash register and cost-tracking system. Although a substantial investment (approximately $30,000), this is money well spent. Research this equipment purchase as you would the brewery and talk to the restaurants that currently use the systems you are considering. Make sure to evaluate hardware and software requirements, training, expansion capabilities, and most importantly, service and support. Open with the best one you can afford.

TIP 8: CAPITAL

Your project will cost more and take longer than you plan. Every dollar you borrow, you must pay back. Every dollar you spend in excess of what you raised will haunt you. If your project costs more than you have, you must borrow more. The greater your debt service, the more sales must increase to meet your original profit projections. While obvious, these points are often forgotten, overlooked, or ignored. Remind yourself of them often.

Not every dollar spent must be borrowed from the bank or investors. Pursue economic development grants, city incentives, equipment leasing, energy conservation loans, and tenant-finish contributions from your landlord. Ask everyone associated with your project if they know of other sources of capital.

TIP 9: FINANCIAL CONTROLS

Have a bookkeeping system in place from the time you write your first check. Your first system may start as a simple manual ledger, evolve into a computerized spreadsheet, and end up in the hands of a professional bookkeeper, but make sure there is a system in place. A shoebox full of receipts is not sufficient. Use the "Standard Chart of Accounts" for restaurants. This is available through the National Restaurant Association or your CPA. Break your budget into specific categories, such as brewery equipment, restaurant equipment, furnishings and fixtures, legal, etc. Keep track of your actual dollars spent versus your budget for each category. If the category is over budget, where will the money come from?

TIP 10: ACKNOWLEDGE WEAKNESSES

To start a brewpub you must have access to capital, restaurant experience, brewery experience and a variety of other talents and expertise. Nobody knows it all. Hire the professionals discussed in tip 5, but educate yourself about the industry. Read trade magazines, attend trade shows, attend the Craft Brewers Conference, read books published for and by the industry, and take classes. Finally, assemble a management team that possesses the knowledge and skills you may lack. ◗

Facility Planning and Operations

AT THE HEART OF EVERY BREWERY YOU'LL FIND the equipment and ingredients needed to make beer. In this section we introduce these elements and discuss issues you'll need to consider as you plan your venture.

We start with a review of the raw ingredients used in brewing with some discussion of how each is procured and handled. Next we talk about brewing equipment and some of the options you can expect to encounter when you go to acquire these items. To wrap these things together, the third chapter in this section looks at the range of issues associated with creating a brewing facility.

Once the brewery is built, you'll encounter a host of demands as you start making beer. From taxes to wastewater, the middle chapters of this section introduce you to some key operating issues and give you tips for managing them effectively.

In the closing chapters of this section we'll take a closer look at the supply process for hops and then consider that part of the brewery that is often the first to fail: its floor.

Of course the arts and sciences of brewing take years to master, so these chapters can only serve as a brief introduction. Nonetheless, once you've finished this section you can move on to the next element of the brewery business. In Section III, we'll talk about getting your beer to the consumer.

Chapter Nine

Raw Materials for the Commercial Brewery

A primer on brewing materials and their acquisition and handling in a commercial setting.

By Ray Daniels

EVERY BREWERY REQUIRES THE SAME BASIC inputs for the production of beer: water, malt, hops and yeast. Here's a brief introduction to these four essential raw materials and some of the issues you'll need to consider in planning your brewery.

Water. As it accounts for more than 90 percent of the finished beer, water is an important ingredient. When planning your brewery consider the source, cost and treatments that will be necessary for brewing with it.

Unless a brewery is lucky enough to have its own water well or other source that supplies water for free, you will purchase water from the local public supplier. Be sure to find out what that water will cost and budget accordingly, considering that it takes at least ten and usually 15 barrels of water to produce one finished barrel of beer in a small brewery. After that, consider the capital and operating costs involved in the various treatments that may be required.

Once you have a source, determine its composition. At the very least, it should meet all standards for safe drinking water and be free of iron. If a public water supply is being tapped for brewing water, chances are it will be biologically sound. For private water sources, you'll probably have to test and monitor the quality as a part of your operations. Otherwise, if a consumer or the press discovers that your beer contains heavy metal or pesticide residues, you might be out of business. Use of an activated charcoal filter for all brewing water can help to ensure that what goes into your beer won't contain surprises between actual tests of the water purity. Beyond that, you'll need to conduct water analyses on a regular basis to monitor the effect of water treatment and to compensate for possible fluctuations in the water supply's quality.

Once safety is ensured, we begin to think about how water influences the flavor of the beer. Public water supplies are commonly chlorinated and that can produce undesirable beer flavors. Here again, an activated charcoal filter works well to remove chlorine and all brewery water should go through one before use.

Next, we need to consider the trace minerals in water that influence beer flavor and the brewing process. Because water composition varies widely, you'll need to consider the exact mineral composition of your water when deciding which beer styles to produce and how to equip your brewery. In many cases, some form of water treatment will be required beyond carbon filtration.

Water with lots of temporary hardness will need to be softened before brewing many beer styles. While other options exist, small brewers commonly use additions of food-grade acid.

After softening, craft brewers often add mineral salts to adjust water composition for specific beer styles. Both food grade acid and mineral salts represent operating cost items to consider in the overall budget for the brewery.

Malt and Other Grains. The Germans have an expression that says "Malt is the soul of beer." Not surprisingly then, malt plays a very large role in the character of your finished product.

"Malt" is shorthand for "malted barley"—the essential raw material for nearly all beers. At most breweries, one pale-colored malt such as a pilsner, pale ale, or 2-row malt will be selected as the "base malt" for nearly all beers brewed. This base malt constitutes up to 90 percent of all the malt purchased by the brewery. In addition to base malt, brewers use specialty malts with specific characteristics to change the flavor, color and body of the finished beer. Beyond this, most craft brewers use some malted wheat and other specialty grains and may occasionally use an alternative base malt for a specific beer style.

Various suppliers offer a full range of malts to small brewers. To the extent possible, you'll want to get most or all of your grain from one source to minimize shipping costs and ordering hassles. Inevitably, however, some specialty grains and other ingredients will have to come from different suppliers. When selecting a malt supplier you'll look at the character and quality of the malt itself, the cost of the malt, the packaging options available (bags, supersacks, bulk), shipping terms and costs and some less tangible issues such as service and support. Other business issues such as minimum order size and payment or credit terms may also play a role in your decision. In certain cases it may be wise to test grains from different suppliers by doing small-scale brews.

Hops. Hops play several roles in beer, providing bittering, flavor and aroma characteristics depending on how they are used. Hop growers offer more than 30 different varieties from several geographic areas and each contributes unique traits to the finished beer. Unless you are making just one simple beer, you'll need to purchase and stock a number of hop varieties at any one time. Once purchased, hops should be stored cold. Most small brewers simply keep hops in the walk-in beer cooler; others use a chest freezer or other dedicated cooler.

Prices from different suppliers generally won't vary greatly, so consider the hop varieties and form (whole vs. pellet) needed as well as your comfort level with the supplier you choose. Also consider the shipping, credit and payment requirements.

Yeast. The specific yeast used in fermentation greatly influences the flavor, body, color and foam traits of the finished beer. To achieve the desired results, brewers must carefully manage the conditions and handling of the yeast before and during fermentation.

One or more yeast strains will be used in your brewery. Some brewers make all of their beers with a single yeast year-around. This has the advantage of simplicity but limits the range of flavors and other traits possible in your beers. Because of this, most craft brewers use several different strains of yeast in the course of any one year. Some strains will be used for just one or a few batches of a special seasonal beer, while other strains may be used year-around to make styles that cannot be made from the brewery's main yeast. For example, a brewery might use a general ale yeast to brew a range of American and British style ales. But when they want to make a lager, a Belgian-style ale or a German-style wheat beer, they will need specialty yeast strains.

After purchasing yeast, it often needs to be propagated via smaller fermentations until you have enough yeast to properly ferment a full-sized batch of beer. After that, yeast can be used numerous times if handled and stored properly—so long as there isn't a significant wait between uses. Finally, even carefully handled yeast needs to be replaced from time-to-time in order to maintain the quality of your finished beer.

As a result of these factors, you should determine what styles of beer you will make—or at least how many different yeasts you want to be able to work with at one time and during the course of the year. From this, you will be able to budget for the equipment needed in the brewery and for the cost of yeast purchases during the year. ◗

Chapter Ten

Professional Brewing Processes and Equipment

Prepare to brew commercial-size batches by understanding the equipment required for every process.

By Eric Warner and Ray Daniels

WHILE MANY WHO ASPIRE TO OPEN A brewery already understand a lot about brewing, you'll make hundreds of decisions while building and operating a commercial brewery. In this section we visit key sections of the brewery (brewhouse, fermentation, packaging, utilities and laboratory) to discuss their functions and highlight some issues you should consider during brewery development. In each section I'll address the considerations of packaging breweries and brewpubs.

THE BREWHOUSE

The brewhouse is the heart of any brewery. Here brewers combine and cook raw ingredients to produce that sugar-rich soup known as wort that the yeast will ferment into beer. The components of the brewhouse begin with grain storage and milling. From there we go to the mashing and lautering steps where we dissolve and separate extract from the grains. Next we get to the boil kettle where the liquid extract is hopped and boiled in preparation for fermentation. Finally we whirlpool the wort to remove hop and protein debris before chilling it in preparation for fermentation.

Grain Storage and Milling. Because you'll buy many brews' worth of grain at one time, you'll need to store it before it gets used. At a certain volume, bulk deliveries to a silo are best. But all small breweries receive some grain in bagged form, so every brewery includes a malt storeroom. Ideally this room should be cool, dry, free of mice and insects and located close to the malt mill. Often grain storage is on an upper level and if so, remember that a pallet of malt weighs anywhere from two thousand to three thousand pounds, so you'll need to plan a way to get the malt up there.

The first thing we do in brewing is mill the malt. Milling influences brewhouse efficiency as well as the time it takes to lauter and thus complete the brewing day. In nearly all cases for a small brewery, a two-roller mill does the job, although four-, five-, or six-roller mills can improve brewhouse performance. With the proper equipment, malt can be crushed wet or be conditioned with steam just prior to milling to improve extract efficiency. But in most small breweries a dry grist, two-roller mill is employed, as more costly alternatives do not yield a large enough increase in brewhouse performance.

Classic brewery design places the malt mill above the mash tun so gravity feeds the grist into the vessel. When this isn't feasible, the crushed grain must be conveyed pneumatically, mechanically or manually into the mash tun. The same options apply to transporting the unmilled grain to the malt mill.

As with all grain, movement and milling creates dust. This dust needs to be isolated from the rest of the brewery for two reasons. For starters, grain dust is a potential explosion hazard. Second,

Process Summary: Grains must be stored under proper conditions at the brewery before use. On brew day, the malts are milled to split them open exposing the starch-rich interior while keeping the husks nearly intact to serve as a filter bed during lautering. Grain dust must be minimized and controlled.

grain carries microbes that can produce unwanted flavors in beer if they get into the process downstream of the brewhouse. For both reasons, grain grinding is best carried out in a separate room isolated from the fermentation and packaging areas of the brewery.

Because of the explosion hazard, building codes usually dictate specific fixtures and structural standards for milling areas. Also, Occupational Safety and Health Administration standards provide guidelines for avoiding grain explosions along with guidelines for protection from the dust and flour that arises during the milling. Always design milling operations to be as ventilated and as dust free as possible. This protects you and your employees and also reduces the amount of time spent cleaning the grist room.

Mashing & Lautering. To initiate the brew, you mix the crushed grains with hot brewing water to achieve a desired mash-in temperature. Many breweries use a specially plumbed mash hydration fixture in the grain chute to mix the water and grist. This approach reduces dust clouds and ensures uniform wetting of the grist. Without a mash hydrator, brewers mix the water and grist in the mash tun. Mixing demands movement of hundreds of pounds of grain and water, making it a very physical job when done without mechanical assistance. Uneven mixing may result in reduced extract efficiency. Overall, the mash-in process should proceed as quickly as possible, so the water lines and mixing section must be amply sized.

Process Summary: During mashing, the malts are mixed with hot water and allowed to rest at specific temperatures in order to extract sugars, proteins and flavor compounds from the grains. Next is lautering where the extract-rich liquid is drained from the grains before they are washed with hot water.

If brewing frequency allows, hot water for mashing can be obtained from the wort cooling process that occurs at the end of brewing. The heated water is stored in a well-insulated warm water tank and may be heated further if needed. This sort of tank is a good application for used equipment. Rather than having a hot liquor tank, many smaller breweries use the brew kettle to heat mash water and transfer the hot liquor for sparging to an empty fermenter until it is needed, thus saving the expense of a tank.

Design the mash tun in accordance with the planned batch size, keeping in mind that a strong special beer can require substantially greater mash capacity than an everyday beer. This is particularly important if a combination mash-lauter tun is going to be used, as too thin or too thick a grain bed will result in less than ideal lautering conditions. Insulate the mash tun well and, in the case of the mash tun that isn't doubling as a lauter tun, equip it with an agitator to evenly distribute the mash across the areas where heat transfer occurs. The agitator blade is usually propeller-shaped and should rotate at speeds that will mix the mash, not purée it.

The lauter tun is made of stainless steel or copper and is also well insulated to prevent a drop in temperature during the run-off. It needs to be perfectly level to ensure proper run-off and maximum yield. The form of the lauter tun is cylindrical and its capacity is sized according to the size of the mash, which is determined by the amount of milled grain. Grain bed depths of one to two feet are common, with the deeper beds used in mash-lauter tuns. Modern lautering technology prescribes grain bed depths of as little as eight to ten inches. The design of the false bottom facilitates a steady, efficient run-off that yields a clear wort. The false bottom is usually made of stainless steel and is laid into the lauter tun on a system of supports. The false bottom is either slotted or holed and the plate(s) of the false bottom is milled or punched. A wire, V-screen-type bottom is also commonly used. In either case, the false bottom should be removable, yet firmly secured in place during usage, particularly if rakes are used in the lauter tun. If the lauter tun is a dedicated lauter tun, then the mash should be pumped into the lauter tun at the bottom to minimize aeration of the mash.

Do not overload the lauter tun, as this will bend the false bottom, resulting in an uneven run-off and decreased yield. To clarify the initial run-off, employ some method of wort recirculation to pump the first runnings back onto the top of the mash so the grain bed filters them. A sparge system above the surface of the mash sprays hot water on the grain bed once the concentrated first wort has been drawn off.

Some lauter tuns use cutting rakes to loosen the grain bed during lautering and facilitate rapid and uniform rinsing of the grains. Rake systems also include a plow parallel to the false bottom that can be raised and lowered to discharge the spent grains from a hole in the bottom of the tun. This automates the process of removing spent grains from the lauter tun and is a real time-saver if there is a large amount of grain. Generally speaking, if your brewhouse is larger than fifty barrels you probably want to have rakes and a spent-grain discharge system. Particularly large systems should also have an automated means of moving the spent grains to a silo or storage vessel.

The sweet wort drains from the bottom of the lauter tun via one centrally located run-off pipe or in larger tuns, via several run-offs evenly distributed on the bottom. From here the sweet wort is either recirculated into the lauter tun or pumped into the kettle by an open or closed wort collecting grant.

Brewhouse Designs: Small breweries commonly use a two vessel brewhouse consisting of a heated kettle/whirlpool and an insulated (but not heated) combination mash-lauter tun. In this system, grains remain in the mash-lauter vessel throughout mashing and lautering and the boiled wort remains in the kettle until it has been whirlpooled and is ready for cooling.

Larger brewhouses use additional vessels to separate the four functions. A four vessel brewhouse would include a mash tun, a lauter tun, a boil kettle and a whirlpool. Here the mash tun and kettle would be heated while the other two would be insulated. Other common additions would be mixing equipment in the mash tun and rakes and grain moving equipment in the lauter tun. The use of additional vessels facilitates rapid brewing of multiple batches in a single day while dedicated vessels improve performance of each step in the process.

Boiling. The brew kettle must have the capacity to hold the lautered wort plus sufficient headroom for foaming during the boil. To avoid oxidation of the wort, lauter-tun run-off should be underlet into the brew kettle. Like the other vessels in the brewhouse, insulate the kettle well. The shapes of the kettles are extremely varied, but the most common form is a cylindrical kettle with a slightly concave or slightly convex bottom. Copper kettles conduct heat better than stainless-steel ones, but the latter are less expensive and easier to clean and maintain. The top of the kettle must have a dome and vent to lead the steam away from the brewhouse. The kettle is fitted with a manway through which the hops are also often dosed.

Kettles can be heated in a variety of ways. The most traditional method is with a direct fire, in which case the flame is directed at the concave bottom of the brew kettle. In larger breweries, steam is a common and useful brewery utility and will be used to heat the kettle. In steam-heated kettles, the steam circulates through jackets in the walls and floor of the kettle. To ensure a rolling boil from steam jackets, offset them in some manner or segregate them into areas having two different steam pressures, resulting in two different steam temperatures. This sort of kettle design is suited to dual use as a whirlpool as well.

Kettles can be fitted with an internal boiler — placed inside the kettle to circulate steam — or with an external boiler. Located outside the actual brew kettle, the external boiler is comprised of plates or pipes where steam and wort circulate. The walls of the plates or pipes separate the two media and serve as the surface through which the heat transfer occurs. With this system the kettle can be fitted with a flat bottom and double as a whirlpool.

Brew kettles have a few, key design criteria, otherwise they are pretty simple. For one, the kettle must be sized so the wort comes to a boil quickly and can maintain this boil for the prescribed time.

Process Summary: Wort is boiled with hops to develop bitterness and extract flavor and aroma compounds. The boil also coagulates excess protein, sterilizes the wort, inactivates mash enzymes and reduces the volume of wort to your desired batch size through evaporation.

Obviously, a good boil is predicated on the heat source being adequate. Steam boilers are generally more efficient than direct fire burners and in either case, it's important to consider factors (such as altitude) that can affect the net efficiency of the system. To this end, the kettle must achieve the desired evaporation rate during the boil (usually 10 percent per hour). Second, the boil must be rolling and vigorous, so that all parts of the wort have equal contact time with the heating surfaces, otherwise off-flavors may result and protein coagulation will be less. Avoid dead zones in the boil to alleviate these problems.

Whirlpooling. After the boiling, we remove the trub (coagulated protein) and hop debris from the wort. Systems designed for using whole hops may include a hop strainer or separator, but in most small breweries whirlpooling handles all the separation chores. In special cases settling, filtration or centrifugation may be used by brewers at this stage.

To establish the whirlpool, the brewer pumps the just-boiled wort into a special tangential inlet pipe in the whirlpool vessel. This pipe directs the wort along the outside surface of the circular whirlpool wall. Soon all the liquid in the vessel swirls around in a circle. When pumping ends and the swirling wort slows, solid particles collect in a pile at the center of the vessel so that clear wort can be drawn off from the outside edge.

For the whirlpool to function optimally, certain dimensions must be observed in its design. The whirlpool must be perfectly cylindrical and the inlet(s) should run tangentially into the side of it. The whirlpool should have two outlets. One should be high enough above the bottom of the whirlpool to remove the first one-half to two-thirds of the wort. The lower outlet should be mounted on the lower side near the edge of the bottom. The height-to-width ratio of the whirlpool must also be within a certain range for the physical forces acting on the trub particles to have their maximum effect. To get the best whirlpooling effect, the diameter-to-height ratio of the wort in the whirlpool needs to be at least 1:1. This is why I'm not a huge fan of combination brew kettle–whirlpools. The design elements of a good whirlpool and a good brew kettle are basically mutually exclusive. The lone exception to this is the combination brew kettle–whirlpool with an external boiler that I mentioned earlier. This design, however, isn't the most realistic option for start-up breweries. Have the bottom of the whirlpool properly designed for complete (as possible) trub removal. Flat bottoms or whirlpools with a slightly raised center sloping toward a trough around the perimeter have proven very effective.

Before fermentation, we must cool the clarified wort and nearly every craft brewery cools wort with a plate heat exchanger. Here the hot wort runs on one side of a stainless steel plate while cold water or another coolant runs on the other. Heat is transferred from the hot liquid to the cold one.

The plate cooler can be single stage or dual stage, with brewing water serving as the coolant in the first stage and cold water, alcohols, or other coolants in the second stage. With this type of system, it is essential that the number of plates be sufficient to cool the entire batch of wort in less than one hour, that the energy recovery from the hot wort be as complete as possible and the amount of hot brewing water obtained in the process be of the proper temperature and amount. I constantly see small breweries with under-dimensioned plate heat exchangers. If your system is designed right, you should be able to cool your wort in less than an hour and have a hot liquor tank full of sparge-temperature water.

Post-boil wort aeration is also critical for a speedy fermentation with the right balance of aromas and flavors. The aeration of the wort can be carried out at any temperature. Venturi tubes, aerating candles made of ceramic or a sintered metal, or

Process Summary: After boiling, the wort is whirlpooled to help separate clear wort from the trub (coagulated protein) and hop debris.

metal platelets can be used to aerate the wort. Use either sterilized air or pure oxygen for aeration, though in the latter case, take precautions to avoid over-oxygenating the wort, which has a toxic effect on the yeast. You may want to integrate a gauge into the aeration device to monitor the amount of oxygen or air taken up by the wort. This gauge helps ensure that the wort is not under-aerated or to simply control more precisely this parameter of the fermentation, especially when using pure oxygen for aeration.

We have discussed the key elements of the brewhouse but many accessories and essential decisions have been left out, including pumps, motors, piping, valves, meters and gauges, analytical devices, hoses, cleaning equipment, a hot liquor tank and a hop-dosing device. Here again, you'll want an experienced brewer on staff to help with these decisions during brewery development.

FERMENTATION AND MATURATION

When yeast is added to the wort, it soon becomes beer. To ensure that the beer has all the properties we desire, the fermentation needs to be carefully conducted in facilities designed for that purpose.

In the US, most breweries use closed fermentation tanks known as cylindroconical fermenters. These cone-bottom vessels facilitate yeast removal and other chores without having to transfer the entire batch of beer to a different tank. Occasionally you see open fermenters in a small brewery willing to dedicate the space and resources to this specialized approach. For our purposes, we'll focus on the more commonly used closed fermenters.

Any room where fermentations take place should be well ventilated, clean and cool. The walls and ceiling of the fermentation cellar should be smooth and devoid of cracks or slits in which microorganisms could grow. Indeed, the local health department inspector will probably insist that you have food-grade surface finishes in most of the brewery areas. The floor should be structurally stable to hold fermenters and aging tanks and be able to withstand water, detergents and other chemicals while being easy to clean. The floor should be sloped to the drains to avoid areas of standing water.

For chilling, fermenters are jacketed and may be divided into zones that can be separately controlled. Coolant circulates through the jackets with the flow rate regulated either manually or automatically to maintain a specific temperature. Of course regulating temperature by hand can be tricky and thermo-

THOUGHTS ON BREWHOUSE DESIGN

As the altar of any brewery, the brewhouse is often ornately designed. If brewpub customers have a ready view of the brewhouse, copper or copper-clad brewing vessels may be a worthwhile investment. Remember that in every brewery, tours often help to sell your beer so the brewhouse should be both neat and accessible. This also benefits brewers in their work. A tidy, roomy brewery facilitates productivity more than one that is crowded and unkempt.

Just because a brewhouse is opulently beautiful does not mean it economically produces great beer. Ultimately, you should give the technical performance of the brewhouse top priority when making a purchasing decision. The two factors that drive brewhouse selection should be the quantity and quality of the wort produced. Quantity is measured by brewhouse efficiency or the effectiveness with which extract is harvested from the malt during brewing. Here, values in the 75 to 85 percent range are common for small brewery systems. And quality comes down to the flavor and consistency of the finished beer—a feature that can only really be assessed by looking at what other brewers accomplish with systems from the same supplier.

Ultimately, you'll weigh the needs of your brewing operation against your brewhouse budget and also consider your company's cost structure. Shelling out a bit more for an efficient brewhouse that will result in a higher extract yield might pay off down the road in reduced malt costs. Spending more money on a more versatile brewhouse will enable you to brew a greater number of beer styles. Buying a used brewhouse can result in lower capital expenditure, but running costs such as malt, energy and repair may be higher.

static controls are nearly universal today. Larger breweries have controllers linked to a PC that captures data and refines fermentation parameters.

Closed fermenters must be fitted with pressure regulators and pressure/vacuum relief valves. Most small breweries use hoses to connect fermenters with other vessels such as the brewhouse and CIP reservoir, but larger breweries opt for hard piping to make these connections. Flat or round-bottom fermenters require stand pipes to prevent yeast and other sediment being carried with the beer when it is transferred.

After primary fermentation, most beers mature for some period of time before being packaged and distributed. Without cylindroconical fermenters, conditioning requires a transfer from the fermentation tank to some kind of storage tank. With cylindroconicals, the beer remains in the same tank throughout fermentation and maturation.

Clarifying the Beer. Even if you choose to serve unfiltered beers they must be conditioned and clarified to some degree. An overly turbid beer can be objectionable to the customer and even classic cask or bottle-conditioned beers show little if any haze. When you want brilliantly clear beers, augment the natural clarification process with filtration. Midway between these options, finings will improve clarity without filtering.

With patience, natural sedimentation clears most yeast and turbidity in your beer. Finings like Isinglass, gelatin, alginate and silica can be added to aid this process. Most beer achieves its luster through filter systems. Describing the variety of systems in depth transcends the scope of this book, but I will highlight the pros and cons of the two most common systems: diatomaceous earth (DE) and sheet filtration.

When used properly, DE filters clarify beers to a high degree of brilliance. The DE filter is relatively easy to operate and maintain, though practice is required. The DE filter is clearly the most difficult piece of brewing equipment to master. In addition to this frustration, there are a few other things to consider when using DE filtration. DE represents a running cost. Low-quality DE can affect beer flavor and disposal of DE can present a problem in the future. DE is also a hazardous material causing eye and lung irritation. The biggest drawback of DE filtration for craft brewers is all the filters come from Italy, meaning that it's a pain in the you-know-what to get spare parts for them!

Sheet filter systems "polish" beer by lowering turbidity and increasing biological stability. Sheet filter systems require an input that has already been clarified to a great degree, otherwise the filter will clog quickly and the increased costs of filter sheets will not justify their use. Both diatomaceous earth and filter sheets are one-use and, at present, non-recyclable products. Low-porosity filter sheets, though beneficial in maintaining biological stability, remove bitter substances and proteins from the beer, which can damage head retention.

If filtered or non-bottle-conditioned beer is going to be shipped long distances (such as out of the States), consider the biological and chemical-physical stability of the beer, as recalls can close any brewery's doors very quickly. Biological stability can be obtained through filtration, pasteurization, or by adding preservatives to the beer. The use of filtration techniques to achieve biological stability is effective provided aseptic conditions are maintained when packaging the beer. Membrane filters are usually employed and over-filtration must be avoided to prevent flavor stripping.

Pasteurization is somewhat controversial among craft brewers. Some breweries advertise that they don't pasteurize their products. Though chamber and tunnel pasteurizers significantly affect beer flavor, the same cannot always be said for flash pasteurization. I think we'll see more and more small brewers flash pasteurizing in the future.

Carbonation. Once beer has been conditioned, clarified and in some cases stabilized, package it as soon as possible. Before getting to that point, make sure the right amount of the beer's "fifth" ingredient is there: carbonation. Beers can be carbonated by several methods, so let's take a quick look at them all.

My least favorite, yet most common, method for carbonating beer is the carbonating stone. Diffusing CO_2 into finished beer takes place in a bright beer tank, which serves as a buffer between the filter and the packaging equipment. Similar in-line carbonation systems carbonate beer as it's moved into the bright beer tank. The other methods of carbonating beer include tank carbonation and package conditioning.

With tank carbonation the green beer is transferred to aging tanks with a small amount of residual fermentable sugar. The aging tank is closed off so that pressure builds as this residual sugar ferments in the tank and the beer becomes carbonated.

Package-conditioned beer achieves its carbonation by adding priming sugar or wort to relatively flat beer just prior to packaging. This beer must have yeast in it for the secondary fermentation to take place. In my opinion, the best beers in the world are tank or package conditioned.

BEER PACKAGING

Craft brewers deliver their beers in three basic containers: the keg, the bottle or the serving tank. Let's talk about last option first, since it will be the only one considered by most brewpubs.

You'll only use a serving tank to serve beer on-premise at your brewery, so it is limited to brewpubs and others with an active retail operation. This approach presents several advantages. For one, the beer is freshest when served in this manner. Next, it eliminates product losses encountered in kegging or bottling. Ditto for the packaging costs such as labor, water, energy, containers, cleansers and disinfectants, depreciation. And the bar staff loves not having to change kegs on a busy night!

However, you should keep in mind a few important points when you dispense directly from a tank. If the beers are pumped to the taps under pressure, the tanks must be rated according to the operating pressure necessary to move beer to the taps. You also have to make sure to clean the draft lines regularly to prevent the spread of microorganisms from the lines into the tanks. Beers which are slow sellers and remain in the serving tanks for extended periods of time also become infection prone.

While serving from a tank has great cost advantages, packaging breweries usually don't have that option and even brewpubs often want to sell some beer off-premise in a packaged form. In these cases, kegging offers the best option. This method fits very well into the cost structure of a brewery with limited start-up capital and product quality is easier to maintain because the larger container size of a keg reduces oxygen uptake. Kegging lines may be entirely hand operated or they can be fully automated systems requiring virtually no human attendance.

These days nearly every brewery uses a Sankey type keg and the few who still own the older Hoff Stevens–type are rapidly eliminating them. At this point, I think that not having Sankey kegs will be a significant liability in the marketplace.

To get your beer into a keg, you have many options. Many small breweries have homemade kegging systems that work fine. If you want to save on labor and maintain high product quality and consistency, I recommend purchasing a more automated kegging line. Remember draft to bottle ratios for craft brewers are about 50:50 so don't underestimate the importance of your kegs and kegging equipment. Once craft beer consumers try your bottled product and like it, they will seek out the draft version because they perceive draft beer as representing your product at its freshest and highest quality.

Most brewers hate bottling, but find it a necessary evil. Without experienced and trained personnel, it can be like opening Pandora's box.

Most brewers hate bottling, but find it a necessary evil. Without experienced and trained personnel, it can be like opening Pandora's box. Additional problems arise if the equipment is of inferior quality, if the packaging container is unsuitable or if the fixed and running costs have not been carefully calculated. Running a bottling line is one of the most complex aspects of brewery operations. Even if everything has been planned and organized, something will go wrong. To minimize the effect this will have at bottling time, it is best for someone with extensive experience to plan, organize and oversee the bottling plant.

Selecting the rinsing, conveying, bottling, labeling and packaging equipment for a brewery is one of the most painstaking decisions since so much capital will be tied up in this investment. Many purchase used equipment when they first start bottling. Of course someone must evaluate and appraise the equipment in a knowledgeable manner. I don't want to digress into a lengthy discussion about packaging equipment, but I will say that I've seen some of the biggest mistakes made by breweries who have purchased inferior equipment or the Rolls Royce when a Honda would have sufficed. If distributing in a one-hundred-mile radius and/or your beer's shelf life doesn't have to be that long, don't be oversold on unneeded technology. Always buy a good labeler. First impressions are critical.

Carefully chose your bottle, as it can affect cost structure and the taste of the beer. The chosen bottle must appeal to the target market as well. Have an experienced person accurately calculate the costs of operating and installing the bottling line. Account for various scenarios and make calculations for all situations, including the worst case, which foresees the packaging line operating at its least efficient state.

In certain cases beer is "packaged" in large dairy-type trucks for transport to a packaging line (contract bottling), or the truck itself can serve as the dispensing unit at large-scale events. Both practices occur commonly in Europe and have potential for small brewers in North America, even though these options are rarely available today.

Aside from the packaging equipment itself, the design of the packaging area must be well thought out. A bottling line requires a lot of electrical power, so install outlets and wiring accordingly. A packaging area can get very warm, so appropriately ventilate or air condition it. Lay out the machines in a sensible manner so product and package flow lines are as efficient as possible. Also, place them in a manner that keeps the noise intensity to a minimum for the workers. Don't forget about warehousing both empty and filled bottles. Like I said earlier, I've seen a lot of breweries underestimate this area's storage space.

POWERING AND COOLING THE BREWERY

A common preliminary budgeting mistake is to plan for all the brewing equipment and even some of the peripheral accessories, but to neglect steam, air, CO_2, electricity, fossil fuels and water which make it all work. When we started the Tabernash brewery, refrigeration equipment, a steam boiler, an air compressor and a water treatment system were 15 percent of the start-up budget. Utilities and CO2 make up well over 10 percent of the variable cost of producing beer. And while larger breweries have made great strides in reducing energy usage, small brewers aren't as efficient. If possible, consider steps you could take to conserve energy, water and raw materials in your brewery. Sometimes this involves a capital expenditure that may seem unjustified, but often the extra expense may be amortized in a short period of time by decreased energy and water costs.

Brewery size largely dictates how it will be powered. A small brewpub might have a direct, gas-fired brew kettle and a hot-water heater and large, multi-million-barrel breweries might have their own power plants. For packaging breweries the best answer lies somewhere in between. A steam boiler is often a good choice, as process steam is needed not only for heating the brewing vessels, but also for packaging lines and sterilization.

> Breweries do a great deal of heating and cooling in the process of making beer. Specialized utilities usually supply the needed thermal resources.

Steam boilers come in a variety of shapes and sizes. Keep a few things in mind when deciding on what type of steam boiler to install. High-pressure steam boilers are more efficient, but they also cost more. In most places local codes require a full-time certified boiler operator be on hand when the boiler is operating. There's no reason why one or more of the brewers can't obtain certification. High-pressure (i.e., high-temperature) steam is also better for sterilizing than low-pressure steam. If you're a brewpub or small-scale brewer, a low-pressure boiler is adequate. Boilers usually require water treatment of some kind, particularly high-pressure boilers. By the time you add in piping, a condensate system, insulation and a chemical feed system, you can easily double the price of what you would have paid for the boiler alone.

Refrigeration systems offer fewer choices because using ammonia as a refrigerant as large breweries do is out of the question.

The brewer has a choice when selecting the condenser, evaporator and coolant. If the cost of water is prohibitively high, an air-cooled condenser is the best option. In Colorado we're obligated to use air-cooled or evaporative systems. Otherwise, water-cooled condensers are standard equipment. Water at the freezing point is a good coolant because it is cheap, chemically inert and can be stored in large quantities in an ice bath. This is advantageous when it is time to cool the wort. Brine mixtures are often implemented and alcohol-water mixtures are a very popular coolant choice among small brewers to lower the coolant temperature well below 32° F (0° C). In either case, take precautions to avoid corrosion of the cooling system. Non-corrosive brines are available, but they are more expensive than the chloride-based brines. Add inhibitors to alcohol-water mixtures to prevent corrosion.

All but the tiniest and simplest packaging breweries will need a source of compressed air. At Tabernash we used compressed air to operate pneumatic valves, to raise and lower our lauter tun rakes, to operate our kegging machine and to aerate our wort. To preserve the life of our equipment we have water coalescers for the compressed air. To preserve the integrity of our beer, we also have an oil coalescer and an in-line sterile filter just prior to wort aeration.

A source of CO_2 is also necessary. CO_2 is used for dispensing keg beer, pressurizing tanks, purging equipment and transfer lines of air, operating packaging equipment and carbonating beer. Unless your brewery is tiny, you probably want to avoid using fifty-pound cylinders. Bulk tanks usually offer a less expensive way of having five hundred pounds on reserve. Some brewers consider tanks larger than this. The investment won't be cheap, but if you use a lot of CO_2, it will pay for itself quickly through lower CO_2 cost per pound. It's also critical to have appropriate gauges and regulators at each point that the CO_2 is used.

THE LABORATORY

No matter how small or simple a brewery may be, some sort of laboratory analyses are conducted. Of course measuring density and temperature are the bare bones minimum that every brewery needs to have and that is quite simple. Some means of measuring pH is also extremely useful. A lot can be done to improve quality and consistency if pH is measured at a few key steps in the beer-making process. Every brewery should also do some basic microscopy to determine the biological quality of its beer. Using culture media to screen for wild yeast and beer-spoiling bacteria is another way of monitoring quality and consistency and is also a good reason to have a basic laboratory. At the bare minimum, use microscopy in conjunction with media tests to evaluate the yeast culture, green beer, filtered beer and packaged beer. Ideally, conduct culture tests at each step of the post–brewhouse production process to ensure the brewery and beer are free from infection.

Also consider malt analyses and if you lack the equipment needed to analyze your malt, independent labs are of service. If even only periodic, these tests help monitor the quality of brewing ingredients and serve as a basis for comparing the lab values that the suppliers provide against those found in an independent analysis. Analyses of the grist are both inexpensive and informative if yields are off or if conversion isn't achieved in the brewhouse. Analyses of spent grains are also simple and very informative in this regard.

If you bottle or keg beer, it is wise to conduct tests to indicate the foreseeable shelf life of the beer, air uptake during the filtering and bottling processes and if the desired degree of carbonation has been achieved. The possible analyses don't end here, but a craft brewery's budget probably won't include more complicated and specific analyses.

CONCLUSION

In this chapter, we have reviewed the common processes of brewing and the equipment commonly used to perform those steps in a craft brewery. While no two breweries will ever be exactly alike, this analysis establishes the basic framework for any new brewery and identifies those topics that need research and attention during the planning and start-up phases of development. In the next chapter, we'll begin to look at broader issues related to the brewery such as site selection, building modifications and staffing.

Chapter Eleven

Building Your Brewery From Site to Staff

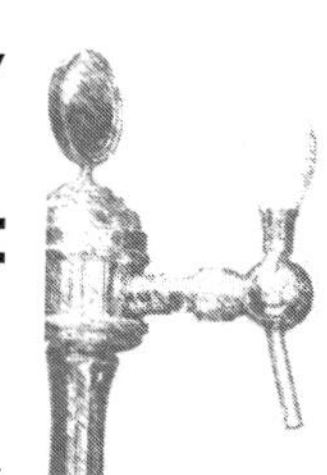

Important details for creating an efficient brewery capable of making world class beer.

by Eric Warner

WHILE YOU CAN'T NEGLECT PLANNING, distribution, marketing and sales, the brewery and the beer you produce remain the cornerstone of any successful brewing company. You must achieve quality and consistency, particularly if the beer is packaged and distributed beyond your own premises. You'll find these goals easier to achieve if you buy the best brewing equipment available. But as with all things, some compromises must be made. As a general rule, I advise people to save money on tanks and peripheral equipment. During start-up of Tabernash Brewing Company we saved hundreds of thousands of dollars on fermentation and storage tanks by purchasing reconditioned stainless steel tanks. We also bought second-hand refrigeration equipment, chemical tanks, fork lifts, etc. Try not to skimp on the equipment that has a lot of moving parts and a direct impact on the quality of your beer. We purchased our brewhouse, filter, pumps, hoses and packaging equipment new.

The same probably holds true for the building your brewery will be housed in. Everybody would love to have a tiled, copper brewhouse with a beautiful pub nestled in some pristine mountain valley. But reality means you'll probably end up renting space in "the up and coming" part of town. Unless you're an expert at balancing unlimited desires, financial reality and what it really takes to make great beer, you'll have to find somebody to help you sort it all out. In order to operate a safe, efficient brewery that makes great beer, you'll need somebody on board capable of evaluating and selecting the right facility, the best equipment your money can buy and the raw materials needed to make your beer. Suppliers and consultants can be of service, but someone within the organization should know brewing and packaging. It helps if this person understands the architectural and engineering issues involved with a brewery. They should also know the laws and regulations governing the brewery and production processes and have some grounding in waste and environmental issues as a bonus. And, if this dream brewer has been through it all once before at another brewery, hire him or her right away.

SITE SELECTION

The physical location of the brewery can influence brewing procedures, equipment choices, process steps and ultimately the quality of the beer itself. If a possible site lies seven thousand feet above sea level, consider the reduced boiling temperature of water at this elevation. Overlooking this simple law of physics can result in improper equipment choices and bad beer. Or let's say you want to start your dream brewery on a tropical island. Water could be very expensive, or you may find you have to desalinate ocean water or build huge catch basins for rain water.

Evaluate a site in terms of water quantity, quality and accessibility, all of which greatly influence production costs. A brewery I consulted with in northern Canada had to truck water from a local river for brewing. In January they needed an ice auger in addition to their tanker truck, hoses and pump.

Ambient microflora cannot be taken lightly. Breweries built near a vineyard or orchard may have infection problems due to high concentrations of bacteria and wild yeast from these crops. Incorporate the area's climate into the evaluation of possible brewery locations. The difference between refrigeration costs for a brewery in Phoenix and one in Toronto are staggering.

Having prior brewery start-up experience on your team will help you get the most bang for the buck. Engineering and architectural expenses can pile up quickly if you have to buy all the expertise you need from consultants. In the worst case scenario architects and engineers overdesign the facility and bill you for the privilege.

If your head brewer capably manages the brewery construction process, including budgeting, working with architects and engineers, managing contractors and selecting the right equipment, you can save money by employing that brewer for six to twelve months before you make your first batch of beer. From another angle, if the brewer must operate the brewery, then it makes sense that he or she designs it. If your expertise is in sales, marketing, finance, or something other than manufacturing, consider investing the money up front and finding somebody who can build a brewery that will require the least amount of capital to make the best beer as economically as possible.

THE BUILDING

In all likelihood, you won't build your brewery from the ground up which means it won't come ideally suited for brewing and packaging. In this case, you'll need to adapt the structure to the brewing process with alterations—sometimes major ones. You should consult with engineers, contractors, equipment suppliers and building inspectors before acquiring a building. They can evaluate the building's stability (remember, one barrel of water at 60 degrees F weighs 258 pounds!), adaptability and suitability as a brewery. They can also estimate the costs for modifying the building in order to brew and comply with building codes.

Some of the points you'll examine when looking at a building include: ceiling height, insulation, door and entryway widths, floor structure and strength, shipping and receiving areas (dock-high doors!) and floor composition. Brewery floors must withstand stress, beer, caustic and corrosive substances as well as traffic. (See related chapter on floors in this section.) Ensure that the building is free of insects and rodents, as these pests are costly to eradicate. Determine the soundness and dimensions of the facility for plumbing, electricity, gas, sewage, etc. In some areas, buildings must also meet the standards of applicable seismic codes.

Don't take the available cubic footage in a building choice lightly. A building with a high cubic to square foot ratio becomes attractive when its rent is lower than other buildings in the area, square footage is somewhat smaller than optimally desired, or when taller pieces of brewery equipment like cylindro-conical fermentation tanks are planned in the brewery design. With a little imagination and reconstruction, a building that seems too small can be modified to better utilize the available space.

Most start-up breweries fall short when planning space for dry and finished goods storage.

Most start-up breweries fall short when planning space for dry and finished goods storage. Once sized, the brewhouse and fermenter space requirements are clear. But projecting the space required by malt, empty kegs, bottles, pallets and finished cases of beer is a much different story. Here a high cubic-to-square foot ration is extremely advantageous. Storing raw materials or finished goods off-site is fine. Companies do it all the time all over the world and it's not a frustrating "gotcha" if you plan for it.

Oh, did I forget the biggest consideration in selecting the best location for your brewery? Rent is crucial. You have to remember that in all likelihood your brewery (I'm talking about packaging breweries, not pubs here) will not be profitable for at least two to three years. The difference between $2 and $5 per square foot over that period for a five-thousand-square-foot facility is $30,000 to $45,000. If you're paying more rent, you should get more out of your facility. It would be worthwhile if it includes refrigeration equipment, floor drains or sanitary finishes on floors, walls and ceilings. I personally believe in using capital to transform a low-rent shell into a brewery rather than taking on a large monthly rent obligation for a ready-made facility.

A lot of this thinking applies to brewpubs, the retail nature of that business must be considered. Location plays a much greater role for restaurants. Thus, high rents can pay off if they enable premium pricing and generate customers traffic. Also, look at brewpub facilities for their aesthetic qualities as well as practical considerations.

Finally, keep in mind future expansion needs—especially for a packaging brewery. Weigh the costs of excess floor space in the short term against the capital costs of building an entire new brewery in the future. Sometimes nearby space may become available from time to time as it did for Tabernash. That brewery was located in a multi-unit building with a lot of month-to-month tenants.

DESIGN AND EQUIPMENT FOR THE BREWERY

In the previous chapter, we reviewed the essential brewery processes and the equipment that gets the job done. As noted there, that description omits scores of important details, so you'll need a lot of additional hard work and diligence to decide which equipment to buy. Eventually you'll start talking to suppliers and face a decision about which one to give your money to. Here I'd like to mention a few issues to keep in mind when working with those vendors.

The most important criterion in choosing a supplier is your faith in their commitment to helping you resolve problems you encounter when using their equipment. Sometimes malfunctions are due to the equipment, but other times your or your brewer's ineptitude or confusion cause them. Most suppliers warranty their equipment, but the guys who will walk you through a problem that is no fault of the equipment are your best bets.

This rule assumes you've decided on two or three potential suppliers. If there's only one game in town for a certain piece of equipment, then your decision is easy. In most cases you will decide between two to three suppliers and the following criteria will help you choose. I definitely recommend checking the equipment manufacturer's reputation. Call breweries who previously purchased equipment from your prospective suppliers. Remember, if you ask the suppliers for a reference list, it is unlikely they will refer you to unsatisfied customers. Do some digging on your own and answer the following questions: Has the equipment been reliable and economical? Are the beers from breweries using this equipment flavorful and clean (although this is not entirely dependent on the brewery itself)? Is the service and support from this supplier good? Are they charging different customers the same price for the same equipment? Are they timely with their production and delivery schedules? Are they truly a turnkey supplier, if they tout that? Does the equipment do what they say it will?

The most important criterion in choosing a supplier is your faith in their commitment to helping you resolve problems you encounter when using their equipment.

Other things to bear in mind are the flexibility or expandability of the equipment or system. A total turnkey brewery or a metrically fitted brewery may not be compatible with future equipment purchases. Spare parts should be readily available for the system. The Italian filters are the worst in this regard — stock spare parts for these filters. Finally, the equipment should meet all electrical, health, construction, plumbing and safety standards before being purchased.

A common question among beginning breweries is whether or not to go "turnkey". This approach leaves the hundreds of small decisions and overall coordination of elements with the vendor rather than putting them on you. The idea is that the vendor delivers and installs a complete system that is ready to operate.

My advice on turnkey systems is this: if you're a brewpub and don't have a knowledgeable brewer on staff, go turnkey. If you're a packaging brewery, you must usually piece together your brewery using various suppliers, just because no one company makes everything you'll need.

A particularly cloudy area concerns accessories like hoses and pumps. Many equipment manufacturers will sell them, but since they are just reselling someone else's products you may save money by going to the source yourself. In either case it's important to make sure that the size of the equipment is matched in each step of the brewing process. Going turnkey, you will usually get a malt mill that matches the mash tun, which matches the brew kettle, which matches the fermenter and so on. Designing the brewery on your own definitely necessitates having someone who is at least familiar with the big picture.

ORCHESTRATING BEER STYLES WITH BREWERY DESIGN

The style of beer you want to brew is largely a decision to make on your own. Market research can give some indication of this style, but cases can be made for brewing ales, lagers, or both. Don't make this decision without considering the costs of both. Common arguments for brewing ales are lower production time and reduced refrigeration costs. Though this is a valid rule of thumb, note that a thoroughly attenuated, high-quality lager beer can be produced in four to five weeks at temperatures only slightly lower than those of top-fermented beers.

What must be clear from the outset are the chosen fermentation parameters. A classically brewed lager could take up to ten weeks to ferment and condition, whereas a more modern fermentation might require only twenty-four days to produce the same style of beer. This difference forces the brewery to consider the capacity of the fermentation and lager tanks. It also means refrigeration costs will differ in these two cases. Though ales generally require less time to attenuate than lagers, fermentation parameters of top-fermented beers must also be matched with projected output in terms of fermentation and storage vessels and the cost structure of the planned brewery.

Also consider brewhouse design when deciding on beer styles. Adjunct brewing requires more intense mashing than all-malt brews. If you want to produce a light Pilsener-style beer, the system should have as little oxygen uptake as possible to avoid unwanted deepening of color and taste. All of these issues should be considered before deciding on the final specifications for the brewing system you need to purchase.

STAFFING THE BREWERY

Craft breweries often begin as small operations without the funds needed to staff each individual department, area of accountability or specific job. Sometimes owners and investors work long hours performing a variety of tasks in every department of the brewery. Ideally this is part of the impetus for owning and operating your own brewery. However, hard work alone is seldom enough to start and maintain a successful brewery. Knowledge and experience are essential for planning and making decisions, not only on the technical end of the brewery but on the business side as well.

Brewing is an art requiring a bit of feeling and touch but is also a science requiring some insight into the technology involved in making and packaging beer.

Brewing is an art requiring a bit of feeling and touch but is also a science requiring some insight into the technology involved in making and packaging beer. Individuals who have little more than extensive homebrewing experience operate many successful breweries. Just as many breweries have encountered difficulties because of inexperience in operating a facility in which hundreds of thousands (if not millions) of dollars have been invested. Just because someone has extensive experience or education as a brewer doesn't mean they are the best person for the job. There are a number of possibilities for staffing a brewery and in the end no one solution may be any better or worse than the next. Do an extensive analysis of what tasks must be performed, what qualifications are necessary, what the labor cost structure of the company can tolerate and most importantly, who will receive a paycheck from the brewery for working there.

If certain tasks in the brewery remain uncovered, someone within the company must augment their knowledge and skill, or you must tap some external source. In this case there are a number of options. For one, equipment suppliers often provide a great deal of support to their customers if they are service oriented and financially compensated for providing this service. Buying more expensive brewery equipment may be justified if the equipment suppliers are helpful and supportive not only during brewery installation, but after the operation is up and running.

Another option is to hire a consultant to help design and install the brewery, formulate the beers, educate the personnel, provide troubleshooting assistance, or locate qualified brewers. Caution must be taken, as dishonest consultants have burned many. Research the background of any consultant or supplier you may employ. A popular option is to hire a "brewmaster" to plan, organize and operate the brewery. As with suppliers and consultants, brewmasters come in all shapes and sizes with varying degrees of education, experience and success. It is best to seek out a brewer or brewmaster who is affordable and best qualified to execute the tasks required.

The craft brewing industry has a high potential for growth, otherwise you probably wouldn't be reading this. You will obviously hand select your first employees, but where a lot of growing companies drop the ball is how and who they hire during the hyper-growth years. I've built the finest production team in the country by using a combination of good draft choices and key free-agent acquisitions. I "scouted" my draft choices by letting people "apprentice" in the brewery for a short period of time. I can see how they work and the other brewers can see what they're like to work with. It's not always easy to build a winning team on draft picks alone, so occasionally I'll pick up a free agent. Sometimes direct experience is great, but other times relevant experience is just as good, if not better. Promoting from within is also something we try to do as much as possible. One of my brewers used to be a delivery driver. They key thing is to select the best people possible who are in strong accord with the mission or goal of the company.

Of course brewers don't work for beer and smiles alone. Usually the best people also get paid the most, but balance this with maintaining production efficiency. One strategy we employ at Tabernash is an employee stock option plan. If departments and the entire company meet certain goals, we grant options. This is a good way of conserving cash, keeping key people and most importantly, giving employees a feeling of being critical to the company accomplishing its goals. What type of wage you pay your brewery personnel all comes down to your business philosophies. Remember, however, that labor will be one of your top three cost areas for beer production. But before you get any ideas of paying your brewers minimum wage, remember it is very expensive to train new people.

The supply of trained brewers is catching up with the industry's demand in North America. Five years ago it was a much different story, but now there's a good crop of journeymen brewers and those who have completed brewing programs at universities or institutes. Take your time, there's a big pool of good people. Ultimately your brewer has to be qualified, a team player and you have to be able to work with him or her.

One final tip: If you run across someone who can weld, has experience as a plumber, carpenter, mechanic, mason and electrician, can fix your car, makes great coffee and knows where all the best fishing holes are, hire him or her on the spot. A brewery is full of all kinds of machines, plumbing and structures that will require repair at some inopportune time. If a full-time and capable employee is on hand at the moment of malfunction, hundreds if not thousands of dollars can be saved.

THE FIRST BREWS

Once you have installed the equipment, placated the building inspectors and can't stand another day of all that money going out with none coming in, experimental brewing can begin. Here you'll design recipes for the system and then modify them based on empirical observations of the initial brews. Recipes should not be scaled upward linearly from small-scale experimental brews, as yields will increase with brewhouse size and sophistication. This is particularly true with hop yields. Our first batch of our assertively hopped helles ended up like a Pils, even after I had compensated for an increase in hop yield. If you buy a small brewery, don't expect to get stellar yields from your malt. If your brewery is larger and has been built by a top manufacturer, you should be able to achieve performance that equals their promised standards.

If you plan to make many different beers, you won't be able to test each one. But you should make a few brews before you plan to produce beer for sale to ensure the production process will run smoothly and that finished beers will be of the desired taste and quality. The type of brewery warrants the intensity of test brewing to a large extent. Even if equipment is able to be cleaned-in-place (CIP), it is best to manually clean as much of the equipment as possible before the first use and initiation of the CIP systems. Some like to conduct water brews prior to brewing.

Common problems to look for in test brews are poor head retention, metallic flavors and a rubbery-plastic taste. A free-standing brewery making one product to be marketed over a large area must perfect the process until product consistency is achieved. The allure of local brewpubs lies in the fact that each brew is a bit different from the next, so the test brews themselves can usually be sold unless they have yielded an undrinkable beer. Touting the beer as the "very first beer ever made from our brewpub" should generate sufficient interest in the product.

Of course nearly every aspect of brewery building takes longer than you think it should or will. Remember this when testing your equipment. If you're lucky, delays may only be a few hours or a day. With bigger systems like a high-tech bottling line, it may take months before the system has all of the bugs worked out of it. The key thing to know is how long it will take before the system is functional enough to do what it's supposed to and produce the quality product you look for.

BREWERY BYPRODUCTS AND ENVIRONMENTAL ISSUES

The brewing process generates many byproducts and wastes in all three physical states: solid, liquid and gaseous. Consider how to use, recycle or dispose of these products. Brewing and packaging beer also requires a great deal of energy. Take measures to recover heat and reduce energy consumption wherever possible.

The most readily apparent brewery byproducts are the solid ones, most notably spent grains, grain dust, hot trub, spent hop cones, excess yeast and diatomaceous earth (DE). Many of these can be used as livestock feed, which is the most common procedure for disposing of brewery byproducts. The spent grains have long been used as an inexpensive source of protein and carbohydrates for livestock. Many breweries sell spent grains to local farmers or feed producers and even if local farmers don't pay for the spent grains, they will at least come and remove them at no charge, saving the brewery disposal costs. Breweries nestled in the midst of urban sprawl may have difficulties with disposal, as farmers are not often interested in a long drive to the city for a small amount of grain. One solution is to store the grains until enough have accumulated to make it worth the drive. A spent grain silo is typically used for storage, but it must be hosed out and cleaned regularly, as rotting spent grains host large, offensive-smelling colonies of microorganisms.

The brewing process generates many byproducts and wastes in all three physical states: solid, liquid and gaseous. Consider how to use, recycle or dispose of these products.

Trub matter from the brewhouse is rich in protein and is a valuable agricultural product. Due to the extreme bitterness of the hot trub, it must be sparingly dosed into the rest of the feed or else the animals will reject it. Some breweries even use the hot trub in the next mash to leach the remaining extract and bittering substances from it. Farmers or the pharmaceutical and cosmetics industries can also use spent or excess yeast. Smaller breweries have to rely on giving the yeast to farmers for it to be meted into the feed in small amounts. An overdose of yeast will give livestock stomach problems and deplete the animals' vitamin supply. Do not simply waste the yeast down the drain as it places an extremely high biological oxygen demand (BOD) on the local waste-water treatment facility. You may get away with it for awhile, but eventually they will track you down and suggest that you start paying for that privilege. If the yeast is put directly into a local stream or lake, it will contribute to the oxygen depletion of these waterways. DE is basically like sand and washing it down the drain is not the best idea. Stock can digest the yeast/DE mixture, or it can be disposed of as solid waste.

One of the most troublesome brewery byproducts is the liquid waste, namely wastewater and beer. The brewing process requires five to ten times more water than the amount of beer produced. An efficient, conscientious brewery strives for five times the water, while a sloppy, poorly managed operation will use ten times. Even if fresh water is cheap and waste water isn't taxed by volume, the brewery should strive for minimal water usage. The day will soon come when water is no longer cheap and bad habits are hard to change. You can decrease water usage without compromising beer quality in a number of ways. An easy way to save water is repair all leaks immediately. "We'll take care of that tomorrow" turns into next week, then next month and so on. Another solution is to avoid oversparging. Also, a properly sized heat exchanger for wort cooling yields only as much water (or slightly more) as the amount of wort being cooled. CIP systems that recycle detergent and rinse water for prewash purposes can reduce usage of cleaning water. The water hog in any brewery is the bottle washer. The water can be recycled for first rinse water, cleaning vehicles, flushing toilets, washing floors, etc. Bear in mind the more fresh water that is used, the higher the effluent will be.

Gaseous brewery byproducts come in two main forms: CO_2 from fermentation and smoke from the boiler or direct fire burner. Carbon dioxide recovery only works for breweries who produce fifty thousand barrels of beer per annum.

When it comes to combustion exhaust, breweries large and small can have an impact. Local and federal laws dictate how clean boiler vapors must be. Natural gas is currently the cleanest fuel used to power breweries, as it produces virtually no sulfur dioxide, a leading cause of acid rain. The boiler should also operate with the proper air-to-fuel ratio in the burn. If it is not optimal, nitrous oxide and hydrocarbon emissions will be higher than needed and fuel consumption will increase. Catalytic converters, filters and desulfurication plants are a few examples of how emissions can be reduced or converted into less harmful compounds.

Ensuring efficient boiler function is only one of many ways to reduce energy usage. Boilers can be designed very efficiently in terms of primary energy usage. Designs that maximize the thoroughness of the burn and use flue gases to preheat the air or feed water are helpful in this area. Brewhouse design has the greatest influence on primary energy usage of any brewery department. Basic insulation of vessels and piping is an easy way to save energy.

Simple designs that either boil under pressure and/or recover the heat in vapors from the brew kettle will reduce primary energy input. Overboiling increases energy usage and only under certain conditions — such as high coagulable protein amounts in the wort, high altitude breweries, or high levels of DMS precursor — should wort be boiled longer than one hundred minutes. Larger breweries may consider a system that incorporates an external boiler with vapor compression. A properly designed wort chiller attains maximal heat recovery. If pasteurization is considered, then flash pasteurization is the clear choice. It is the most efficient form of pasteurization in terms of heat recovery and is the least detrimental to beer flavor.

With increasing public awareness of environmental issues, every brewery must be concerned with public reaction to the facility and soundness of the brewing procedures. It also makes good bottom-line sense to operate as efficiently as possible.

CONCLUSION

This chapter concludes our overview of brewery planning and operations. In subsequent chapters in this section, other brewers and technical specialists review key issues in further depth to help expand your knowledge of the many details involved in a new brewery installation.

Chapter Twelve

Uncle Sam Comes Calling

An orientation to Federal brewery regulations and how to get started acquiring the needed permits.

By Pete Johnson

ONE OF THE MOST IMPORTANT INITIAL understandings any new brewery/brewpub owner needs to come to, is that the alcohol industry is one of the most highly regulated industries in America. This chapter focuses on the federal regulatory authority known as the Alcohol and Tobacco Tax and Trade Bureau (commonly referred to as TTB), and is meant to provide a summary overview and introduction of the regulatory role of the agency for those planning to open and operate a brewery. And even though TTB's authority covers issues related to alcohol, tobacco and firearms, I'll only refer to alcohol in this text even though certain authorities span all three areas.

The information in this article was largely drawn directly from TTB, specifically from the web site www.ttb.gov. That's good news for you, because it means that most of the information you'll need is easily accessible, including easy-to-use online forms. At the end of this article is a list of specific web resources within the TTB site.

One other note before we begin. Just as every business situation will be unique, laws, regulations and court interpretations constantly change the legal landscape through which any business must navigate. This is not meant to be a blueprint to follow blindly, but rather an overview of the major areas any brewery operator will need to be familiar with. As you get into the process, you will find it necessary and invaluable to establish a dialogue with TTB personnel. You will want to be a regular visitor to the TTB web site which in addition to being an excellent resource is an essential news source about changes in the legal and regulatory landscape.

The Homeland Security Act of 2002 created TTB as a new and separate agency under the Department of the Treasury, splitting its functions from the Bureau of Alcohol, Tobacco and Firearms. In its own words, TTB's mission is "to collect taxes owed, and to ensure that alcohol beverages are produced, labeled, advertised and marketed in accordance with Federal law. Our objectives are to protect the revenue, protect the consumer and promote voluntary compliance." TTB headquarters is located in Washington, DC, and the other major location is the National Revenue Center (NRC) in Cincinnati, OH. TTB also maintains seven field offices and laboratory facilities in several locations.

In a nutshell, the Bureau ensures tax and trade compliance with the Federal Alcohol Administration Act (FAA Act) and the Internal Revenue Code (IRC), the two primary governing statutory authorities outlining the responsibilities of the TTB.

The FAA Act provides for regulation of those engaged in the alcohol beverage industry, and for protection of consumers. To ensure the integrity of the industry, the FAA Act includes provisions to:

- Require a permit for those who engage in the business as a producer, importer, or wholesaler of alcohol beverages;
- Issue, suspend, and revoke permits;
- Ensure the integrity of the industry by preventing persons who are not likely to operate in accordance with the law from entering the trade; and
- Protect the revenue and consumers by ensuring the integrity of the industry members.

To protect consumers, FAA Act provisions:

- Ensure that labeling and advertising of alcohol beverages provide adequate information to the consumer concerning the identity and quality of the product;
- Require that alcohol beverages bottlers and importers must have an approved certificate of label approval (COLA) or an exemption certificate before the product may be sold in the United States; and
- Prevent misleading labeling or advertising that may result in the potential for consumer deception regarding the product.

The FAA Act also includes provisions to preclude unfair trade practice:

- Regulate the marketing promotional practices concerning the sale of alcohol beverages; and
- Regulate practices such as exclusive outlets, tied house arrangements, commercial bribery and consignment sales.

Under the IRC, Chapter 51 provides for excise taxation and authorizes operations of alcohol producers. Specific provisions include:

- Classification of alcohol products for excise tax purposes;
- Permits methods of operation for breweries, wineries, distilleries and industrial alcohol producers and users;
- Regulation of the operations of breweries, wineries, and distilleries; and
- Regulation of the production, packaging, bottling, labeling and storage requirements related to these commodities.

Finally, TTB also administers and enforces the Alcohol Beverage Labeling Act (mandating that a government warning statement appear on all alcohol beverages for sale or distribution in the U.S.) and the Webb-Kenyon Act (prohibiting the shipment of alcohol beverages into a state in violation of the receiving state's laws).

> You will want to be a regular visitor to the TTB web site which in addition to being an excellent resource is an essential news source about changes in the legal and regulatory landscape.

GETTING STARTED WITH THE TTB

So, you want to establish and operate a brewery. Your first stop is the National Revenue Center in Cincinnati. Upon request (the NRC's toll free number is 1-800-398-2282), TTB will send you a packet of information and forms that will get the ball rolling. There are about a dozen items (depending on your particular circumstances) that you will need to provide in this initial round. The key items you'll be concerned with are the Brewer's Notice and the Brewer's Bond.

Brewer's Notice (Form 5130.10) - Basic information about location, type and size of operation, business structure, diagram and legal description of brewery premises, and a statement describing security at the brewery. Additionally, the following forms must also be included with the filing of an original notice:

Supplemental Information on Water Quality Considerations (Form 5000.30) – Relating to water discharges.

Personnel Questionnaire (Form 5000.9) – Used to determine eligibility and suitability of applicant to engage in the TTB-regulated business.

Environmental Information (Form 5000.29) – Information relating to heat and power (types and sources), solid and liquid waste and noise.

Brewer's Bond (Form 5130.22) or **Brewer's Collateral Bond** (Form 5130.25) - The bond represents the brewery's and the surety's (basically, an insurance company that provides the bond and ensures payment of the brewery's liability) promise to pay the applicable taxes on all beer, including any penalties and interest that may become due.

Your first stop is the National Revenue Center in Cincinnati. Upon request (the NRC's toll free number is 1-800-398-2282), TTB will send you a packet of information and forms that will get the ball rolling.

The bond amount equals 10% of the maximum tax liability for a calendar year, with a minimum of $1,000 and a maximum of $500,000. TTB offers assistance in determining the proper amount of the bond at 1-877-882-3277.

In filing a Brewer's Bond, you agree to the following conditions appearing on Form 5130.22:

Liability as a brewery: I am liable for taxes on all beer removed for consumption or sale, including beer that I:

- transfer from this brewery to other breweries or pilot brewing plants that I control;
- import in bulk and remove from customs custody for transfer to my internal revenue bond;
- remove without payment of tax for export or for vessels or aircraft supplies but which is not exported or used as authorized; and
- remove without payment of tax for authorized research, development or testing relating to beer I brew, produce or receive.

You must also attach a power of attorney from the surety company. TTB also suggests a Department of Treasury resource for identifying a surety company at www.fms.treas.gov/c570/index.html

OTHER ITEMS

You may have to file one or more forms or documents pertaining to corporate structure, how you decide to handle signing authority, if the brewery will be part of a controlled group and if your brewery premises falls under the National Historic Preservation Act. Finally, if your business has not already done so, you will need to apply for an Employer Identification Number (EIN) with the Internal Revenue Service.

Once you've received TTB approval on these items, you will have to file other applications and forms depending on the types (e.g. formulas) and number (e.g. COLA's) of products you brew and also regularly complete excise tax filings.

Formula and Process for Domestic and Imported Alcohol Beverages (Form 5100.51) - Formulas are required whenever a brewer intends to produce a fermented product that will be treated by any processing, filtration, or other method of manufacture that is not generally recognized as a traditional process in the production of a fermented beverage designated as "beer," "ale," "porter," "stout," "lager," or "malt liquor." This information consists of both a detailed and specific quantitative list of each ingredient in the product and a step-by-step description of the production process.

Some examples of non-traditional processes that typically require the filing of a formula:

- removal of any volume of water from beer;
- filtration of beer to substantially change the color, flavor, or character;
- separation of beer into different components;
- reverse osmosis;
- concentration of beer; and
- ion exchange treatments

Some examples of traditional processes for which, generally, no formula is required:

- pasteurization;
- filtration prior to bottling;
- filtration in lieu of pasteurization;
- centrifuging for clarity;
- lagering;
- carbonation; and
- blending

Additionally, formulas are generally required for:

- any fermented product to which flavors or other non-beverage ingredients (other than hop extract) containing alcohol will be added;
- any fermented product to which coloring or natural or artificial flavors will be added;
- any fermented product to which fruit, fruit juice, fruit concentrate, herbs, spices, honey, maple syrup, or other food materials will be added; and
- saké

At a minimum, information on the volume and alcohol content of the malt beverage base, identification and source of any flavoring material used in the product, the maximum volume and alcohol content of each flavoring material used in the product, the percentage of alcohol contributed by the flavor(s) to

FURTHER RESOURCES:

Alcohol Rules and Regulations:
www.ttb.gov/rulesandregulations.htm

TTB publications:
www.ttb.gov/publications/

TTB forms (online and by mail):
www.ttb.gov/forms/index.htm

Sample Brewer's Report:
www.ttb.gov/forms/pdfs/5100/
51309worksheet.pdf

Electronic Tax Payments (Pay.gov):
www.ttb.gov/epayment/epayment.htm

To contact TTB's Brewery, Wholesaler, & Importer Applications Branch directly:
1-877-882-3277
National Revenue Center
550 main Street Suite 8002
Cincinnati, OH 45202-5215
(513) 684-3337
Fax: (513) 684-2242
ttbquestions@ttb.gov

the finished product, a specific description of when flavoring material is added in the production of the product, and the total volume and alcohol content of the finished product must be included.

Two copies of this form must be submitted for each formula. TTB also provides assistance in making a determination if you are unsure if a particular situation will require a formula filing, and for an exemption from the formula requirement.

Certification/Exemption of Label/Bottle Approval (COLA) (Form 5100.31)- A certificate of label approval authorizes the certificate holder to bottle and remove or import alcohol beverages that bear labels identical to those shown on the certificate of label approval.

There is no fee to apply for label approval. If you are applying for label approval for the first time, you will need to send a copy of your approved brewer's notice (or basic permit, depending on your business). You must also submit your application in duplicate with the labels attached to the front of the form. TTB has 90 days to take action on applications for certificates of label approval.

You may submit applications electronically at www.ttbonline.gov/colasonline. This site also gives you the ability to check the status of your application (you may also call the Alcohol, Labeling, and Formulation Division Customer Service Team toll free at 1-866-927-2533).

Brewer's Report of Operations (Form 5130.9)- This report must be filed if you produce more than 5,000 barrels of beer a year, or if you produce less but bottle or keg your beer.

Brewpub Report of Operations (Form 5130.26) - File this report if you produce less than 5,000 barrels per year and you do not bottle or keg your beer.

Excise Tax Return (Form 5000.24) - The regular federal excise tax rate on beer is $18 per barrel. However, a reduced rate of $7 per barrel is in effect on the first 60,000 barrels for brewers producing less than 2 million barrels annually (the rate reverts to $18 per barrel with barrel 60,001). Additionally, if your excise tax liability was less than $50,000 in the previous year, you may be eligible to file and pay on a quarterly rather than on a bi-weekly basis. More information on this program can be found at www.ttb.gov/main_pages/small_alcohol.htm

These are only some of the most common federal forms and issues associated with operating a brewery. The sites listed below under "Further Resources" provide a much broader perspective from which you can explore your relationship with TTB, and you are strongly encouraged to take some time early in the process to familiarize yourself in detail with the information contained in www.ttb.gov. And, of course, each state (and some local jurisdictions) also has its own alcohol regulatory agency, each with its own unique requirements, rules and regulations.

Recall what was said in the first sentence of this article – this is a highly regulated industry. Now you have an idea of what that means, at least on the federal level. But, you also have some idea of the personal and professional rewards that come with owning and operating a brewery or you wouldn't have taken the time to read an article like this one! Yes, there are many rules you need to follow and many forms to be filled out, but you only help yourself by understanding those rules and being careful and accurate with your filings. Hopefully, this primer has started you down that road. Cheers!

Chapter Thirteen

Dealing with Rules and Regulators

A pioneer of the craft beer industry talks about challenges and road blocks from government officials and their codebooks.

By Peter Egelston

Peter Egelston's experiences opening the Northampton Brewery in 1987 put him on the cutting edge of the craft brewing movement in his community. But despite the fact that the average American now lives within 10 miles of a brewery, some regulators still don't understand what our industry is all about. We include Egelston's experiences here for the valuable lessons they still convey for those looking to start a brewery. – Editor

WHEN WE STARTED OUR BREWERY, WE TOOK a proposal to the planning board of the city for initial approval, which we received pending further information. Then we acquired a site, went back to the planning board for a formal hearing, and secured approval for the project. We extensively renovated our building and installed our brewery over about an eight-month time and then opened. This all sounds very easy, but there were a few stumbling blocks and pitfalls along the way. You will likely encounter some of the same challenges we ran up against.

From the outset, I want to emphasize the need to educate your regulators. Most problems you encounter with regulatory bodies come from misconceptions about what you are doing. Despite the fact that there are more than 1500 small breweries operating all over the country these days, many people still envision huge mass-market breweries when they think of beer production. In that situation, they see a brewery as a huge industrial plant belching out noxious fumes and other pollutants. Your job is to educate them.

One way to do this is with a press packet. Collect articles about breweries in various parts of the country. Get photographs of operating brewpubs and small breweries. Your role first and foremost is educating people to prevent problems rooted in misconceptions.

One of the first questions you'll encounter with regard to your facility will be about zoning. Zoning is an important issue for brewpubs, especially because they are usually located in a commercial district zoned for retail business and restaurants as opposed to an industrial district. On the other hand, breweries producing a strictly wholesale product are usually located in an industrial district, since there is no sense paying the high rent charged in a commercial district for an industrial operation.

The main problem in dealing with the planning board or zoning commission is how to convince them to let you set up a business perceived by almost everyone as industrial in a commercial setting where industrial uses are prohibited. The tactic that a number of brewpubs employ is the analogy of a restaurant with an on-premise bakery. This is a very useful analogy to draw, and it holds true for the most part. Many restaurants operate their own bakeries, and their raw materials are similar to those used in breweries. Likewise, bakeries' waste products are not unlike the waste products produced in breweries.

> From the outset, I want to emphasize is the need to educate your regulators. Most problems you encounter with regulatory bodies come from misconceptions about what you are doing.

After zoning, the second issue most likely to cause problems is waste — solid and liquid. During our start-up, I had just gotten the brewery online and was running my first test batches. I thought I was home free. Everything had been taken care of, I thought. Midway through my brewing, a large man with a red face came storming into the brewery waving sheets of paper under my nose, telling me my operation was illegal. He was the manager of the municipal wastewater treatment plant, who had been notified by a friend that a brewery was opening in downtown Northampton. Before the manager came in, however, he had called the manager of the wastewater treatment plant in Merrimack, New Hampshire, where Anheuser-Busch operates a 3.5-million-barrel-a-year brewery. So our local treatment plant manager came to our 1,000-barrel-a-year brewery expecting to find an operation similar to Anheuser-Busch.

He had in hand applications for industrial wastewater discharge permits and told me that I would have to test my own wastewater four times a month at my expense, send the results to the municipal plant for approval, and dig a manhole over the sewer outlet at an estimated cost of $3,000 so he could install an electronic testing device to test the effluent at the point of entry into the sewer. This would have been fine if I was opening a Coca-Cola bottling plant, but in our case it was rather ridiculous.

Once he looked around the brewery, he realized what he required of us was overdone. But he had painted himself into a corner. He had notified the city authorities, and there was no easy way for him to back down. Finally, we went to the mayor, fortunately a great fan of our beer and a supporter of our project, and he arranged a compromise whereby the wastewater treatment facility sent an engineer to the brewery to watch me clean the mash tun. She took samples of our effluent and reached the conclusion we had told them all along: "Yes, our wastewater is of a very high potency, but the volume we put down the drain is a minuscule quantity and is not any way significant to the wastewater problems of the city." They let us off the hook. However, we were lucky to have a friend in city hall, or we could have been in grave trouble.

When starting your project, keep constant contact with the people in charge of treating wastewater. At our original zoning hearing, the head of the zoning board was responsible for inviting every person with an interest in the project (i.e., electrical and building inspectors, the city attorney, etc.), but he had neglected to invite the superintendent of the wastewater treatment facility. The superintendent regarded it as a personal slight, and it became our problem. So seek out these people. The element of surprise does not work in your favor. People in charge of regulating your brewery do not like surprises.

Regarding building codes, expect to be dealing with a number of inspectors, whether you're renovating an existing structure or building something new. Although most municipalities have adopted a uniform code, inspectors have a certain amount of latitude in interpreting that code. With respect to building codes, your first task is to educate yourself. You do not need to be an expert; just be familiar to the point where you can identify unreasonable requests. Inspectors are not always right. There will be times when some negotiation is required.

Here's a tip: do not let your contractor serve as your proxy in negotiating with your local code enforcers because your contractor's interest may not always coincide with your interest. He or she is bound to think first and foremost of preserving a good working relationship with city hall and will be more than happy to spend your money accommodating the building inspector, rather than fighting for your rights. Our electrical inspector required that all of our brewery wiring be in hard conduit as opposed to PVC flexible wiring. All the junction and switch boxes had to be rated for high-moisture, wash-down areas and were extremely expensive. Also, because we run a brewpub, our code has a very high standard. But this is an area where we didn't want to cut corners.

Fire regulations are another area of concern. Are the entrances and exits adequate? Is there a sprinkler system? This is generally dictated by code. Is there handicap access? Your contractor should be familiar with local building codes and know the specific requirements for these.

> Here's a tip: do not let your contractor serve as your proxy in negotiating with your local code enforcers because your contractor's interest may not always coincide with your interest.

Beyond building codes come miscellaneous issues that may or may not apply to your operation. Grain dust is one. At our original zoning hearing, one member of the zoning board had read an article about a grain silo that exploded and was worried about grain dust explosions. Finally, in order to satisfy this person, we offered to purchase preground malt or mill the malt off-premise. He was happy, and we left it at that. By the time we opened, we showed him our wash-down procedure, and he relented. Consequently, we mill our own grain on-premise and don't have any problems with the city.

Noise is another public concern. When applying for your initial zoning, you may have a public hearing, and your neighbors may ask about noise. Get information about noise from other operating brewpubs. As far as I know, noise hasn't been a problem with a brewpub beyond that of a typical bar or restaurant.

People will also ask about odors. I was asked recently to write a letter for a brewpub opening in another city attesting that no one has complained about odors from our brewery. People have a perception of a brewery as a large industrial operation with foul odors. This is certainly not the case with breweries.

Volatiles such as steam coming out of the kettle may be a problem. Greg Noonan, owner and brewmaster at the Vermont Pub and Brewery in Burlington, Vermont, had to bend over backwards to address that issue when people questioned the volatiles coming out of his kettle. What Greg did was to reroute the steam coming out of the kettle into the kitchen so it could be released through the hood over the stove and grill. Consequently, he has the cleanest hood of any restaurant in the state, maybe in the country.

Health codes vary in different localities. Your health inspector may be very interested in what you do or may be totally mystified by it. In our case, the health inspector is very interested in our kitchen. He comes in with a white glove and thermometer and checks out the kitchen temperatures. Then he walks into the brewery, looks around, scratches his head, and leaves. But you may not have the same experience, so be prepared to address health issues. Brewing pretty much monitors itself from the health standpoint. You're not likely to poison anyone when you're making beer. If your sanitation procedures aren't up to snuff, your beer won't sell.

To recap and also give you my suggestions for dealing with individual inspectors, let me point out again that you must educate people. Don't wait until misconceptions have already been formed. Most regulators have an alarm signal that goes off when they hear the word brewery. For example, Greg Noonan had leased his site but hadn't received his zoning approval when he ordered his brewery tanks from England. He had no place to put them when they arrived so he stored them in the space he had rented. The superintendent of the planning commission just happened to drive by, see brewery tanks in the window and got into a snit because no one had consulted him. As a result, he forbade having a brewery in downtown Burlington. That was the point that Greg had to start from and he ran into stumbling blocks every step of the way. To give you an idea of what he went through, he had to put a sprinkler system inside his walk-in refrigerator.

Do your homework. Don't be caught by surprise because you don't know enough about something. Depending on how far along you are, a surprise could be very inconvenient or costly.

Don't depend exclusively on someone else's knowledge of codes and regulations. For example, don't depend solely on your contractor's knowledge of the codes. Remember, contractors are not spending their own money. Get to know the codes yourself.

Also, get to know the people who have the control over regulations affecting your brewery: inspectors and decision-makers. Northampton is a small city with one electrical inspector, one building inspector, and one health inspector. This is both an advantage and a disadvantage. It might be better to be in a very large city where you're dealing with a large, faceless bureaucracy, rather than individuals.

Let all the concerned parties know about your project from the very beginning. You want to create good will. Do this by telling people what to expect. You sometimes have to play politics but do so carefully. Many inspectors and regulators operate autonomously. They have their own little fiefdoms and they don't like to be told what to do. Remember that what your building inspector approves may not be approved by your electrical inspector. Get to know the jurisdiction of each inspector. A colleague of mine says that his philosophy is "We don't ask for permission — we beg for forgiveness." While that may work in some cases, in general, I think it is a risky way to conduct business.

Learn who influences whom. As a last resort, you may have to go over people's heads. We've had to do that sometimes, but it doesn't create good will. In two situations, we've had to run straight to the mayor and say, "You'll have to fix this if you want any more beer."

Understand your regulator's point of view. A fire marshal has opinions about what is safe and what isn't — ditto for the electrical inspector and the wastewater treatment people. Think about why they want you to do something; often there is a good reason for it.

Try to avoid adversarial positions. This brings me to the point of whether or not to hire an attorney. I recommend having a good lawyer in the wings. But I've found that most of the time, I'm better off talking to the regulators myself. I've been in front of the Alcohol Beverage Commission more times than I care to think about, both with lawyers and without. I usually get what I want when I talk to them person to person. Lawyers can be helpful; they can also create an adversarial situation just by their presence. Use the services of an attorney with some common sense.

Accept compromise. You may not get everything you want and you may have to spend some money. If it is a choice between paying extra money and jumping through hoops to get your project done or being stubborn and not, then the answer is obvious.

> Finally be ready for anything. In the very last stage of our project, the city attorney refused to let us use the word "brewery" in our signs or advertisements.

Finally, be ready for anything. Sometimes even after you have done everything right, things come up. In the very last stage of our project when we were ready to open, we hired a sign maker to design a nice sign for Northampton Brewery. The city has very strict sign codes, and the city attorney refused to let us use the word "brewery" in our signs or advertisements.

The city attorney's rationale was if we were going to operate a bar and restaurant where the brewery would only be an accessory, then we wouldn't be able to promote ourselves as a brewery because people would complain about an industrial use in a commercial district. It came down to the fact that the attorney didn't want people calling her office and complaining about our zoning.

We went to the mayor and explained the problem, but he wouldn't overrule the city attorney. Instead, he suggested a compromise wherein we would call our company the Northampton Brewery at the Brewster Court Bar and Grill. Now everyone simply calls it "The Brewery."

In situations like this, it helps to retain a sense of humor about it or you won't be able to tell these amusing horror stories in the future.

As I review these thoughts many years and two brewery openings later, it seems to have held up pretty well, even with the enormous changes that have taken place in the craft brewing industry. In some respects, things are easier today than in the past, mostly because there is so much more information to draw from.

One point that I will add now is to prepare for growth and all of its ramifications. A brewpub that was originally designed for nine hundred barrels of annual production may someday evolve into a three-thousand-barrel facility. This may require some reassessment of the issues covered in this chapter, especially disposal of wastewater. If that happens, you can wind up making some very expensive changes to accommodate the growth. ◗

Chapter Fourteen

Down the Drain But Not Forgotten

Local authorities fret about brewery wastewater but you can prevent major problems with this background information and some practical pointers.

By Michael J. Pronold

IN EVERY BREWERY IT TAKES FAR MORE water to make beer than just what winds up in the product itself—five to ten times as much in fact. And because a lot of that water is used in one way or another for cleaning, much of it winds up as wastewater carrying along various chemicals and organic materials.

Most of us don't think much about where water goes when it disappears down the drain. But as a brewer, your wastewater can set off alarms at the local water treatment plant for a variety of reasons. As a result, you'll need to be aware and pay attention to what you will send downstream long before you begin to operate your brewhouse. In this article, we'll familiarize you with key wastewater issues so you'll know where to start in planning your brewery and working with local water authorities.

The wastewater generated from brewing and cleaning operations by small breweries must be discharged to a wastewater treatment plant, thus subjecting it to the restrictions and/or regulations of the local sewerage district through local ordinances or a pretreatment program. The purpose of these restrictions and programs is to control discharges of harmful pollutants from industrial and commercial sources which interfere with the wastewater treatment plant, collection system, and sludge disposal operations. The program also protects worker safety, the public, and the local environment. Brewery wastewater is a concern because of the pH of the wastewater (cleaning solutions, beer wastes) and high total suspended solids (TSS) and biochemical oxygen demand (BOD) which may interfere with the wastewater treatment plant's ability to adequately treat wastewater.

We'll begin this review by looking at the sources and character of wastewater in a brewery. Afterward, we'll detail common control programs that breweries may be required to follow.

SOURCES AND CHARACTERISTICS OF WASTEWATER

The sources of wastewater in a brewery come from two different general operations. One source is from production operations, which includes spent grain and yeast; filtering media; and the heels of fermenters, conditioners, brew kettles, and whirlpools. Small amounts of spilled beer also come from bottling and kegging operations and spent beer in returned kegs. At times there may even be a need to dispose of a bad batch of beer. These wastewaters from the production process contain product or by-product at some stage in the brewing process. Wastewaters generated from these operations are generally very high in TSS and/or BOD, with a low pH. The suspended solids from heels of brewing vessels can be well over 1,000 milligrams per liter (depending on the amount of yeast

WASTEWATER TERMS

BOD (biochemical oxygen demand). The quantity of oxygen utilized in the biochemical oxidation of organic matter over a period of five days at a temperature of 68 degrees F (20 degrees C) and usually expressed in milligrams per liter.

COD (chemical oxygen demand). COD is a measure of the oxygen equivalent of the sample's organic content that is susceptible to oxidation by a strong chemical oxidant.

pH A measure of the acidity or alkalinity of a solution on a scale of 1.0 to 14.0, decreasing with increasing acidity and increasing with increasing alkalinity.

TSS (total suspended solids). Solids that are suspended or floating in a liquid and measured by removal through a specified filter size and usually expressed in milligrams per liter.

and trub). BOD of finished beer is approximately 80,000 milligrams per liter, and the pH of finished beer generally runs around 4.2. In comparison, wastewater from households has TSS and BOD in the 150 to 300 milligrams per liter range with a neutral pH (6.0 to 8.0).

The other source of wastewater comes from the cleaning of production equipment. This includes washing of tanks, kegs, bottles, and other equipment with a caustic cleaning solution. Wastewater generated from cleaning is reflective of the high caustic solution used to clean the equipment. These cleaning solutions by themselves are generally low in TSS and BOD but may be high depending on the amount of product in the wash water. They are also very high in pH (10.5 to 13.5). If captured, this caustic solution may be reused until the pH drops to approximately 10.0 to 10.5 or becomes unusable due to contamination by other materials. It is then generally discharged to the sewer. Acidic sanitizers used to disinfect equipment is often made up of phosphoric acid and iodine. This wastewater is low in TSS and BOD and has a low pH (3.9). Acidic cleaning solutions are used for bright tanks and are a combination of phosphoric and nitric acid.

WASTEWATER PH

The pH of wastewater is regulated by the sewerage district and has limits that vary from locale to locale. Typical limits are 5.5 to 11.5, but could be as restrictive as 6.0 to 9.0. These limits are set to protect the wastewater treatment plant and the collection system. Wastewater at the treatment plant is treated biologically by organisms which thrive in a neutral pH range. Wastewater with a low pH may be corrosive to the sewage-collection system and be a worker health and safety concern. In fact, wastewater with a pH less than 5.0 is a prohibited discharge by federal regulations. The wastewater generated by the brewing process and cleaning operations can fall outside the acceptable pH range if discharged by themselves without pretreatment. The possibility of this happening is common in breweries. Larger breweries may have cleaning and brewing operations occurring simultaneously which may dampen the pH range of the wastewaters as the low pH brewing wastes combine with the high pH cleaning wastes. Nevertheless, it may be necessary to install pretreatment or BMPs for the control of wastewater pH.

PH CONTROLS

One option for controlling of pH is to collect the various wastewaters into a collection vessel and adjust the pH if necessary. The low pH of beer wastes, sanitizing solutions, and acidic cleaners and the high pH of the caustic cleaner waste may result in a pH that is within the permitted range. The collection vessel would need to be sized according to the volume of wastewater, and this may present space constraints for some facilities. Space constraints may necessitate that a facility install a continuous collection/treatment system with a smaller capacity.

Also, supplemental pH control may be necessary to adjust the pH to an acceptable range. This would require adding an acidifier (sulfuric acid, CO_2) or a caustic (spent caustic solution, lime product) either manually or automatically to a batch system or through an automated pH control system that continuously monitors and adjusts the wastewater pH. Operation and maintenance of the system and the cost of chemicals incur additional expenses.

Also, hazardous materials (acids, caustics) on-site must be stored and handled accordingly.

Another pH control mechanism is to control the pH of the wastewater at the source. Prior to discharging the heel of a brewing vessel, caustic (used on-site for cleaning) can be added to raise the pH to the acceptable range. Practical experience or bench testing can determine the appropriate amount of caustic to add.

Control of caustic wastewater can be made cost effective for the brewery by installing cleaning-in-place (CIP) units. These units are made up of a receptacle for the caustic solution used in cleaning vessels. The solution is pumped to the vessel and used in cleaning and returned to the CIP unit. The solution can be used numerous times until the pH falls to below 11.0. The solution then needs to be disposed of; but, the pH may now be in the acceptable range.

Care must be taken when combining waste streams in an effort to achieve a pH in the allowable range. If chlorinated caustic cleaners are used, neutralizing with a strong acid will liberate chlorine gas. If iodine solutions (acidic sanitizers) are made too alkaline, the iodine can plate out, in effect scaling the tank.

WASTEWATER TSS AND BOD

TSS and BOD may or may not be regulated by the sewerage district. If the brewery represents a significant amount of the TSS and BOD loading at the wastewater treatment plant, or poses a threat due to a slug load, the district may put limits on the amount that the brewery can discharge. Whereas the treatment plant is designed to treat biological wastes, it can become overburdened with high-strength wastes. Wastewater that is inadequately treated by the wastewater treatment plant may be discharged to the receiving stream, resulting in the treatment plant violating its discharge permit. This concern rises as the wastewater treatment facility decreases in size and the strength and amount of brewery wastewater discharge increases. In addition, if the brewery is located near the treatment plant, it may pose a threat due to slug loads. Breweries located further from the treatment plant may have their flows diluted from other wastewater in the collection system and reduce this concern. If the strength of the waste is high enough, local conditions may necessitate that a brewery install pretreatment for the control of TSS and BOD.

TSS AND BOD CONTROLS

The control of TSS and BOD can be accomplished through pretreatment and/or source control. Pretreatment can be accomplished in several ways, including centrifuges, filters, screens, settling basins, or an activated sludge system. The first four methods are designed to remove settleable solids from the waste stream. An activated sludge system is similar to a wastewater treatment plant where biological treatment is used to reduce the TSS and BOD. The result is a sludge which must be handled and disposed of in some manner. An activated sludge system can reduce TSS and BOD significantly, but are expensive to install and operate and are not very common except in large breweries. However, as more breweries start up operations and existing ones grow, it is inevitable that some will be required to install these systems. It may also be cost effective to install a treatment system to reduce the surcharges that a brewery may incur.

Source control through good housekeeping is a very effective way for a brewery to control TSS/BOD and the associated higher sewer bills. Spent yeast can be killed by cooking, and when added to grain it can be given away as feed. Killing the yeast is necessary to maintain the health of the animals consuming the spent grain. Waste beer from returned kegs can also be heated and disposed of in the grain or separately in a tank for transporting liquids. Filtering media and the associated yeast can be cleaned "dry" and disposed of as a solid waste. If it is removed with water, the solids may be able to be removed through settling and the liquid discharged to the sewer. A large portion of the extra-strength charge is generated from dissolved BOD (i.e., dissolved sugars and carbohydrates). Removal of solids will not reduce this source of BOD.

SUMMARY

Wastewaters generated from breweries can be a concern to the sewerage district that the brewery is located in because of the pH, TSS, and BOD of the wastewater. The brewery may need to be permitted and also possibly implement controls for pH, TSS, and BOD. The permit requirements and control measures may add significant costs for the brewery through higher operation costs and/or sewer fees. The requirements will vary depending on the local sewerage district. These issues should be addressed prior to starting any brewing operation by contacting the sewerage district you will be located in.

CONTROL PROGRAMS

Programs that a local sewerage district may implement to restrict the wastewater discharge from a brewery can vary. These types of programs include: (1) a rigid permitting program; (2) a discharge authorization; (3) informal agreements; and (4) a surcharge program.

Pretreatment permit. A brewery may be required to obtain a wastewater discharge permit from the control authority and be subject to the same discharge limitations and permit requirements that regulate other industries in the sewerage district. If the wastewater discharge is 25,000 gallons per day or more, the brewery is required by Federal regulations to obtain a wastewater discharge permit. A permit may include any or all of the following:

1. Applying for a permit and paying an appropriate permit fee. The permit application generally requires schematics of all sewer lines, sewer connections, and floor drains on the site, water usage, facility layout, production records, chemical storage areas, and general information.
2. Installation of a sampling manhole so the control authority has access to take random samples of the wastewater from the facility.
3. Monitoring and reporting requirements where the facility must sample the wastewater, have the samples analyzed, and report results to the control authority.
4. Creation of an accidental spill prevention plan that must be approved by the control authority.
5. Allowing on-site inspections of the facility by the control authority.
6. Meeting discharge limitations set forth in the permit.

Violations of any of the permit requirements can subject the brewery to enforcement that can include compliance orders, requirements for the installation of pretreatment equipment, additional monitoring and reporting requirements, and fines.

Discharge authorization. A discharge authorization program may include a formal written agreement between the sewerage agency and the brewery. These are generally less stringent and have fewer requirements than a pretreatment program permit. Actions required of the brewery could include a plan to keep spent grain out of the sewer, control the rate of discharge, and other best management practices (BMPs) to limit the impact of the wastewater on the sewer system.

Informal agreements. If the brewery's wastewater discharge is deemed to have a minimal impact on the sewer system, the sewerage agency may only request that certain BMPs be implemented. These may be in the form of requests, directives, or educational brochures which are given to the establishment.

Surcharge program. A surcharge program is a vehicle used by sewerage agencies for recovering the cost of treating wastewater that has high TSS and/or BOD. Whereas the treatment plant is designed to treat biological wastes, it costs the facility more money to treat high-strength wastes. This is due to the increased solids that must be handled or disposed of and the increase in operating costs for things such as blowers that supply oxygen to the bacteria that feed on the high-strength wastes. This fee may be referred to as an extra-strength sewer charge. These charges can be in addition to the permitting programs described above.

The costs are based on the poundage of TSS and BOD calculated using the amount of flow and the "strength" of the waste (concentration of TSS and BOD) in excess of the level of ordinary domestic wastewater. Sometimes a chemical oxygen demand (COD) test is substituted for a BOD test. This substitution is made because a COD test only takes two hours, whereas a BOD test takes five days to perform. For samples from a specific source, a COD can be empirically related to a BOD. These costs can be significant and should be evaluated when starting a brewery.

The type of program implemented by the local sewerage agency depends on the perceived impact of the brewery on the sewer system. Breweries with a greater impact will be subject to more controls. The impact is site specific and will depend on many factors. The closer the brewery is to the treatment plant, the greater the impact will be on the sewer system. In addition, the impact of a brewery will be more significant on a smaller wastewater treatment plant. ◗

Chapter Fifteen

Better Brewery Floors

Build your brewery on a solid foundation that will survive wide temperature fluctuations, harsh chemicals and extreme physical abuse while holding multi-ton brewing vessels.

By John Mallett

IN THE LATE 1980S I FOUND MYSELF WORKING at a Boston brewpub; one of the first in New England. That facility was originally built on a shoestring budget and flooring was not a priority item. After a year of operation the flooring situation had deteriorated to the point where we had an abundant crop of mushrooms that would sprout from the wood floor under the serving tanks on a regular basis.

Eventually the situation was remedied with a generous application of concrete but being able to solve existing flooring problems is not always inexpensive or even possible. The cheapest time to fix the floor is before the doors open.

Floors provide a base upon which we work and set very heavy equipment. Brewery floors must also maintain their surface and structural integrity, be easily cleanable, waterproof and hopefully drain any stray liquids to an appropriate drain.

When you go to build a brewery, you'll see a whole world of flooring systems. An uninformed decision can bring you years of frustration (and squeegeeing). And if you talk flooring with brewers you get a lot of different opinions.

CONCRETE IS THE BEST BASE

Breweries go into many different building types and on to many different floors—with varying success. One brewery installation I worked with placed ten 40 barrel unitanks on a second story, wood-based floor. The loading and unloading of over 10,000 pounds of beer per tank caused flexing of the floor despite the installation of some serious structural steel. This was a very difficult flooring application and truth be told the floor did not stand up to the task. Great flooring requires a very stable base to prevent flexing and eventual cracking of the top waterproofing.

In my experience the best (only) *base* worth talking about for brewery floors is concrete. Concrete is by far the most commonly used building material in the world. It is light, strong and easy to work with. So what is it?

Concrete is a mixture of three basic ingredients: Portland cement, water and aggregates such as rock or sand. Portland cement (a type of cement, not a brand name) is a closely controlled chemical combination of calcium, silicon, aluminum, iron and small amounts of other ingredients. When the concrete ingredients are mixed, the water and cement form a paste, which coats and binds the aggregate together. In essence the aggregate acts as filler in the mixture. Water also acts to hydrate the cement, which will then harden into a rock-like mass. In 1999, U.S. Portland cement consumption reached 104.9 million metric tons.

You will find many nuances in the formulation and application of concrete. Although you could simply call up the ready-mix plant and order up a truckload you may want to at least talk to the technical person at the plant first. Concrete can be formulated with a wide range of options. One factor is strength, which depends on variables such as percentage cement in the mix, size and type of aggregate, water/cement ratio, and curing temperature, conditions and time. Mixes can go much higher, but will commonly have 2500-4000 psi of compressive strength—ample to support vessels of up to 40 barrels in capacity.

> Brewery floors must also maintain their surface and structural integrity, be easily cleanable, waterproof and hopefully drain any stray liquids to an appropriate drain.

Mixtures may also have other ingredients. All cement has some gypsum that is added to help regulate the setting time. Steel or nylon fibers add strength to a concrete with or without the use of reinforcing bar or wire. Additives can help accelerate curing, control moisture, retard microbial growth and even color the concrete.

When using concrete, make sure that what you are laying it on will not shift or move excessively. Soil type and compaction are both very important. You must make sure the concrete is poured thick enough to resist cracking. In my experience, the absolute minimum pour depth is one-and-a-half inches.

When you pour the concrete for your brewery floor you have an opportunity to slope the floor towards the floor drains. The standard slope is one-quarter inch of fall per foot of run (one inch : four feet) One eighth inch per foot is as flat as I would go and my preferred flooring specification is three-sixteenths of an inch per foot which seems to be a good compromise. Just remember that if you pour a floor thinking that you will rely on some minimum wage worker to squeegee your water to the drain, there is a good chance that he will be looking back at you from the mirror as you brush your teeth every morning.

After pouring, the concrete must be surfaced. The finishing procedure involves a rough screed and then increasing levels of floating and troweling. Final finishes may include hand or machine (power) troweling or perhaps a simple brush finish for enhanced slip resistance. This is also the time to think about control joints which allow the floor to expand and move without random cracking. These joints are often saw-cut in at a later point.

If the concrete is to be used in public areas, one interesting treatment is "stamped concrete". This procedure uses rubber mats to decoratively texture the surface in a variety of patterns simulating brick, stone and even wood. In combination with colorants this can be an inexpensive, attractive and hard-wearing surface.

The next step is curing. Proper curing delays the drying shrinkage until the concrete is strong enough to resist shrinkage cracking. Concrete that is moist-cured for 7 days is about 50% stronger than concrete exposed to dry air for the same period. If the concrete is not properly cured it may develop cracks that would not otherwise have occurred.

One standard method of multi-story building construction uses steel beams supporting metal decking (called "B" deck) into which lightweight concrete is poured. This building design flexes and may cause eventual problems with maintaining a good waterproof floor.

A standard mix of 3000 psi concrete costs about $450-550 per nine-cubic-yard truck load at the time of this writing—check with your local supplier for current costs.

FLOOR TOPPINGS

The next part of any flooring system is the surface treatment. You can spend a little or a lot here as the top layer can be as simple as no treatment or as bombproof as stainless steel. Lets take a look at some different options.

No Treatment The first option is no treatment at all. You can't beat the initial cost for this option, but you'll find a big delayed expense as the underlying layer degrades. In the case of concrete, beer (which is acidic) and cleaners will begin to dissolve the cement right out of the concrete. Most aggregate will be unaffected and you will eventually end up with a disintegrating, unsightly and uncleanable mess. This may be a good option where floors are not exposed to much abuse but then again we are talking about a brewery environment. **Advantages**: Minimum cost. **Disadvantages:** Will breakdown quickly in a brewery environment.

J-17 This product comes up a lot in discussions among brewers and they seem to have a range of opinions. A quick call to the manufacturer, Dayton Superior Corp., confirmed that this product is not a waterproofing sealer but a concrete hardener/dust-proofing additive. This water-based product chemically reacts with the free lime (CaOH) in the concrete to produce Calcium Silicate Hydrate, which is the jell that binds concrete together. Concrete treated with J-17 is more dense but not more chemically restive. The increased density slows but does not stop penetration of water and chemicals into the concrete. This product is quite liquid and can be applied with a squeegee. **Advantages:** Minimal cost. **Disadvantages:** Not designed as a waterproofing agent.

Penetrating water repellants Some may be tempted to use generic water seals on brewery floors. These compounds block pores in the concrete to repel water, but they are not very durable. Unfortunately they also don't usually allow application of other flooring products. The wide range of products on the market includes silicone-based options and others based on more appropriate silanes and siloxides. These products were developed for weatherproofing protection on concrete highway bridge decks. In the right environment they bead water and protect the concrete. The question for a brewer is " is my brewery the right environment?" Personal experience shows that these products will bead water, for a time. Regular reapplication of these products will increase the life of the floor but it is not an ideal solution. **Advantages:** Minimal cost, easy application **Disadvantages:** Not designed to last in a brewery, needs to be regularly reapplied.

The Epoxy Family I love the epoxy salesmen: "This is a fourth generation, high-solids, engineered polymer that the US military has approved for tank traffic. It is ideal for brewery floors. As a matter of fact we have this product in many breweries worldwide." Statements like this make you think that this product would actually work as a reasonably priced floor coating. However, in my experience, these treatments do not always work well in the brewery.

Epoxy flooring materials come in many forms and thicknesses with various application techniques. The simplest is a paint form that may be spray, roll or squeegee applied. As thickness increases the application methods change toward hand or machine troweling.

In my experience, these coatings can fail where they bond to the underlying substrate. Moisture from the free water contained in concrete frequently contributes to this bond failure. As discussed previously, curing concrete is in part a drying process. And, since concrete is porous, water can travel through it. Non-porous epoxy systems don't allow your concrete to sweat water. Water buildup between the concrete and the epoxy causes the bond to fail and then you will start to pull up epoxy material in sheets. Once the floor fails it is very difficult to stop, the water continues to travel through the system resulting in more failure. Many can be patched but the entire area needs to be allowed time to dry. Unfortunately this is not a reasonable request in a working brewery.

Physical failure can also occur. Drop a valve on a thin material and you may poke a hole through the coating and compromise the flooring system. Common sense would dictate thicker applications for a working brewery.

Hot water running on a brewery floor expands the floor topping and can break the concrete-epoxy bond.

Heat shock can also cause failure with an epoxy floor. Heated materials tend to expand. Epoxies tend to expand at greater rates than the underlying concrete. Hot water running on a brewery floor expands the floor topping and can break the concrete-epoxy bond. Once this occurs other cracks can develop in the epoxy and floor failure is not far off. Up to one-quarter inch epoxy can be lifted by heat shock. One way to help prevent this is to increase the depth of the epoxy compound so that it has sufficient thermal mass to resist such a failure. Unfortunately this can quickly raise the price of these options to an unacceptable level.

Epoxy compounds have been developed that are better suited to the brewery environment. Ucrete HF made by Selby/Harris Specialty

Chemicals is one such product. It was specifically formulated to replace tile-flooring systems in food processing, dairy and brewery applications. It is a bit unique in that it is a water-based mixture of highly modified epoxy, concrete and urethane and because of this it has a coefficient of expansion close to that of concrete. As with any flooring system the preparation of the concrete is very important. Because it releases water as it cures, the concrete will need to be typically poured four weeks prior to epoxy application to achieve a low enough moisture content for proper bonding. Additionally the cement surface should be shot-blasted. The product is applied one-quarter inch to three-eighths inch thick. The manufacturer has a one-year warranty and claims that it bonds to itself well and is easy to patch if required. They recommend saw-cutting the underlying concrete near walls and drains to prevent the spread of moisture in the event of a system failure.

The New Belgium Brewing Co. has used Ucrete in the brewery. According to Dennis Shippey at the brewery, they have had some problems with the system, however, he attributes the problems to the installer, not the product. He feels that the adhesion of the product to the concrete is very good. It exhibits excellent resistance to common brewery chemicals, however, some discoloration can occur. Attempting to Ucrete in around legs of existing equipment can cause problems. If you need to anchor equipment to the floor then a chemical (epoxy) anchor has given good, durable results. Dennis mentioned that he would ask how many installations a potential contractor had done and would want to see some of them firsthand before committing to any deal. This is good advice for any flooring installation. **Advantages:** Seamless systems available in a variety of colors. **Disadvantages:** Susceptible to thermal or mechanical damage. If water gets under it you will be removing it in sheets. **Cost:** Epoxy systems range in price a great deal. Quality systems such as Ucrete can run upwards of $12 per square foot.

TILE TALK

Like any effective brewery flooring system, tile protects the underlying concrete from physical abuse, heat shock and cleaning chemicals. Tile is fireproof, fadeproof and dentproof, good looking, rugged, repairable and has a great history of use in the brewery. It is also expensive to install and can cause problems in some installations. Most tile contractors will be familiar with the range of options for tile floors. You must properly match tile grout and adhesive to brewery requirements. Brewery appropriate tiles include the standard quarry tile, clinker tile or paving tile. The main difference between these tile types is in their physical sizes and installation methods. Tiles are formed or extruded from high quality shale and fired at extreme temperatures in a slow moving tunnel oven, a process taking nearly nine days. The finished product is uniformly dense and made in various surfaces. Pavers can reach a compressive strength of 24,000 PSI. Unglazed quarry tile is resistant to stains but not stainproof. Light colors tend to show staining more than dark colors and red is the most resistant to the staining compounds found in the brewery.

Tile is fireproof, fadeproof and dentproof, good looking, rugged, repairable and has a great history of use in the brewery.

Pavers, also called acid brick, are four inches by eight inches extruded brick tile and come in thicknesses ranging from one inch to 1.375 inches for brewery use. They are not a precisely finished tile but are the most durable floor covering available. They are used where extreme chemical, heat shock or forktruck traffic might cause a thinner tile system to fail. Pavers are usually laid using a thinset epoxy adhesive. Pavers are available in the standard brick red color. Despite the mass of this product it is not much more expensive than quarry tile. The main price difference that you may see is in the cost of shipping.

Clinker tile is also a four inch by eight inch tile used commonly in Europe. It comes in both half-inch and three-quarter inch depth. This tile is commonly set using two inches of a Portland cement and sand-based mortar bed. The tile is laid on the bed and then set into place using a vibrating machine. This is a very smooth and attractive flooring system and the gaps between individual tiles are fairly small. Due to this small gap the replacement of individual damaged tiles my be very difficult. It is similar in thickness to quarry tile and should offer similar resistance to brewery damage. Some installers will offer a 5-year warranty on this type of flooring.

Quarry tile is the standard for use in many kitchens and breweries. It comes in a variety of colors and many tradesmen have experience installing it. Quarry is a six-inch by six-inch tile available in half-inch or, less commonly three-quarter inch, depth. It is installed with a quarter-inch spacing between tiles and set using a variety of methods.

ADHESIVES AND GROUTS

The tile used for the flooring system is important but the adhesive used to bond the tile to the floor and the grout used to seal between tiles are critical. Various materials are used and many times the same product may be used for both jobs.

Broadly the two ways that tiles are set are the "thick setting bed" method and the more standard "bond-coat" or "thin-set" method. Each has advantages. Thick beds are used with vibrated-in-place flooring systems. Some floors with a slight flex to the underlying substrate may use an industrial brick system which has a membrane between the tile and the base floor and thus provide an ability to bridge cracks. These are complicated systems for use with specialized duties. On all types of thicker flooring systems, expansion joints in the base floor should have a corresponding control joint in the installed flooring system.

The most common adhesive for general tile work is a cement and sand setting mortar which may have additional ingredients added to the mixture. These mixtures may include modified latex or even a small percentage of epoxy. The mixtures may be formulated for use in a thick bed, self-leveling or thin-set application. In general these cement-based adhesives are unsuitable for a bond-coat brewery flooring application and a better specification would be a 100 percent solids type of epoxy system.

Epoxys are a two-part system made of a resin and a hardener. The resin is the base liquid and the hardener is a catalyst. There are many different types of epoxies and additives are also often used to provide flexibility, add color or lower the cost through the use of fillers such as sand, carbon or silica. Epoxy adhesives are commonly laid using a quarter-inch-deep v-notch trowel. This will give an excellent bond to the floor and provide a nominal one-eighth inch adhesive layer.

One widely specified epoxy grout is the furan based epoxy type. This system has been used in harsh, wet, hot, sanitary applications for over 50 years. Furan based grouts can withstand service temperatures up to 300° F. Application presents some challenges as they are fairly volatile compounds and have a very short working time—as little as 15 minutes after mixing. The adhesive qualities of this grout require the use of tile that has had a topcoat of wax applied to prevent the excess grout from remaining permanently bonded to the tile. One widely known maker of Furan based grouts is Atlas.

In recent years new high-grade epoxy formulations have been developed. These have better chemical resistance, lower odor, and easier cleanup procedures than furan based systems. Additionally they are available in a variety of colors and a lower skill level is required for installation so lower installation costs may be seen. Light duty commercial grade epoxy grout exists but they may not stand up to brewery requirements. The better grades of epoxy are not much more expensive. One such product line would include Latapoxy 300 adhesive and Latapoxy 2000 Industrial Epoxy Grout. These products meet or exceeds the ANSI specifications for both epoxy and furan grouts. Coverage of adhesives applied with quarter-inch v-notched trowel is about 18 square feet per gallon.

Tile costs per square foot:
Tile only
Quarry tile: $2.04
Acid Tile: $2.55
Furan Epoxies
Adhesive: $1.31
Grout: $0.60
Epoxies
Adhesive: $3.49
Grout: $2.05

Total costs of materials for quarry tile with Novaloc epoxy: $7.58 per square foot.

Total costs of materials for quarry tile with Furan epoxy: $3.95 per square foot.

Advantages: Durable proven system that can be repaired

Disadvantages: Cost is high, some systems can be difficult to repair. Like all flooring jobs, quality is subject to the skill of the installer.

Costs: Installation costs for quarry tile are widely dependent on the size and difficulty of the job. Large open areas will get you the best pricing, but in general you could see an installed price of about $11-18 per sq. foot. Installed cost for Clinker tile is quoted as being close to $11 per square foot. As with any installation, requiring skilled work, the system is only as good as the installer. Larger breweries make use of companies working on a national scale. Inexperienced installers may suffer problems utilizing materials that are more difficult to work with.

STAINLESS STEEL

When Kyle Carstens at the Wynkoop Brewing Co. in Denver Co. decided to repair/replace the brewhouse floor, no contractor was able to guarantee that the floor would not continue to leak. The brewhouse at the Wynkoop sits on a wooden subfloor and as such it flexes with the changing weights of the brewery tanks. Tile, epoxy and membrane were bound to fail so he eventually decided to have a fully welded 1/8" thick stainless steel floor installed. The installer first laid marine grade plywood to make the floor consistently pitched and then laid and welded the floor. The material has a raised non-skid tread plate pattern.

Advantages: Cool as Christmas.

Disadvantages: Unproven, Expensive.

Cost: About $70 per square foot.

CONCLUSION

What should I do about my floors? Many brewers ask that question, but to answer it you first must determine what performance you need from your floor. One store of the Capitol City Brewpub in Washington DC is located directly over the US postal service museum. You can bet that they have some pretty stringent flooring requirements. On the other hand, the malt storage area of a 500 barrel per year brewpub hardly needs to be tiled. I think that for a must-not-leak application on cement I would look at a tile based system installed over a waterproof membrane. For a new production brewery brewhouse, paving tiles may be the best choice. For a good looking and cost effective floor the quarry or clinker tile would be a good choice. If you have a limited budget, a simple concrete floor with a regularly scheduled application of sealer might be best. What is not appropriate? I would stay away from thin epoxies, untreated concrete and oh yes, wooden floors that grow mushrooms.

WEB RESOURCES

Ucrete
www.selby-ucrete.com
Monolithic epoxy flooring

Stonehard
www.stonehard.com
Many flooring products

Atlas Minerals
www.atlasmin.com
Furan based epoxy

Laticrete
www.laticrete.com
Novaloc based epoxy

Dayton Superior Chemical
www.daytonsuperiorchemical.com
Concrete water repellants

Summitville Tile
www.summitville.com
Tile manufacturer

Argelith
http://argelith.com
Clinker tile manufacturer

ACSS
www.acss.de
Clinker tile installer

Niece Eckard Waterproofing
www.nieseggert.com
U-crete installer

Stogsdill Tile Co.
www.stogsdilltile.com
Paving tile installer

Concretenetwork
www.concretenetwork.com
Great Concrete website

Chapter Sixteen

Hopping From Farm to Fermenter

Details on hop growing and distribution that can save you money on this essential raw ingredient.

By Ralph Olson

FARMERS GROW HOPS; BREWERS USE THEM. But few brewers buy their hops directly from farmers. Given the simple nature of the commodity, this may seem odd. After all, by the time most hops leave the farm, they are suitable for brewery use. Thus, compared to corn flakes or automobiles—or even malt—hops seem rather simple. Yet despite this, a long-established and worthwhile intermediary serves brewers and growers in the space between the oasthouse and the brewhouse.

Hop dealers play an important role in facilitating orderly commerce. Let's take a brief moment to examine some of their roles.

Inspection and Testing – The hop dealer inspects hops received from the farmer for pests and damage that may reduce their value to brewers. They also test for alpha acid percentage, moisture content and in some cases things like beta acids, total oils and other physical properties.

Warehousing – While brewers use hops throughout the year, growers harvest the entire crop during a few scant weeks in late summer. Dealers warehouse the hops in cold warehouses to help preserve them until they are shipped to brewers. This relieves both brewers and growers of the need to have sufficient storage capacity for an entire year's worth of hops.

Processing – While some breweries still use whole hops, most brewers prefer at least some of their hops in other forms such as pellets, plugs or extracts. The dealer manages production of these products. In some cases, they merely process hops already selected by a brewer as when a specific lot of hops needs to be pelletized. In other cases, they may select part of their inventory for processing into other forms based upon their assessment of the likely market demand for those other products.

Development – Dealers support research and development in a number of areas. This ranges from the development of new hop varieties designed to address the needs of both growers (e.g. disease resistance) and brewers (e.g. higher alpha acid content) to research on new hop forms (e.g. extracts) that can be useful in the brewery.

Communication – Hop dealers serve as an efficient channel of communication between growers and the brewers. Since they talk to many people in both communities, they can describe market conditions and trends on both the supply side and the demand side. This allows a brewer to get a sense of what is going on with hop supplies by talking to their dealer rather than having to call up ten or twenty hop growers.

Marketing – Of course hop dealers sell hops as well. In this sense, they play a critical role for the growers, helping to ensure that the marketplace buys what growers produce. Ultimately, the dealer determines the best way to market all of the hops while considering things such as quality, composition and variety. When all is said and done, at the end of the day the goal is to have everything sold and have the breweries be happy with what they have bought.

Other Services – Some major breweries will buy hops directly from a grower and there is even an American brewery that grows some of its own hops. Here, the dealer's role is to help receive, inspect, weigh, warehouse and ship the hops for the brewer. A fee is charged for these services. Many brewers take hops in the whole hop form, but many brewers want to take their needs in the form of pellets, extracts, and other downstream products.

Aside from buying hops from growers, dealers can facilitate sales between brewers while preserving the anonymity of each party. Market conditions and recipe changes can lead a brewer to have surplus hops. When this happens, brokers facilitate a sale without either party having to surrender their identity to the other.

INDUSTRY STRUCTURE

One thing that impacts the structure of the hop industry is the nature of hop growing. As most brewers know, hops are produced in a small number of special geographic regions around the world where the necessary combinations of soil, climate and daylight are found. Let's look briefly at the major hop growing regions and their characteristics.

Overall, the biggest producers of hops are the United States and Germany, which together account for about 70 percent of worldwide production. Overall the production of the two countries is about the same, although one may be a good bit bigger than the other in any one year based on crop and harvest conditions. Historically, the US has been seen as a grower of bittering hops and Germany as a producer of aroma hops, although this has changed to some extent in the past ten to twenty years.

Overall, the biggest producers of hops are the United States and Germany, which together account for about 70 percent of worldwide production.

As a brewer, you need to understand the structure of the hop industry so that you have a better idea where and how to purchase the hops you want while getting the quality you need at a reasonable price.

In Germany today, there are still a few thousand growers. These growers generally have small areas under cultivation. As a result, hop sources from Germany come in small lots. German growers commonly form small groups that will have a spokesperson who is responsible for getting the hops sold.

In contrast to this, the American industry is more concentrated. Today in the US we have around 80 hop growers. We have seen a continued decline and are now to a point where we can ill afford to lose any more of these producers. When I started in 1978, there were approximately 180 growers. Total US acreage has remained somewhat consistent. However, in 1978 the average farm size was around 200 acres. Today it is more like 450 acres.

The other hop producing areas that export significant amounts of hops include the Czech Republic and England in the northern hemisphere and Australia and New Zealand in the southern hemisphere. While Germany and the US account for about 70 percent of all hops, none of the remaining growing countries accounts for more than 10 percent of worldwide hop supply.

Today hop dealers appear in a number of forms. Some are privately owned by individuals or investors with no ownership ties to individual buyers or brewers. Others are cooperatives owned by groups of hop growers. In line with these different forms of ownership, we find both locally-owned operations and brokers who are part of large international organizations.

As a brewer, you need to understand the structure of the hop industry so that you have a better idea where and how to purchase the hops you want while getting the quality you need at a reasonable price. Let's now look at the hop dealer structure today and how it operates.

Most major dealerships over the years have been owned or influenced by companies in Germany. This only makes for good sense given the dominance of German brewing philosophy worldwide over the past 150 years or so. Only when one considers that the main (but not the only) role of the dealer is to act as a go-between for the grower and the brewer, does the German influence become clear. In previous times, dealers had ties to a specific brewery that went back many decades. Through time, however, many individuals or groups of growers have organized dealers to perform the basic role of selling hops to breweries.

While most brewers purchase hops from hop dealers as we have defined them here, some buy from other types of organizations that might be defined as wholesalers or even retailers of brewing ingredients. While wholesalers and retailers usually inventory hops to be shipped to the brewer, they do not purchase them directly from growers. Also, they are unlikely to perform any of the testing or processing roles offered by dealers. Because dealers generally have a minimum quantity purchase for each variety, brewers who purchase small quantities of some hops may find it advantageous to purchase from wholesale or retail organizations.

In addition to hop dealers, you may encounter hop marketing organizations. These groups focus on promoting the hops grown in a specific region or by a specific group of growers by publicizing the hops and arranging contracts for their sale. While some fill all the roles of a dealer as we have defined them here, others focus primarily on promotion while leaving the actual warehousing, testing and processing of the actual hops to other organizations.

As we have discussed, sound companies and consistent performance are important in hop marketing so that a dealer can reliably deliver hops to brewers. A dealer needs good supply, production, and storage capabilities. It also needs to be able to read what the market is doing through good research and statistics. When all these things come together, the production of hops each year matches the needs of brewers around the world, good beer gets made and everyone is happy. ◗

Section III

Marketing and Distribution Programs

NOW THAT YOU HAVE SHARED THE DREAMS of successful brewers and gotten a grasp on practical issues in making beer, let's consider how to connect with consumers. Here you'll find that most chapters focus either on packaging breweries or brewpubs. Distribution is the fundamental difference between these businesses and this section can help you better understand the implications of each business model.

At the beginning of this section we start with a global view, looking at the demographics of craft beer drinkers and an overall strategy for building customer loyalty in brewpubs.

From there we jump into practical details of craft beer marketing from mug clubs and distributor margins to public relations and on-premise promotions. Through these articles we cover the various aspects of marketing and distribution to give you practical insights as well as a starting point for creative thinking about your own unique promotional programs.

By the time you finish this section, your vision for a craft beer business will probably be taking shape. In the final section of the book, we'll begin to look at financial issues including preparation of a business plan.

Chapter Seventeen

The Converging Consumer Profiles For Beer And Wine

Increasingly, drinkers of good beer look like drinkers of good wine according to a national beer survey.

By John P. Robinson, Ph.D.

HISTORIANS TELL US THAT BEER AND WINE developed from parallel production processes based on the availability of fermentable materials. Beer evolved in northern grain growing cultures, wine from southern fruit growing cultures. From this, one might conclude that the two beverages would share more features than differences.

In America however, we know that beer and wine have vastly different consumer images. Wine is viewed as upscale, with rare vintages fetching hundreds if not thousands of dollars. Wine growers and connoisseurs devote countless hours to develop, cultivate and appreciate subtle differences in flavor and texture. Much effort is expended to find the proper "pairing" of wines with expensive meats, cheeses and other delicacies. In brief, wine connotes class.

Beer on the other hand is considered plebian, a mass consumption beverage requiring little subtlety or imagination for appreciation. A Napa Valley wine grower may admit that "It takes a lot of great beer to make a great wine," but where is the brewer who could get any mileage (or credibility) out of stating the reverse?

It comes as some surprise then to contemplate results from the first national survey comparing American wine and beer consumers, particularly craft beer consumers. Conducted in 1999 and 2001 with 1389 respondents aged 21 and older across the country, this National Beer Survey finds less distinction between wine and beer consumers than might be thought. This is especially true in relation to drinkers of craft brews.

For example:

- The proportions of beer and wine drinkers are virtually identical, at just about 50 percent of the population for each.
- Beer and wine drinkers are more often than not the same people. More than three-quarters of the wine is consumed by people who drink beer and nearly three-quarters of the beer is consumed by drinkers of wine.
- Both products are consumed by people who are more affluent and educated than non-drinkers and who are more active Internet users and museum visitors.
- Usage of both is higher among residents in the Northeast and West coasts than in the South or Midwest.

However, many of these similarities come into sharper focus when craft beer drinkers are separated from more traditional mass-market beer drinkers and when premium wine drinkers are similarly separated from drinkers of mass-produced wines. Indeed, craft beer consumers in many ways appear more upscale than typical wine drinkers.

SURVEY DETAILS

The National Beer Survey reported here is the

fourth in a series of surveys conducted to monitor trends and characteristics of craft brew drinkers. The first was conducted in 1995 and reported in *American Demographics* magazine, with subsequent 1996 and 1998 survey results presented in *The New Brewer* (Sept/Oct 1998). All surveys were conducted as part of omnibus national probability surveys conducted by the Survey Research Center of the University of Maryland. The Center typically was able to complete interviews with nearly 60 percent of designated respondents using Random Digit Dial (RDD) techniques—far higher than in typical marketing surveys.

In each of these surveys, respondents are first asked if they have consumed any beer in the previous 12 months. As in previous surveys, about half of respondents in the latest survey said they had. Those who answered "yes" were then asked to estimate how many 12-ounce glasses of beer they consumed in a typical week. Consumers were then asked two questions to determine if they had consumed an American craft or micro beer—first, whether they had consumed a beer on premises in a brewpub and second, if they had consumed a national or locally-produced craft beer bought in a store.

In this year 1999-2001 National Beer Survey, more than a quarter of American adults overall (27 percent) answered yes to one of these two questions and thus qualified as a craft beer drinker. Among beer drinkers, then, just over half (53 percent) said they had at least sampled one craft beer in the last year—either in a brewpub (32 percent) or bought from a store (47 percent). Twenty-eight percent had beer from both types of places. Put another way, almost 90 percent of those who had a beer in a brewpub had also consumed a store-bought micro, while only 60 percent of those who bought a craft beer in a store also had one in a brewpub.

That estimated 27 percent of the American public who experienced a craft beer in a year's time is the highest proportion in any of the previous National Beer Surveys and is up about seven percentage points from our earlier surveys. Still, this group is not completely dedicated to craft beers, since in our next follow-up question, we find that less than 20 percent of craft beer drinkers (or about ten percent of the adult public) claim that half or more of the beer they drink are micros. Thus, in this analysis, we define craft beer drinkers to include those who estimate that at least two percent of their beer consumption is from craft beers.

For purposes of this discussion then, the population of craft beer drinkers includes about 16 percent of the adult population in America versus 34 percent who almost entirely drink mass-market beers and 50 percent who drank no beer at all in the previous year. Throughout this report then, these are the groupings of beer drinkers that we contrast with parallel groups of America's wine drinkers.

WINE CONSUMERS

In this 1999-2001 edition of the National Beer Survey virtually as many respondents said they had consumed wine in the past year (50 percent) as beer (50 percent). When asked how many six-ounce glasses of wine they averaged in the previous week, about half said less than one and another quarter said only one. Averaged across all wine drinkers, the average was about one-and-a-half glasses per week. In contrast, beer drinkers said they averaged about five 12-ounce servings of beer per week. The typical wine drinker, then, consumes only about a third as many equivalent portions as the typical beer drinker.

That beer and wine drinkers are hardly distinct segments of the public is indicated by the finding that almost two-thirds of beer drinkers are also wine drinkers. Moreover, they average more wine servings than non-beer drinkers. That is even more true among microbeer consumers. Put the other way, 73 percent of wine drinkers are also beer drinkers and 29 percent are craft beer drinkers. In contrast, only 32 percent of non-wine drinkers drank beer and only seven percent of non-wine drinkers are craft beer drinkers.

DEMOGRAPHIC AND LIFESTYLE CONTRASTS

The survey results distinguish three parallel groups of beer and wine consumers in this study: 1) nonusers (about 50 percent of both groups), 2) mass consumers who consume only less expensive or mass-market versions of the product and 3) premium consumers who consume more upscale and presumably more complex versions of the product (about one-sixth of each group). In the latter category are more frequent drinkers of craft beers for beer and those who pay $10 or more for their typical bottle of wine.

Table 1 contrasts the six groups in terms of their demographic and psychographic or lifestyle makeup.

Table 1: Demographic/Lifestyle Differences in Beer/Wine Consumption

	Beer			Wine		
	None	Mass	Micro	None	<$10	$10+
Overall Population	50%	34%	16%	50%	34%	16%

Demographics for each type of wine or beer drinker

	Beer			Wine		
	None	Mass	Micro	None	<$10	$10+
Family Income	$36K	$40K	$54K	$34K	$44K	$58K
Education (yrs)	13.2	13.4	15.0	12.9	14.0	14.8
Art Museum (1)	29%	31%	55%	24%	42%	49%
Email hours/wk	1.3	1.1	3.6	1.2	2.3	3.3
www hours/wk	1.9	2.1	4.7	1.7	2.8	4.1
Age (yrs)	48	45	39	45	48	42
Male %	35%	56%	63%	48%	45%	49%
White %	75%	82%	87%	76%	85%	88%
Married %	61%	58%	56%	58%	60%	56%
Children %	41%	45%	36%	42%	47%	40%
Employed %	58%	65%	75%	62%	58%	71%
Work Hours	41	41	44	43	46	42

1-Percent who visited a museum in the last year.

Distribution of each type of wine or beer drinker by geographic region

	Beer			Wine		
	None	Mass	Micro	None	<$10	$10+
Northeast	20%	19%	21%	17%	20%	29%
Midwest	23	28	21	26	22	24
South	40	37	27	40	36	25
West	18	15	30	16	22	23

Work and lifestyle attitudes by type of wine or beer drinker

	Beer			Wine		
	None	Mass	Micro	None	<$10	$10+
Always Rushed %	34%	34%	30%	37%	30%	32%
No Wasted Time %	55%	56%	63%	55%	58%	61%
Moderate+ stress%	65%	66%	69%	64%	67%	61%
Enjoy job (0-10)	7.4	7.1	7.5	7.3	7.3	7.5
Want day off %	54%	41%	54%	52%	44%	54%
Free time prefer %	48%	48%	53%	44%	52%	54%
Tired after work %	24%	19%	17%	23%	18%	15%

The first set of figures are for the factors of most interest to marketers, namely the socio-economic background of respondents for each category of beer or wine consumption. Here it can be seen first that as the average annual family income increases, they move from nonusers to mass market beer/wine users to premium product users (which, of course, do cost more money). In the case of beer, the average family income of non-beer drinkers is $38,000 per year, of mass-market beers $42,000 and of micro-drinkers $55,000. The parallel figures for wine consumers are more distinct—$35,000, $45,000 and $58,000. That would put the micro-drinker at about the average income of those who consume $8-plus bottles of wine, which is the mark of a rather upscale consumer.

In terms of the highly related factor of years of education, the craft beer consumer is actually higher—14.8 years versus 14.5 years for premium wine drinkers. Moreover, micro drinkers score at least as high on several indicators of cultural and media sophistication: attending art museums (50 percent vs. 45 percent among premium wine drinkers), use of email (2.6 weekly hours for each group) and use of the World Wide Web (3.4 weekly hours vs. 3.3 hours). On each of these indicators of cultural participation, of course, the micro consumers also score higher than drinkers of mass-market beers and wines.

Please note that these cultural differences are not simply a function of craft beer drinkers having more education or income. When these factors are equal, micro drinkers are simply more active culturally.

AGE, GENDER, RACE

On the factor of age, on the other hand, both micro drinkers and premium wine drinkers are somewhat younger than either nonusers or consumers of less expensive products. That is surprising since younger consumers generally make less money than older consumers, and we have seen how micro consumption increases with income. In terms of amounts consumed, however, there are contrasting patterns: older beer drinkers drink less beer, while older wine drinkers drink more wine.

While both mass and micro beer drinkers are disproportionately more likely to be male than the rest of the population, women are more likely to be wine drinkers than men, either for premium or low-priced wines. Put the other way, 36 percent of men but only 20 percent of women are micro drinkers; in contrast, 52 percent of women are wine consumers vs. 48 percent of men. However, in terms of amount consumed, contrasting patterns appear again: male beer drinkers drink more beer, and male wine drinkers drink more wine.

Beer and wine are also more likely to be disproportionately consumed by whites, with only 10 percent of blacks being craft beer drinkers (vs. 31 percent of whites) and 7 percent premium wine drinkers (vs. 20 percent of whites). On the other hand, other minorities are about as likely as whites to be premium beer and wine drinkers. In terms of amounts consumed per drinker, the figures are relatively equal across race and ethnic groups unlike the age and gender differentials above.

LIFE-STYLE AND OTHER FACTORS

In terms of other demographic factors, however, there are few differences across the three groups of beer/wine consumers. Premium wine drinkers are slightly less likely to be married, but otherwise marriage and children are equally prevalent among premium users and the rest of the population. Rates of employment are higher among premium product users (because they are younger), but hours of work per worker are not much different than the rest of the population.

However, on the subjective side of employment, some interesting differences emerge. Fewer premium beer or wine users say they are very tired at the end of their workday and more say they enjoy their free time more than their time at work. At the same time, they enjoy their work no less than the rest of the sample and they are not much different in their desire to get time off from work.

More generally, premium users are less likely to describe their lives as always rushed, although they are also more likely to describe themselves as having unwanted time on their hands. Overall stress levels are about equal across the three categories of both beer and wine drinking.

Finally, in terms of regional differences, one again sees parallels across serious beer and wine consumption. Both are bi-coastal, with greater consumption of more expensive beers and wines on the East and West coasts than in the middle or Southern states. In the case of microbeer drinkers, higher proportions are found on the West than the East Coast; in the case of premium wines, more are found on the East Coast. For both beer and wine, higher consumption is found in the Midwest than in the South.

CONCLUSION

The growing audience for craft beers (which has now reached more than half of beer drinkers across the country) has a market profile that mirrors that of wine consumers (both for low and high priced wines), in particular having higher income and education levels than the rest of the population. Indeed micro consumers emerge as slightly more serious art museum patrons and computer/Internet users independent of their higher income and education.

Moreover, premium beer and wine drinkers share the feature of being younger than the rest of the adult population. They also report slightly lower levels of stress and psychological malaise than others. Both serious beer and wine drinkers are found on the coastal rather inland sections of the country. At the same time, neither group is particularly distinguished in terms of their employment, marital or parental status.

On some other factors, however, there are notable differences between beer and wine consumers. In particular, men are much more likely to be beer drinkers and to drink more beer if they do drink. Perhaps being more calorie conscious, women are more into wine, although less into serious wine than men.

Overall, however, it makes little sense to treat beer and wine consumers, both premium and not, as distinct groups. There is considerable overlap between the two, with micro drinkers being far more likely than mass market and non beer drinkers to drink wine, and to consume more expensive wines; in much the same way, premium wine consumers are far more likely than average to drink craft beers.

Perhaps more importantly, there are several ways in which micro drinkers seem more open and sophisticated than consumers of fine wines. Maybe, there is more to be gained by telling premium wine drinkers about new craft beers than by advertising to mass market beer drinkers. ◗

Chapter Eighteen

Creating Customer Connections To Build Your Brewpub Business

Think of your brewpub as a brand to build a loyal consumer base.

By Kevin Finn

TODAY'S CONSUMER SELECTS FROM AN infinite range of restaurant choices. As brewpub operators we often compete against large restaurant chains with muscle-bound marketing departments. They start out by locating in high-visibility, high-traffic locations, control costs through scale economies and then use large marketing budgets and a regional or national presence to build huge brand awareness. When facing that kind of competition, brewpubs have to know how to fight back.

Brewpub operators can strengthen their competitive position—not by focusing just on beer or just on food—but by building the entire business into a strong, local brand. A brewpub's ultimate goal is to create such a strong image in the consumer's mind that they think of our brand *every time* they decide to dine at similar mid-priced, casual restaurants.

WHY BRAND?

Brands help consumers in their buying decisions. First, brands segment the market, helping consumers make purchasing decisions based on a price/value relationship. For instance, Gap, Inc. segments the clothing market using Banana Republic, The Gap, Old Navy, Gap Kids, etc. They have a variety of brands that appeal to different markets by price point and image.

Brands create economies of scale in marketing. A known brand is easier to market than many lesser-known brands. In addition, brands also have "revenue leverage" based on the total number of buyers. Even as a wider variety of people purchase a brand, current users also use them more often.[1]

A familiar brand allows consumers to become so comfortable with a brand that they come to trust the brand. Consumers generally choose a known brand over an unknown brand, even when offered a high-quality or high-value unknown brand.

When choosing a casual place to dine, consumers often use habitual evaluation, or their past habits, to choose a restaurant. Consumers also use brand loyalty when evaluating a brand. In 40 percent of purchase occasions, consumers engaged in habitual evaluation and relied on brand loyalty over price and promotions.[2] Both play a role in bringing customers back to your brewpub on a regular basis.

THE PRODUCT

Brands give products or services a distinctive image, characteristic or association in the consumer's mind. Your brand's image includes all physical and conceptual contacts that consumers have with your brewpub.

In Figure 1, the small inner circle represents the physical aspects of a brand. Because you can see, touch and feel it, this is what most people generally think of as being the product. Whenever consumers physically contact your

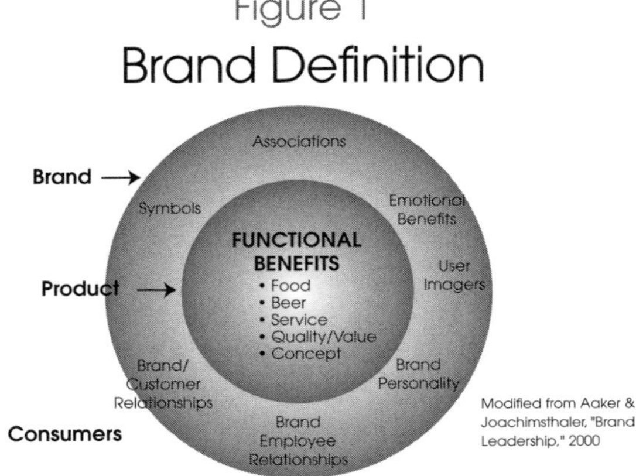

Brands are products or services that have a distinctive image, characteristic or association in the consumer's mind.

brand they have entered this inner circle. The outer circles are conceptual, non-product related attributes of your brand.

In this article, we'll explore that outer circle to discover what brand essence is and talk about the techniques you can use to build a strong brand for your restaurant-brewery. But before we discuss these techniques you should understand what your product is and how it relates to your customer's understanding of your brand. When consumers think of your brand, what images do you want your product to convey to your customers? A brewpub can be a variety of things to a variety of people but your brand's essence or conceptual identity should be aligned with your physical product and your overall brand goals. For the most part, you and your staff have control over your product and for the purposes of this article we will assume that that your product is aligned with your brand.

THE BRAND

Why do customers walk into your brewpub for the first time? Usually because someone has planted an image of your brand in their mind. Otherwise they would not be walking through your door. Where did those images come from? They generally come from your current customers, the media and your own marketing efforts.

So, the first way to get more customers is to insure that your current customers have a great experience. This creates positive word-of-mouth advertising. Then by using marketing in a variety of ways including advertising, promotions and public relations, you can create a positive image of your brand.

The brand's essence is based on the outer circle in Figure 1. These are the links that your marketing, the media, your customers and your staff have to your brand. The personality of your brand can be conveyed to your customer in a variety of ways including your staff, your product and your marketing. Is your brand casual, fun, upscale or a combination of these traits? Relationships can be established with your brand through marketing and then reinforced through product usage. What type of relationship do customers have with your brand? Do they come because they want a great beer, or that they like the atmosphere or that your location happens to be convenient?

Emotional benefits are possibly the strongest link your brand has to its customers and are often the hardest to establish. For instance, consumers often choose a brand because it validates their lifestyle. Your brand can validate your customers' lifestyle as beer aficionados, as consumers who dine at the "hottest" restaurant, or as consumers who want a friendly, local pub. To provide those links your brand can be associated with a variety of things including a beer-smart serving staff, beer related events, media personalities or non-profit and charitable organizations.

BRAND EQUITY

Consumers choose brands that have strong brand equity. Brand equity incorporates all knowledge that consumers have of your brand. That knowledge comes from all the images and associations acquired by contacts with your brand. Obviously then, to build brand equity your goal should be to make all customer contacts with your brand a positive experience.

A brand's image is a mirror reflection of the brand's identity. You create a brand's identity first by creating a product and then using marketing to create the links to your customers. On the other hand, each consumer will have a unique image of your brand. They must filter all the information they come in contact with regarding your brand. You provide some of that information, but additional information comes from other sources including the media, your customers, your vendors and everyone else who has been exposed to your brand. All of those messages go into building each consumer's unique image of your brand. You want those links to provide clear benefits, positive associations and intense and powerful relationships that motivate them to use the brand. Those links come from your brand messages, contacts and associations.

Brand messages include concepts, ideas, symbols, colors and marketing messages used to persuade customers to come to your brewpub and spend money. They tend to be formal and controlled by the marketer and include things like advertising, promotions and public relations.

Brand contacts include the informal images or information-bearing experiences consumers may have with your brand. They include word-of-mouth comments, personal experiences, news stories and reviews and even your employee opinions of your brand.

Brand associations can be product or non-product related.[3] Product related associations go back to that inner circle—physical interactions. All brewpubs share similarities, but each concept differs somewhat. Differences come by way of the types of beer, the types of food, and the level of service that we provide. Different concepts elicit different associations for each consumer.

Non-product associations include emotional benefits, attitudes, symbols, user imagery (or who uses the product) and usage imagery (how the product is used). These images result from how your brand contributes to the consumers' lifestyle. For instance, one set of customers may be business people who want a more upscale image (user imagery) and their usage (or usage imagery) may be based solely on the lunch and happy hour day parts.

Finally, symbols constitute the visual associations your marketing creates for your brand. You display these symbols in many ways including your menus, signage and uniforms. In addition, awards or positive reviews of your restaurant provide validation of your current customer's emotional benefits and reinforces your brand image to other potential users.

BUILDING BRAND IDENTITY

To create a strong brand identity, you must first establish a clear understanding of the brand throughout your organization. Do you truly understand what your brand should communicate to your customers? This sounds easy, but isn't. And without this understanding you may create confusion in your consumer's mind regarding the true image of your brand.

Next, make sure your brand identity doesn't conflict with your customer's image of your brand. This ties directly to your concept. For instance, if your concept is upscale but your customers tend to be young, your identity may always be in conflict with your customers' image of your brand. If your customers are business people but your concept is a pub with little emphasis on food, your identity may be in conflict with what your customer's image of a brewpub should be.

> When building a brand we have a variety of tools that we can use to communicate our brand to consumers as shown in Figure 2. They include: 1) symbols & marks, 2) public relations, 3) advertising, 4) promotions, 5) events and sponsorships, and 6) employee relations. The messages you communicate with these tools should be aligned with your brand's identity so consumers get a unified image of your brand. Let's look at each of these in turn.

Figure 2
Iron Hill's Brand Communications

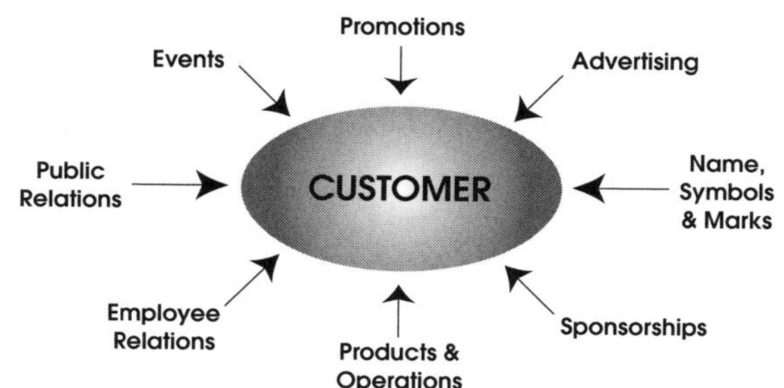

Brand communication includes all of the ways that customers gain information about your operation.

In addition, different types of customers can have different images of your brand. As brewpub operators, many of us have been able to make the transition from restaurant to bar, but if this conflict is not managed it can create identity problems that will distort your brand.

Finally you should establish brand goals. Those goals will be different depending on where your brand is in its lifecycle. Your branding strategy will be directed at three customers: competitive customers (customers who use other casual restaurants), new or emerging customers, and current customers. New brands need to gain market share by attracting competitive customers. Once open, you should increase your visibility and differentiate your brand from your competitors. Once you have become established the goal should be to increase sales to current customers by giving them additional reasons to visit your brewpub as well as adding new and competitive customers. Older or declining brands generally want to maintain or increase profit margins by cutting costs and retaining customers.

SYMBOLS AND MARKS

When creating a brand one of the first things you will do is create your brand's name. Your brand name should sound familiar but still distinctive enough to break through the competition. We chose Iron Hill because it was masculine, was a local historic landmark but also could be used as we expanded into different markets. "Hops" is good example of a name that uses ingredients to create an image, while "Thirsty Dog" is an example of using a product's attribute to create memorable associations.

Your brand mark or logo creates visual associations that can lead to instant recognition and legal protection via trademark restrictions. It may be the first image a customer acquires in association with your brand. Iron Hill's mark (Figure 3) is easily recognizable and relates to the architecture of our brewpubs. We designed our interiors in the "Arts and Crafts" architectural style—a style that borrows elements from Japanese culture. Adapted from Japanese motif, the bird incorporates barley and hops within the wings. It's simple elegance is distinct, unique and recognizable. The font was chosen because it has a solid, masculine and iron-like quality to it.

Some of the uses of our mark include an iron weather vane sculpture (Figure 4) that can be found behind all of our bars. The mark and logo carry through to many of our in-house materials: menus, place mats, coasters and napkins (Figure 5).

Figure 3
Brand Mark

IRON HILL
BREWERY & RESTAURANT

When creating a brand, one of the first things you will do is to create your brand's name. Your brand name should sound familiar but break through the competition. Your brand mark creates memorable associations.

Figure 4
Brand Mark

Some of the uses of Iron Hill's mark include an iron sculpture we call the "weather vane" that can be found behind all of our bars.

PUBLIC RELATIONS

Public relations allows you to communicate to consumers outside of advertising to achieve your overall branding goals. The field of public relations includes community relations, publicity and media relations. At Iron Hill, we place an emphasis on publicity because of its importance in branding.

In community relations you interact with neighborhood organizations to create images and goodwill for your operation and your brand. We try to pick three or four major events a year and really get behind the events. The goal is to create stories that are interesting. As an example, we became a major sponsor of West Chester's bicentennial cele-

Figure 5

Logo

The logo is placed on our menus, uniforms, pens and napkins to reinforce our brand mark.

Figure 6

Public Relations

Iron Hill Brewery says it will produce Bicentennial brew

WEST CHESTER – Iron Hill Brewery & Restaurant Monday announced it will brew Bicentennial Lager for the West Chester 200 celebration.

As an official sponsor of the event, the brewpub will donate 10 percent of the sales of the Bicentennial Lager to West Chester 200.

The beer will be released on four of the five major celebration weekends throughout 1999 and the Bicentennial Ball. The first batch will be released April 16 in conjunction with the West Chester Kickoff Weekend.

Bicentennial preparations

West Chester Mayor Clifford DeBaptiste (above) taps the first Bicentennial Beer made for the borough's 200th birthday Thursday as Iron Hill Brewery General Manager Sean Caviston and John Featherman of the bicentennial committee watch. Below, Steve Pavlo of D. Malloy Paving surfaces a parking lot A map of Sunday's parade route appears on Page A3.

Community relations is a great way to generate publicity and create goodwill for your brand.

Figure 7

Public Relations

To support a local soup kitchen, we had a local DJ create and serve a soup at the restaurant. Photo opportunities are an important part of public relations.

bration. We agreed to brew a Bicentennial beer four times throughout the year and to donate 10 percent of our beer sales to the community every time we brewed the beer. As a result of this program, we received press coverage each of the four times we brewed the beer (Figure 6).

At another event, we had a local DJ create and serve a soup at the restaurant the week prior to Christmas and donate profits to the local soup kitchen. We kicked off the event by serving the soup at the shelter. The idea was to create a photo opportunity for the press (Figure 7).

The simplest way to generate publicity is through the use of a press release. We send out dozens of press releases each month to various media sources. Some are simple and regular and include: upcoming beers, food specials and an entertainment calendar. Others occur because of special events, new hires, a new menu or awards.

With media relations, the goal is to be a source of information for the press. If they have questions regarding craft brewing, the brewpub industry, the restaurant industry or local business developments, you want to be a source for their needs.

ADVERTISING

Advertising has been the traditional way to create and establish national brands, particularly television advertising. The goal of advertising is to continue the existing dialogue between your brand and your customers. Advertising's strength is its ability to reinforce your brand's identity. It should support the existing relationship between your customer and your brand. Advertising's weakness is that it is ineffective at changing a brand's image in the short term.

When advertising an existing brand, a relationship already exists between customers and the brand and the goal is to continue the dialogue, therefore reinforcing the image. We constantly use print and outdoor advertising to reinforce our image as an upscale brewery/restaurant. Much of our advertising is directed at our core demographic of dining customers and uses lifestyle magazines. Additionally, we create an identity through associations with local radio personalities that have a following among the under-30 crowd. Here we target a younger demographic that is harder to reach. They are usually bar customers who come during our late night day part, but may become dining customers in the future.

Figure 8
Advertising

Much of Iron Hill's advertising is directed at our core demographic of dining customers. We advertise in lifestyle magazines such as *Delaware Today*.

Figure 9
Promotions

Music adds value without discounting. It also distinguishes us from the other national mid-price chains.

New brands must capture the targeted consumer's imagination. The goal may be to establish your brand as the local or niche brand versus the national chains. As local owner/operators we can make personal connections to customers that are not possible for large brands.

PROMOTIONS

Promotions are generally discounts, or an added incentive that immediately drives traffic to your brewpub. Where advertising is long term, promotions are generally short term, with the goal of increasing sales immediately. We often use promotions in conjunction with advertising and public relations to further build our brand. Unfortunately promotions are often based on discounts and can eventually devalue your brand and as a result customers will come to expect a discounted price. We try to use promotions that add value to our brand.

The brewery creates lots of opportunities to create promotions that add value. As brewers we have a unique marketing opportunity that we need to use to our advantage. Brewery promotions can include a variety of events. Some events that we have had success with include: 1) inviting guest brewers from other local microbreweries to showcase a limited release beer, 2) mug club, 3) special tappings of seasonal or reserved beers, 4) and inviting a local celebrity to brew a beer.

We also use promotions to drive sales on a slow night. Simple promotions include discounts on pints, pitchers, wings, nachos, etc. These are generally geared toward a younger audience that comes in later in the evening after our dining customers have left. We have also had success with combining food and beer into special promotional packages. By packaging two or more products you can create a higher perceived value for your customers but in doing so increase your average check per customer.

EVENTS AND SPONSORSHIPS

Sponsorships allow you to create associations to organizations that may have broad appeal. For instance, we sponsor the local minor league baseball team and the university basketball team and both are highly regarded within the local community. In addition, we sponsor numerous events to help promote our brand, including many local charities.

Food and beer events allow a wide range of consumers to sample your products at very little cost. Consumers come in direct contact with your brand in situations that allow you to create strong associations. At events, we put a great deal of effort into presenting our product so the brand contact is positive.

EMPLOYEE RELATIONS

Your employees are involved in most of the contacts that consumers have with your products. Training is essential so that your employees understand your brand's essence and how they can create positive experiences when customers use your products. Our training program is extensive and includes training in food, beer, service and our culture, allowing our staff to gain knowledge about our products and brand.

To reinforce the importance of craft beer to our employees we take one employee each year from each restaurant, at our expense, to the Great American Beer Festival. We also encourage all of our employees to attend the event. Employees earn points toward the trip throughout the year, and every August we throw a party to announce the winner at each restaurant.

CONCLUSION

Building a brand includes much more than just creating a great product. It encompasses your brewpub's personality, the benefits and emotional links it provides to your customers, your brand name and mark, and the positive associations your marketing creates for your brand.

You can create links between consumers and your brand in many ways including symbols and marks, public relations, advertising, promotions, events, sponsorships and employee relations. All of these links should take into account your brand's goals and reinforce your brand's position in the market. To be successful you need to position your brand so that it takes into account your brand identity and then communicates that identity to consumers every time they come in contact with your brand.

Brand building is an important tool that can be used by any brewpub of any size. Remember your brand image is built on every contact that your brand has with consumers. Positive contacts increase your brand equity and negative contacts will decrease your brands equity. As brewpub operators, we want to ensure that every contact is positive and ultimately builds brand equity.

[1] Anschuetz, Ned (1997a), "Building brand popularity: the myth of segmenting to brand success," *Journal of Advertising Research*, 37 (Jan-Feb) 63-6

[2] Murthi, B.P.S. and Kannan Srinivasan (1999),"Consumer extent of evaluation of brand choice," *The Journal of Business*, 72 (April) 229-231.

[3] Keller, Kevin Lane (1993), "Conceptualizing, measuring, and managing customer-based brand equity," *Journal of Marketing*, 57 (Jan) 1-23.

Chapter Nineteen

Mug Shots: Using Mug Clubs to Build Business

Larger servings and other privileges of membership help to build customer loyalty.

By Greg Kitsock

A MUG CLUB IS AN EXCELLENT WAY TO create an inner circle of loyal regulars and give your clientele maximum bang for the buck.

Details vary from one brewpub to the next, but the basic deal is as follows: For a nominal fee (generally between $20 and $50 a year), the customer gets to drink from a special vessel, and can buy beer at a discount—sometimes a substantial one—over the regular price. Other perquisites of mug club membership may include:

- Free t-shirts, or a discount on merchandise with the brewery logo.
- Admission to special events like beer dinners or the tapping of new brews.
- Reduced prices on food items. For instance, Gritty McDuff's in Portland, Maine rewards its mug club members with a free lunch on their birthday.
- Raffles and giveaways. J.T. Whitney's Pub & Brewery in Madison, Wisconsin randomly picks a number each day and posts it on the brewpub's web site. The lucky customer whose mug club membership number corresponds to that figure gets to drink free that day.

From the restaurateur's point of view, a mug club offers at least four distinct benefits:

- It makes casual customers into regular ones and persuades regular customers to visit even more often.
- It's a great way to fill your restaurant on nights that would otherwise find you half-empty. By holding mug club nights on "a relatively slow night like Thursday, we can guarantee that the whole upstairs will be packed," says brewer Kevin Litchfield of the Lake Placid Pub & Brewer in Lake Placid, NY.
- It gives you the opportunity to compile a database of your most loyal clientele.
- For areas unfamiliar with the concept of a brewpub, a mug club is an effective tool for weaning customers off of mass market brands and on to your house beers. "We had a hard time in the beginning—this is a serious Coors and Budweiser population here," comments Alyssa Marsh, general manager of the Three Rivers Eatery and Brewhouse in Farmington, Colo. By aggressively promoting its mug club (house brews available for $2 a 20-oz. mug at any time), Three Rivers has reduced in-house sales of Coors Light and Budweiser to negligible amounts.

Mug clubs are not a new promotional tool. McGuire's Irish Pub in Florida, which opened in Pensacola in 1989 and added a branch in Destin in 1996, has long been offering its customers the same deal: buy a 14-oz. ceramic stein for $19.95, and we'll number it, stencil your name on it, and store it behind the bar. The holder can stroll in at any time and get a mug of beer for the happy-hour price of $1.50.

McGuire's is unusual, if not unique, in that there is no renewal fee, and members can keep their mugs at the brewpub for as long as they like. The Destin location so far has accumulated 2,000 mugs, lining the ceiling above the horseshoe-shaped bar and filling a series of Plexiglas cases along the walkway to the restrooms. The Pensacola pub is adorned with over 5,000 personalized drinking vessels.

As brewmaster Madison Roane explains, McGuire's draws a large part of its clientele from the military. "Almost every Navy pilot has to come through Pensacola, and Destin isn't far from Eglin Air Force Base. Our customers can be stationed abroad for 4-8 years, come back and find their mugs still hanging here."

At the Bandersnatch Brewpub in Tempe, Ariz., joining the mug club isn't merely a financial transaction; it's more of a fraternity initiation.

At the Bandersnatch Brewpub in Tempe, Ariz., joining the mug club isn't merely a financial transaction; it's more of a fraternity initiation. Applicants are seated in a barber chair in the backroom, where they have a mug of beer hurled in their face. "People do it for special occasions like birthdays and bachelor parties," laughs bartender Joy Saltsman. Victims can choose a favorite bartender or server to douse them with beer. But no outsiders, please. "We don't want the mug to slip out of the thrower's hand," notes Saltsman. Clearly, this is a job for professionals.

Once initiated into the Beer-In-Your-Face club, customers receive a free t-shirt, and a plaque with their name is added to the brewpub's "wall of shame." There are about 600 plaques, estimates Saltsman, dating back to Bandersnatch's opening in April 1988.

Of course, beer drinkers who don't want to be subject to this indignity can simply pay the $20 entrance fee, receive the 16-oz. logo mug, and obtain the same benefits.

All Rock Bottom restaurant breweries feature a mug club unless prohibited by local law. But the offer differs from location to location. At the Rock Bottom in King of Prussia, Pennsylvania joining the club is absolutely free. Once signed up, the customer is entitled to receive 20 ounces of beer for the same price a regular customer pay for a pint. Each member receives a credit-card-like ID, which is swiped every time he or she orders a brew. After ten visits, the mug club member gets a free t-shirt and pint glass. After 125 beers, "we cut a keg in half and mount it on the wall with their name on it," says head brewer Jon Thomas. After 250 beers, the customer receives a major upgrade: he or she gets to drink from an elaborately-decorated, 22-oz. ceramic Gerz stein with a tree-branch handle.

Most mug clubs, for obvious reasons, attract only local customers who can take full advantage of the privileges. But the Rock Bottom-King of Prussia mug club, because the benefits are indefinite and accrue to other locations, is enticing more casual customers. "We signed up 800 in three weeks," boasts Thomas. "Giving members an extra four ounces of beer is still quite profitable for us," he adds. "And it makes people feel a little special."

Rock Bottom is the nation's largest brewpub chain in terms of volume, and economies of scale enable the company to be especially generous. But single-unit brewpubs can also be competitive. The Three Rivers Eatery and Brewhouse, for example, has formed an alliance with four other independent brewpubs in Durango and Dolores, Colorado. All use a common vessel for their mug clubs—a 20-oz. stein decorated with the logos of all five participants—and all offer a heavily discounted 20-oz. pour, good at any time. A card issued by any one of the breweries will be honored at all the other locations.

The Colorado brewpubs are very promotion-minded. Every mug club night, held on a Wednesday evening, brings a different event. It might be a bowling tournament in which the participants try to knock down miniature liquor bottles with golf balls. It could be bobbing for apples in a tub of beer. Each winter, Three Rivers holds "Freeze Your Ass Off Night." For this, mug club members enjoy dollar beers as long as they sit on the outdoor patio. "We wait until there's a big storm coming to hold that one," laughs general manager Alyssa Marsh.

This past fall, Three Rivers and its partner brewpubs organized a golf tournament for staff and mug club members at a nine-hole course in Ignacio, Colorado. The event featured plenty of beer and barbecue, plus limo and van service so the participants didn't have to worry about driving home. "It was a blast," asserts Marsh. "We hope to make it an annual tradition."

Mug clubs can be fun, but they do require a lot of planning. First of all, check your local ABC laws to make sure the promotions you have in mind are legal. We know of no state or locality that specifically bans mug clubs as such, but many states do restrict price promotions and giveaways. Alaska, for instance, bans happy hours. California allows drink night promotions but they cannot be advertised. Arizona requires prior approval for bar contests, while Georgia prohibits such events entirely. If in doubt, consult your attorney or ABC representative.

If you intend to let customers customize their mugs and hang them behind the bar, the $64,000 question is: How much space do I have? The Bitter End Brewery in Austin, Tex. didn't plan very well, admits manager Travis Gaters. "We initially thought we'd get 100-150 members," he recalls. But the prospect of a lifetime membership for $20 was too good for residents of the Texas capital to pass it up. "When we ran out of allotted room, we had to build more shelves," continues Gaters. "Our entire front bar is double-stacked with mugs!"

Having reached 250 memberships in only three months, the club is now officially sold out. "We're knocking our heads, trying to find space to expand the club," adds Gaters.

McGuire's, which houses the granddaddy of all mug collections, has yet to place a cap on membership, states brewmaster Madison Roane, "but it may happen sometime down the road." It helps that both McGuire's locations are fairly large restaurants, accommodating 400-450 guests.

Even if you have plenty of wall and ceiling space, bear in mind that your assortment of drinking vessels will require periodic maintenance to keep them clean and dust-free. At some point, customers' mugs will have to be arranged in numerical or alphabetical order for easy retrieval. "Sometimes a manager will spend 20-30 minutes looking for a mug that's been misplaced," warns Roane.

Periodically, brewpub staff will have to weed the collection of inactive vessels that are gathering more cobwebs than beer. One obvious way to cut down on clutter is to encourage members to take their mugs with them when they move away from the area. Brewpubs can also charge biannual or annual renewal fees, and enforce the due dates strictly. Gritty McDuff's, which currently has a one-year-waiting period to join its mug club, gives three notices to delinquent members. If they haven't paid the $40 annual renewal fee within six months after it comes due, they're out.

Gritty McDuff's, which currently has a one-year-waiting period to join its mug club, gives three notices to delinquent members. If they haven't paid the $40 annual renewal fee within six months after it comes due, they're out.

You can also offer a monetary incentive. McGuire's charges $19.95 if a customer wishes to keep his mug on the premises, but only $16.95 if he or she agrees to take it home. That extra $3, says Roane, is earmarked for maintenance and building new cabinets to store the vessels in.

As a last resort, you can do away with personalized drinking vessels entirely. Grizzly Peak Brewing Co. in Ann Arbor, Mich. provides special 25-oz. vessels to mug club members, but these remain the property of the brewpub. General manager Rob Bennett keeps twelve of these mugs behind the bar, with a couple dozen extras stashed in the basement in case a large contingent of members shows up.

Bennett, however, is the one source we contacted who complained of an inability to recruit members. "We started a year ago, and we have a little over 35 members," he estimates. "I would have liked to have a couple hundred by this time." Bennett isn't saying that the use of common vessels is the main cause for the lack of interest, or even a major cause. (He tends to blame his small bar area, which is equipped with only 12 stools and five tables.) And yet, he is considering individualized mugs as part of a revamp.

There are no hard and fast guidelines on what to charge members. Entrance fees ranged from zero dollars for Rock Bottom--King of Prussia to a whopping $125 a year for the Monarch's Rest Brewpub in Yuma, Ariz. Yet both these establishments report a tremendous response. The trick may be to offer benefits commensurate with the cost. Rock Bottom's mug club gives you an extra four ounces of beer per pour. But at Monarch's Rest, the first 20-oz. mug of beer is on the house. "After you've had 32 beers, it's paid for," calculates bar manager Kevin Eddy.

As membership grows into the hundreds, your wait staff will find it impossible to recognize every member by sight alone. Some brewpubs, like Rock Bottom and Monarch's Rest, issue laminated ID cards. Many assign numbered mugs to their customers. Invariably, however, a patron will leave his membership card at home or forget his number. That's why it's useful to keep an up-to-date membership directory behind the bar.

Finally, a brewpub owner must be concerned about responsible consumption of alcohol. Even if you run a tight ship, the prospect of cheap beer may alarm neighborhood activist groups—and these groups can cause a lot of trouble when your license comes up for renewal. (For example, in the Georgetown neighborhood of Washington, DC, where this writer lives, the neighborhood advisory council has pressured almost all local bars into dropping happy hours and ladies' nights.)

The brewpubs we queried, however, reported few or no problem arising from excessive drinking.

"It's more of a restaurant scene, not a bar scene," says Kevin Litchfield, brewer at the Lake Placid Brewpub, of his establishment's Thursday-night mug club gatherings. "The mug club brings in a lot of middle-aged, professional people. The average age is 30 to 40, compared to the younger college crowd that drinks at the downstairs bar. A lot of members come in with their wives after work, enjoy a mug or two and have dinner."

"We aggressively train our staff in alcohol awareness," maintains Rob Bennett of Grizzly Peaks. "We have no problem with cutting people off."

"Our members are very well-behaved," adds Alyssa Marsh of the Three Rivers Eatery and Brewhouse. "This is their local hangout; they're not going to do anything to get themselves eighty-sixed."

Some brewpubs specifically limit mug club discounts to normal-strength beers. The Bandersnatch Brewpub offers a 9.3 percent-abv barley wine, but that beer is served only in snifter glasses, insists bartender Joy Saltsman. Similarly, McGuire's brews a potent (9.5-11 percent abv) barley wine ominously named "I'll Have What the Gentleman on the Floor Is Having." But this high-test beer is sold off the wine menu, in bottles only. Mug club members receive no discount.

In conclusion, a mug club is a tried-and-true method to bring more warm bodies through the door. You might make a little less profit from beer, but increased sales of appetizers, entrees and non-discounted drinks will more than offset the cost. You can tweak the bylaws and benefits of your mug club to fit your specific legal situation; the size and configuration of your brewpub; and the spending habits of your clientele.

"Ours is always growing, never decreasing," says Litchfield of Lake Placid. "It gives you a 99 percent possibility of repeat customers," adds Madison Roane of McGuire's. "I think it's a big plus all the way around." ◗

Chapter Twenty

Distribution For the Start-up Brewery

Packaging breweries must manage their sales through the three-tier system in order to succeed.

By Tom McCormick

DISTRIBUTION IS ONE OF THE MOST important, yet commonly overlooked components in the operation and success of a craft brewery. A common misconception by those entering the craft beer industry is that once the beer is brewed, packaged, and shipped to a wholesaler, the brewer can essentially forget about it, leaving the sales, marketing and promotion to the wholesaler. This is not the case, since beer distributors function primarily as a delivery and warehousing mechanism. Most distributors do little, if any, selling and promotion of the beers in their portfolio, with the exception of the top selling two to three brands. Hence, it is imperative that the craft brewer know and understand the second tier of the business — distribution — in order to ensure their products are adequately marketed.

SELF-DISTRIBUTION

One option most brewers have available to ensure good distribution is to distribute themselves. This practice is not allowed in some states and is only practical within the local market area. Self-distribution should be limited to within about a one-hundred-mile radius of the brewery (depending on market density) in order to maintain cost efficiencies. The local market is both your most important market and also the easiest to gain recognition and retail placements because of the "local appeal." Self-distribution has the advantage of personal, hands-on selling that beer distributors cannot give to most products, given the extent of their product portfolios. The disadvantages are the time and resources involved in running a company within a company. Distributing yourself requires a focus from management, additional personnel and equipment and an investment in time and money.

Some small brewers have initiated self-distribution for the first few years to gain good product representation and placement, and then turned the distribution over to a beer wholesaler to further penetrate the marketplace.

SELECTING THE RIGHT DISTRIBUTOR

Eventually craft brewers must select and secure distributors. In most markets you can choose from a number of distributors. Normally, each market will contain two to three major brand houses (distributors are often referred to as a "house"), one each for Anheuser-Busch, Miller and/or Coors. Major brand houses are the largest and most dominant beer distributors. They have a very high level of service, do business with virtually all licensed retail accounts, and are aggressively competitive. They have excellent contacts within the retail trade, including important chain store buyers. The disadvantage for the craft brewer is that he or she is a small fish in a very large pond with these major brand distributors. First and foremost, these distributors are selling their primary brand and are therefore often unwilling to provide much attention to the smaller brands in their portfolio. Major brand houses are also very selective in choosing new brands.

Many markets may also contain a miscellaneous brand house. A miscellaneous brand distributor carries many products other than one of the big three such as regional breweries, popular imports, and non-alcoholics. Although they do not dominate the marketplace like a major brand house, they usually have a high level of service and can be a good home to the small brewer.

In some markets, you'll also find small specialty distributors who specialize in imports and domestic craft beers. These small distributors typically offer great enthusiasm, have a sales staff that knows and cares about beer in general and will take the time to hand-sell your products. The downside is that these small distributors may be understaffed and usually tend to highlight the account base, only servicing the "A" account base.

Liquor/wine distributors can also offer an option to small brewers. Wine distributors will customarily cover a much broader territory - often statewide - while beer distributors commonly confine themselves to a metropolitan area. Wine distributors are good at product knowledge and hand selling but have very large portfolios, and their main focus and interest is in high margin wine and spirits. Because of the slow pull-through of wine and liquor products compared to beer, they may call on retail accounts only every two weeks, whereas a major brand house may call on a high-volume account as often as five to six times per week. Specialty houses ordinarily have a call frequency somewhere in between.

Due to franchise laws imposed in most states, it is often very difficult to terminate a brewery/distributor agreement. Once you enter an agreement with a distributor, franchise laws protect the distributor from suppliers terminating at will. When shopping for a distributor, choose one that not only suits your needs now, but that will also be appropriate in five or even ten years. Spending time in the marketplace in which you are searching for distribution is the most effective way of selecting a distributor best suited to your needs. Obtain a price sheet from each wholesaler so you know which distributors carry the various brands in the market. Talk to retailers to gain insight into which distributor they prefer dealing with. Ask questions about call frequency, draft service, product knowledge, enthusiasm of the salespeople and which distributor understands and sells craft beers the best. Look around the retail accounts to find out which distributor seems to put up the most POS, has the most draft handles and best shelf positioning for craft beers. Talk with other craft brewers in that market to get their opinion from the supplier side.

When shopping for a distributor, choose one that not only suits your needs now, but that will also be appropriate in five or even ten years.

Once you narrow it down to two or three distributors who you feel might best suit your needs, call each one and set up an appointment to present your products. Most distributors are very selective in looking at new brands. Make sure you are well prepared and have a convincing proposal when meeting with the distributor for the first time. You should know your pricing, shipping costs and arrangements, what your advertising and promotion plans and budget will be, post-off and/or incentive programs, and demonstrate how you will assist the distributor in selling the brand.

Be sure to take samples of both product and point of sale (POS) into the interview. Try to also gain some insight about the distributor during the interview. Some questions to ask are: Do they know craft beers and how to sell them? Do they carry other specialty brands, and what has their success been with those? Do they have a brand manager or specific person responsible for your product line? Are they willing to carry all of your line extensions and draft? Do they have refrigeration space for your brand? Do they have good draft support and service? Do they seem financially strong?

Pricing is a key topic with distributors. Although you cannot dictate to a distributor what they will sell your beer for, you can get an understanding of what margins the distributor will be working on prior to signing a contract. Typically, distributors work on a 25 to 28 percent gross margin for craft beers. Additionally, it is very important to choose a distributor that you feel comfortable with. The "comfort factor" should be high on your list when you make the final decision. Each beer wholesaler has its own personality, and you will want a company you can trust and feel confident with so that a lasting, mutually beneficial relationship is built.

Once you have chosen a distributor willing to carry your products, be sure to have your attorney draft a contract agreement. As the product supplier, it is your responsibility to provide such a contract.

WORKING WITH THE DISTRIBUTOR

Once you both sign the contract, you begin to work together on the product roll out. The wholesaler's sales staff is essentially the brewery's sales staff, so it is imperative that they are excited and educated about your brand. You should hold a "kick-off" meeting with the sales staff and tell them the story behind your brands, how they are made, how they are unique and different, and how to sell them. Remember that the sales staff has a lot of other brands to sell so it is vital that you communicate how your brand will provide value to the retailer and why your brand will sell once it is placed in the account.

Brewery sales representatives commonly do "riders" with the distributor's sales staff. They spend a day with one salesperson on their daily route to help present your products and discuss them with the retailers.

In today's competitive craft-beer market it is essential to keep in touch with each of your distributors on a regular basis. Many small brewers fail to realize how much time and effort this requires. Each distributor should be contacted on nearly a weekly basis to make sure they have adequate POS, discuss inventory levels and ordering projections, progress in key accounts, etc. Brewery sales representatives commonly do "riders" with the distributor's sales staff. They spend a day with one salesperson on their daily route to help present your products and discuss them with the retailers. Brewery representatives should also spend time in the market independent of the distributor's sales staff, to make new placements and generally promote the brand.

One of the most difficult tasks is to maintain appropriate "mind share" from your distributor. If your brand only accounts for perhaps 2 percent of the distributor's revenue, it is very difficult to get more than 2 percent of their time. By staying in touch with the principles of the company, spending time with the sales managers and staff, and spending ample time in the market yourself, you will help ensure adequate representation of your brand.

STATE BY STATE REGS

The rules and regulations pertaining to the distribution and advertising of beer products are highly regulated and are enacted and enforced at the state level. Therefore, each state has its own laws and the brewer is responsible for knowing and abiding by them. Regulations often dictate what a brewer may or may not supply to both retailers and distributors, payment terms between brewer and distributor, and very specific, often restrictive terms for terminating a distributor. Contact the state regulatory agency and beer wholesaler trade organization for the specific laws before doing business in that state.

SUMMARY

Beer distribution — with its own personality, language, and terms — is very different from the brewing business. It is, however, intrinsic to the beer industry. As essential as distribution is to the success of a brewery, it is important to learn this unique industry so that you are comfortable and knowledgeable enough to make it work for you. You can brew the very best of products and have great packaging, but without good distribution, it will be not be enjoyed by the end consumer.

PRICING CALCULATIONS FOR BEER DISTRIBUTION

These example calculations provide a model for understanding beer pricing from the brewer to the consumer through the traditional three-tier distribution system. ***In order to determine your own selling price, you must begin by estimating what it will cost you to produce beer.*** From there, you can add the desired brewery gross margin, freight charges and state liquor taxes to arrive at the price the brewery will charge the distributor for beer. In the Distributor and Retailer sections, you will see the calculations needed to determine the mark-up at these segments of the distribution chain. By adding the distributor and retailer margins to the laden brewery cost and dividing by four, you can arrive at the likely retail price for a six-pack of your beer.

Please note that distributor and retailer margins vary widely and may be affected by the size and type of account as well as the nature of your own brand in the marketplace. Higher margins may be required early on in order to entice distributors and retailers to carry your brand.

Please note that this example is based on a potential off-premise sales scenario. On-premise packaging, pricing and margins may vary, but the sequence of calculations will be the same.

Brewery Economics		
Brewery Cost of Production:	$8.00 /case	Includes direct costs, but not overhead or profit. *Use your projected costs.*
Gross Margin:	32 percent	This is the margin needed to cover overhead and provide a profit, usually 20-50%.
FOB (Free On Board) Cost:	$11.76	=Brewery Cost / 1-gross margin %*
Add: Taxes for the state	$1.50/case	Based on tax info in state you are shipping to
Add: freight cost to distributor	$1.25/case	Based on shipping information for the state you ship to
Laden Cost:	$14.51/case	Distributor's Price or what they pay the brewer for the beer
Distributor Economics		
Distributor buys beer for:	$14.51/case	Price brewer charges for the beer
Distributor Margin requirement:	28 percent	Varies by distributor from 24 to 30%.
Distributor price to retailer:	$20.16	=Wholesaler Cost / 1-margin %
Retailer Pricing		
Retailer Cost for Beer:	$20.16/case	Price wholesaler charges for the beer
Retailer margin:	27.5 percent	Varies by retailer and type of account, for off-premise assume 25-30%.
Retail price per case:	$27.81	=Retailer Cost / 1-margin %
Price per six-pack:	$6.95	Case price divided by four

* These examples assume that the gross margin percentage is expressed as a decimal in calculations. Thus 40% becomes 0.40.

Chapter Twenty-One

Introducing Consumers to Your Beer

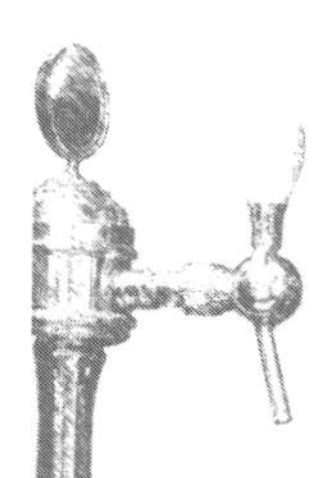

By the pint or by the bottle, retail placements drive the growth of packaged beer brands.

By Pat Meyer

WHENEVER BEER SALESPEOPLE GATHER, they talk about brand building. Usually this means putting a new beer in front of consumers so they will try it, like it, and become a regular customer. A common point of debate asks whether brands are built on-premise (in bars and restaurants) or off-premise (in liquor and grocery stores). Since we usually sell draft beer on-premise and bottled beer for off-premise, the discussion revolves around selling draft versus bottled beer to generate brand loyalty.

Both draft and bottled beer sales pose unique challenges and offer unique benefits. In this article, I'll try to acquaint you with techniques you can employ as you begin formulating a sales strategy for each of your packages.

Before you launch your brand in a new market, you must have a clear strategy. Because while creating a detailed launch plan requires a lot of work, you will find that it is much easier than reviving a poorly launched brand. Whether the initial sales will be made by your distributor or by your own sales people, you should have some clear goals involving both key accounts you want to capture and the total number and type of accounts you hope to gain.

SELLING DRAFT BEER TO CREATE BRAND AWARENESS

Draft beer accounts for about 15 percent of all the beer sold in the United States. For craft beer, the percentage is usually much higher, perhaps in the 30 percent range. But you can't expect to get new draft accounts simply by walking into a pub and asking the manager to put your beer on tap. Draft lines generate a significant portion of the profit for every bar and restaurant. And while the number of lines is limited, there seems to be no limit to the number of competitive salespeople trying to capture them.

Given this competitive structure, you have to add value to what you offer the retailer. Retailers want to maximize sales and profit. Fortunately, as a craft brewer your interests and theirs generally mesh well.

Most retailers will encourage you to engage in brand building activities on-site. This helps them sell your product and realize a profit from putting you on tap. So offering specific brand-building programs when you make your presentation will improve your chances of success. The number and type of programs you offer are limited only by your imagination, time and state liquor laws. To give you an idea, let's look at some of the most common things that might be done.

Enlisting wait staff volunteers. Bartenders and wait staff sell to the consumer and some are very good at it. If you can get the wait staff excited about your product, you have an upper hand in competing for consumer attention. If you can do it, brewery tours get wait staff excited and in touch with your product. The time spent and free beers poured can really pay off. Unfortunately, you can't always gather a large wait staff at one time that works a variety of hours. But if you can't get the wait staff to the brewery, bring the brewery to them. You can often conduct a staff seminar prior to shift changes when you have two separate shifts in the building at the same time. Use your imagination to make these informative and fun.

If local laws allow wait-staff incentives, use them to ensure delivery of your messages to the consumer.

If local laws allow wait-staff incentives, use them to ensure delivery of your messages to the consumer. You might be surprised at how little you have to offer to get the staff excited. Simple wearables or free food and drinks can go a long way. Above all, if you use your imagination to make things fun and exciting for the wait staff, they will treat you right.

Interaction with the consumer. Sometimes you have to take your information directly to the final consumers. Promotional nights give you an opportunity to meet the people and introduce your product. The basic premise of all promotional nights is to have an attractive price for your beer and a giveaway item to capture customer interest. The most effective programs promote interaction between you and the patrons. Also, make sure the information you convey makes consumers want to buy your product at regular price once the promo is over.

Brand presence. No matter how effective your promotions and wait-staff training, you can't reach every customer personally. You also have to use other means for getting your message across. Most restaurant patrons don't ever see your tap handle, so you've got to find some way to get your logo in front of them. You can do this with screened glassware, coasters, table tents, and neons. Since each retailer has different policies and attitudes regarding point-of-sale, you should offer a variety of items. Also, try to supplement your logo with a few words of text or a catchy phrase. Next, try to find a way to let the customer know what to expect when ordering your product. Also, make sure you're the one to put up all your point-of-sale-items—don't count on distributors, bar owners, or on anyone else to do it. And be prepared because you will always go through at least twice as many point-of-sale materials as you thought you would.

SELLING BOTTLED BEER TO CREATE AWARENESS

Bottled beer accounts for the majority of beer sold. Generally speaking, you can more easily gain distribution off-premise than on-premise. While this helps you gain accounts, it is usually not so great for brand building. Off-premise retailers offer so many different products they have less incentive to help you generate sales. It doesn't cost them a great deal to put your product on the shelf and if it doesn't sell, something else will.

For the most part, brand building off-premise comes down to good salesmanship, price positioning, packaging, and thank goodness, a good product. A large percentage of sales and consumer sampling in the off-premise initially comes from impulse buys. Good brand building in the off-premise means putting your product in a position to get those impulse buys. Besides flashy packaging, there are some basic mechanics you can focus on to encourage those impulse purchases.

Pricing can be used to make retailers more receptive to your product and your goals. But laws vary from state-to-state, so you'll have to devise a program that works for each specific market.

Shelf positioning plays a key role in off-premise sales. Many stores use un-refrigerated shelves for beers as well as their traditional refrigerated displays. Ideally you want to be at eye level: you want people to see your product without really looking for it. And you want to be in the right segment of the cooler. Your product should be displayed with beers that are your direct competitors in terms of flavor and price.

Getting as much shelf space as possible has two benefits. First, the "billboard effect" gives your product more visual presence. Second, it helps you avoid out-of-stock situations during busy periods. Focus on these items on both the cold and warm shelves, but pay the most attention to the cold shelf. Cold beer is what sells. The more you accomplish these goals, the more people will try your beer.

Floor displays offer a powerful brand-building tool. A floor display gives your product a large visual presence in a store. By examining the natural traffic flow in a store, you will find the best location for your floor display. Ideally, you would like everyone who shops in the store to pass by your display. A display in a corner of the store that no one ever sees is really just a stack of beer. Always remember to make your displays shopable so that customers can easily grab a bottle or a six-pack. Also, a good display gives the customer information about your brand. Displays are natural billboards for getting a message to the consumer. Find short, concise sentences or phrases to explain to the customer just what they are looking at.

Cooler point-of-sale material. Once you have established a good shelf position, make the most of the attention you receive from the customer. Display the price of your product so consumers can decide if it is in their price range. Cooler statics or channel strips are inexpensive and easy ways to convey this information. If your product is offered at some type of temporary price reduction, make sure customers know they are getting a bargain. People will buy almost anything if they feel they are getting a value. If you can, add some sort of accolade at the point of purchase: a medal, tasting quote, etc. Many consumers need the extra information provided by a couple of lines of text as you often see for wine. Any positive information you can put in front of the customers at this critical juncture when they are about to make a decision is going to weigh in your favor.

In states that allow for in-store tastings, you may have the opportunity to talk personally with potential customers while letting them taste your beer.

Handselling. In states that allow for in-store tastings, you may have the opportunity to talk personally with potential customers while letting them taste your beer. I view this as the strongest method of brand building in off-premise accounts. Here you can tell people your beer's story and let them taste it for themselves. If you can't do tastings, you still may be allowed to come into the store and set up a handsell. While not as effective as a tasting, it still lets you deliver your message to the public.

Handselling can also ingratiate you to the retailer. To achieve the most success, you should have something to catch the customer's eye or something to give away. The cost of giveaway items can be a small price to pay for the opportunity to get people to try your beer and listen to your story.

PROFIT CONSIDERATIONS

Your brewery's profit on different packages of beer can be a vital question when planning your sales strategy. Draft beer appears more profitable than bottled beer on the surface. But I would argue that when draft beer is sold effectively, it is roughly at parity with bottled beer in terms of profit per barrel. Your cost structures will be unique to your operation and economies of scale. Your revenue structures will vary depending on wholesale and retail margins in your particular market. That said, I'll offer some generalizations based on averages I have observed in different markets around the nation.

While bottled beer has higher packaging costs it also offers great revenue per barrel. When you add the extra costs of supporting your on-premise sales, the gap between keg profit and case profit is very small.

Typically a 15.5-gallon keg of beer is sold to retail for around $80. At a 27 percent wholesale margin price, the keg, not including shipping and tax, is $58.40. Gross profit per barrel, depending on economies of scale, is in the neighborhood of $80 per barrel. For a case of six-pack bottles, sale to retail is around $18. At 25 percent wholesale margin price, the case of six-packs, not including shipping and tax, is $13.50. Gross profit per barrel, depending on economies of scale, is in the neighborhood of $70 per barrel. The on-premise market is very expensive to support in terms of sales effort and expected point-of-sale support. The extra dollars of revenue that you gain selling kegs can easily be invested in maintaining your draft lines.

PUTTING IT ALL TOGETHER

While most beer sales professionals agree with the basic brand-building premises outlined above, they usually disagree on how much focus to put on selling bottled beer versus selling draft beer. Lacking unlimited resources, you'll have to make choices about where to focus your efforts. Two schools of thought tend to emerge. The first argues that bottled beer in off-premise should be the main focus. The second argues that on-premise draft should be the main focus.

> The trick comes in deciding how to balance your focus so your sales efforts in on-premise do as much as possible to promote your off-premise sales and vice versa.

The arguments for a bottled-beer, off-premise approach center on the number of places you can put your product and the number of customers who will be exposed. More people visit a liquor or grocery store every day than go to a bar or restaurant. Furthermore, the presentation of brands in off-premise increases the number of people who will notice your brand presence. Usually, it also takes less effort to get distribution in the accounts that really matter.

Advocates for a draft beer approach argue for the high quality of brand building that can be accomplished. Retailer support for brand-building on-premise comes more easily and consumer sampling happens more readily. People are more receptive to trying something new when they are out and they can purchase a single serving.

Both these lines of thought are valid. The trick comes in deciding how to balance your focus so your sales efforts in on-premise do as much as possible to promote your off-premise sales and vice versa. No one has patented a formula for accomplishing this. You have to do your homework to find out how your particular market functions. Get out on the street and talk to retailers and consumers. Examine your costs and make a realistic assessment of how much time and money you are willing to invest. Create target lists of the top accounts in your area and what you would like to accomplish in each of them.

But above all, remember that even though it seems hard, selling your product to retail is the easy part. Selling it to the ultimate consumer is the essential part.

Chapter Twenty-Two

Seven Ways To Help Bars Sell Your Beer

For packaging breweries, connecting with consumers requires a mix of efforts.

By Stan Hieronymus

STOP US IF YOU'VE HEARD THIS ONE before: Two women walk into a multi-tap; they ask the bartender for advice on what beers to order.

"What do you normally drink?" asks Pat Klinedinst, the bartender at KClinger's Tavern in Hanover, Pa.

"Yuengling Lager," says the first woman.

"Pale ales," says the second.

"You might want to try the Victory Lager," he tells the first. "It's a great beer and it's a great beer for people who don't want too much hops."

"I've got this Stoudt's pale ale on draft. It's made just down the road," he tells the second. "You want to try that?"

For a brewery, bars like KClinger's—and bartenders like Pat Klinedinst—are better than gold. What does it take to get that kind of support at the point of sale? That's what we want to look at in this chapter.

As a starting point, let's see what the big guys are doing. It never hurts to check with companies who have money to spend on research and then on marketing.

A few years back, a lot of attention in the beer arena was focused on flavored malt beverages or FMBs. One year, during the NCAA basketball tournament it seemed like there were times when commercials for Smirnoff Ice, Bacardi Silver and SKYY Blue ran almost back-to-back-to-back. But the spending didn't end with television ads. Teresa Zepeda, brand marketing director for SKYY Blue, said: "We are going to follow the highly successful SKYY vodka formula, which is to have a presence and be on-premise in the key accounts where our target consumer is. Our strategy is all about on-premise visibility."

Michael Ward, director for FMB brands for Guinness-Bass Import Co., whose Smirnoff Ice leads the field, also made it clear that on-premise is an essential part of its plans. "Quite simply, the US beer market is a very cluttered landscape to cut through," he said. "In order to have our brand message heard, we have to be on television, in print media, and have to be a real presence to consumers in bars and stores and everywhere else."

On-premise presence matters to breweries of all sizes. Granted, small breweries aren't competing with FMBs at KClinger's Tavern in Hanover, Pa., or KClinger's Publik House in Etters, Pa. Yes, the amount of beer a brewery can expect to push through a tap or three at the Falling Rock Tap House in Denver may not equal what's sold in a busy restaurant at a ski resort. Likewise, the impact of a tap handle at one of three Summits Wayside Taverns in the Atlanta area can't be measured by kegs sold in a week. Still on-premise presence affects off-premise sales.

"We like being at the point where we feel we can influence off-premise choices as well as on-premise,"

Summits' president Andy Klubock said. Bar owners like Klubock have long championed craft beers. Klubock himself will happily entertain customers with stories about the genius of Rogue Ales head brewer John Maier and the marketing genius of president Jack Joyce.

The Map Room in Chicago, Rich O's in New Albany, Ind., and others of this ilk give craft brewers places where they can compete without reaching for their checkbooks. It doesn't hurt to make it easier for craft-beer-friendly establishments.

"I've never asked anybody to help me sell. I figure that is part of my job," said Rich O's owner Roger Baylor. "I'm happy if I have up-to-date handles for the taps. It would really be nice to have a Sierra Nevada handle newer than from 10 years ago."

So it seems like it wouldn't hurt to occasionally check with publicans for suggestions. For this chapter, I did just that. The publicans tended to make the same points—and though the ideas may seem basic it seems that many microbreweries fail to take advantage of these simple ideas.

MAKE GOOD BEER

"The number one thing that promotes the product is the product itself," said John Clinger of KClinger's. "You can paint something as pretty as you want and it won't sell if the quality isn't in the beer.

"We are fortunate here to have nearby breweries like Victory, Dogfish, Troegs and others," he said. "It seems like every time Victory brings out a new beer it is great. The people who drink their products don't know anything about the awards they've won. They just know the beer."

Because specialty beer drinkers are serial samplers, brewers may get the impression a new product is more popular than it will turn out to be once the pipeline is full and everybody has tried it once.

> First it has to pass a basic quality test. "I start with the premise that we only sell good beer," said Laura Blasingame of the Map Room.

"It's up to the beer to keep the customers coming back," Clinger said. "You do that by making it unique. How many ambers and pale ales do we need? You have to carve your own niche. Something unique will tend to stand out."

First it has to pass a basic quality test. "I start with the premise that we only sell good beer," said Laura Blasingame of the Map Room.

SEND SPECIAL BEER

Bar owners appreciate the importance of promoting a flagship beer just as much as breweries—they make more money when kegs move quickly. They also want beers that will set their establishment apart from others.

"If BBC (Bluegrass Brewing Co. in Louisville) has 60 accounts, there are going to be a couple of us that will want that small batch of smoke beer they just made (for sale at BBC's brewpub)," said Baylor. "It gets the geeks on your side."

Baylor can use that word because he is about as opinionated and pro-specialty beer as any publican in the country. "I'll be talking to Ed Herman at Upland (in Bloomington, Ind.) and he'll say, 'I'll hold a keg (of something special) back for you.'

"It fits in with what we are doing, trying to develop and appeal to the broadest palate possible."

"It takes an interesting beer to stick out on the wall just by virtue of what it is," said Falling Rock Tap House manager Chris Black. "People come here looking for something different.

"It doesn't have to be high alcohol or strange ingredients," he said. "Last summer, John Harris (Full Sail Brewing Co.) sent us some beers that stuck out because of the interesting things he was doing with dry hopping."

A good name also helps. "Weyerbacher (Brewing) sales went up when Dan Weirback started giving his beers better names," Clinger said. "If he'd called it Weyerbacher Barley Wine I don't think it would have sold as well as 'Blithering Idiot.'

"Believe it or not, people will sample something just because of the name."

THE PRICE IS RIGHT

"Price is certainly a factor in deciding what to stock," said Clinger. "Anderson Valley Hop Ottin' is $130 for a 50-liter keg. That's a lot, but we do it and we're the only place around here that will."

It's a way for KClinger's to set itself apart. Black and Tom Peters of Monk's Café in Philadelphia are two owners who like to cellar beers and serve them months or years later. They'd rather pay a little more up front, knowing the keg they end up with is special.

Owners are more likely to hurry cheap beer out the door. "I don't want free beer," Peters said. "When they start cutting the price, that makes me nervous."

It can also make a bar owner wonder what kind of deal the pub down the street is getting.

GET A GOOD HANDLE

Since the three Summits Wayside Taverns have 114, 166 and 225 taps, respectively, it's understandable that Klubock puts a premium on good handles. "It's the only way the customer sees your beer," he said. "Companies don't spend enough. Yes, I know they are expensive."

The Falling Rock lines 69 taps on the wall behind the bartenders. "Fancy shapes and designs are not as important as picking one shape and putting the name of the style and the brewery on it as large as possible," Black said. "I learned in wine and liquor sales that you should put that handle against the wall and go stand 20 feet away."

At Monk's, handles sit on tap towers on the bar. "Thin is in," Peters said. "The one thing I ask is for a reasonably attractive tap marker that's not too wide. I hate it when it's so fat that when you pull it you end up pouring two beers at a time. Tall is OK, as long as the handle isn't so long that you bop yourself on the head."

MAKE THE CONNECTION

This is almost every owner's favorite subject. "The best thing the brewers can do is just hang out," Blasingame said. "They don't have to be buying people beer. More than anything, it's people getting to know the brewer."

Nick Floyd of Three Floyds Brewing is a regular at the Map Room. "His beer is so good that I couldn't take it off anyway, but because he's here and people know him I couldn't even think about it," she said.

Summit Brewing founder Mark Stutrud put in an appearance last spring. "Customers just loved it. He has that Minnesota accent; they thought he was so cute," Blasingame said. "And their sales have taken off ever since."

Black says it's as important for brewery sales staff to spend time in the bar. "Get to know the bartenders, find out what they like," he said. "Once you get some of the staff involved, they are the best sales people."

Both Black and Blasingame point out the way to a bartender's heart is not through his or her pocketbook. "It's not money or the swag," Black said. "If you get them enthusiastic at all, it's going to move your beer. A customer may ask, 'What's new. What have you been drinking?' "

That's good for Black's business as well. He takes his staff on field trips to breweries. "It's all part of the touch and feel part of this job, really caring about the product," he said. "And from the standpoint of an owner, it's much harder to say no to somebody in person than on the phone. When push comes to shove, if I know what you look like it's not going to be your handle that comes off."

KNOW THE MARKETPLACE

Spending time in the bars is also a way to find out more about consumers. Brewing companies "need to know who they are selling to," Klubock said. "I think the idea that 'I'm going to brew the beer I want' and people will want to drink it is stupid. They need to get out and see what drinkers do and don't like and listen to them."

Klubock's view of the future should cheer brewers who are willing to do the legwork.

"Mass marketing is dead," he said. "You market within the four walls.

"Your average customers will travel 3-5 miles when they go out to eat. You know where they are coming from and you can market to them on that basis."

What works in one bar or restaurant may not work in another. "You have kids—each one is different. When you treat them different they do better," he said. "It's the same with each account. If you get out and get to know the customers then you can adapt to the marketplace better."

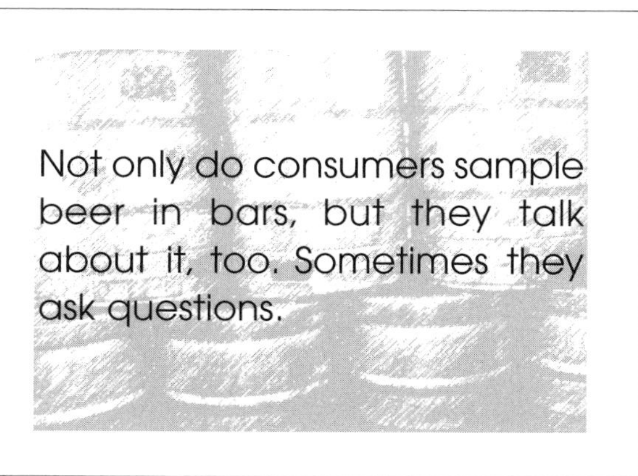

INFORMATION, PLEASE

Not only do consumers sample beer in bars, but they talk about it, too. Sometimes they ask questions. Owners, bartenders and waitstaff like to be able to provide accurate answers.

"There's no shortage of junk I could get to display if I chose to sell some of those products," Baylor said. "I don't expect (micros) to hand those things out. They can make up for that by getting me information.

"Nothing annoys me more than if I can't get information."

That means details about the beer being served, but also beers in the works. Some brewers hesitate to discuss future beers because they don't want bars hounding them for the beer, as if having somebody wanting to sell your beer is bad.

"What we are trying to do here (at Rich O's) is have an intelligent dialogue about beer," Baylor said.

It sounds like common sense, but most of the suggestions from bar owners are just that. "If they are in touch with us and they are in touch with the customers, all they have to do is stop and think about it," Klubock said.

CONCLUSION

Selling beer isn't easy—we all know that. But you sell a lot more of it when you create enthusiasm and support for your products among the people who have to sell it when you aren't there. By deputizing bartenders, wait staff and owners you can leverage your own effectiveness and have the chance to promote your product and sell your brewery scores if not hundreds of times every hour. True, the multi-tap owners we talked to in this article may not be typical of every establishment where your beers pour. Nonetheless, they represent the true motivations and potential of the marketplace. By following their advice, you can save money on fancy swag and meaningless discounts and focus on selling what they—and their customers want.

Chapter Twenty-Three

Using Public Relations To Build Your Brand

Media stories keep your brewery in the public eye.

by Ray Daniels

MANY PEOPLE SEE PUBLIC RELATIONS AS a simple process of sending out press releases. But those who understand its full potential define PR more broadly and harness this marketing tool as a substantial and cost-effective means for building their brand and their business.

For the past 25 years, I have worked on one side or the other of public relations. In corporate life, I used PR techniques to influence opinions about products and educate consumers. As a public relations consultant, I helped companies respond to crises, communicate with customers, regulators and investors and, of course, launch new products. And as a business owner and manager for the Brewers Association, I have harnessed PR techniques to promote events and specific products.

Finally, as former editor of two magazines (*The New Brewer* and *Zymurgy*) I have been on the receiving end of a lot of PR. Some of it is from breweries and other alcoholic beverage producers and the rest comes from suppliers to the brewing industry. Based on my past experience as a producer and practitioner of PR as well as my recent experience as an editor, I'd like to share with you some of my thoughts on how to use PR effectively for your brewery.

ALL ABOUT PRESS RELEASES

First, if you aspire to increase your sales, whether as a strictly local on-premises brewpub or as a nationally distributed craft beer brand, you need to be sending out press releases as often as possible. As a PR consultant I used to preach the need for high frequency of contact with the media, but it wasn't until I became an editor that I truly saw the effectiveness of this strategy.

A number of brewers and suppliers send me media materials 15 to 20 times a year. I hear about every award they win, every new product they introduce, every clever event they create and every significant business milestone they achieve.

Does that mean I publish all of their press releases? Certainly not. But you have to remember that press releases have two purposes: the first is to get messages out to the reading or viewing public so that they will buy more of your product or think better of your brand. The second, and equally important objective, of *media relations* is to communicate with the media.

Each press release I receive effects my perception of the issuing brewery or supplier and reminds me of their activities. Thus frequency of communication has several effects. First, the sheer frequency of communication creates the impression of significance. Simply stated, if I hear from a company often, it seems to me like they have got a lot going on, that they are a "player," and therefore worthy of coverage. Of course this isn't the only factor that influences which breweries get coverage—far from it. But it does have a real effect.

Second, a lot of what goes into media coverage is selected not because it is the most compelling or newsworthy item that occurs during the publication cycle but because it is convenient or colorful. Like everyone else, the media have a job to do and a big part of it is filling up a certain amount of air time or pages on a regular basis. As a result, certain sections of some publications come largely from press releases. When it is time to create a section like that, the editor opens his or her file of press releases and starts looking through them for things that will fill the bill. If you communicate regularly with the media, you are more likely to have something in their files when they go through them and thus more likely to get coverage. (See sidebar on The Editor's Decision Process.)

Rarely does a press release result in a big feature story on your product or company. But frequency of contact with the media does something that's more important by keeping you top-of-mind. As a result, you are more likely to be either featured or at least included in larger stories that get assigned to staff or freelance writers.

Early in my tenure as a magazine editor, we did a feature on a trend toward lager brewing. At the time a number of traditional ale brewers seemed to be adding a golden lager to their lines and the story examined that trend. How did we know the trend existed? Certainly general knowledge of the industry and regular contacts with brewers helps. But press releases often make a story idea like that coalesce. And when a trend story is researched, we don't go out and talk to a random sampling of 20 breweries to see what they are doing. We call the folks who have issued the press releases!

SUBSTANCE COUNTS

OK, so having argued for frequent communication with the media, I must issue an important caution. When you communicate with the media, you need to have something of significance and relevance to say!

Just as I can think of several breweries who send me good press releases frequently, I can think of some others who send me junk time after time. And guess what? The junk hurts their case.

As the editor of a bi-monthly magazine, my copy deadline is 45 to 60 days before readers see the content. If a company routinely sends me announcements for events that are occurring in the next 30 days, I quickly learn not to read them! Then when they send me something that I *can* use, chances are that I will immediately discard it thinking that it is another installment of irrelevant material. (A change in formatting can help to avoid this . . .)

For a national trade magazine, examples of things that get immediate attention from the

THE EDITOR'S DECISION SEQUENCE

When an editor receives a press release, she or he quickly assesses its potential for use. Either explicitly or implicitly, two questions guide their initial decision.

1. Is it relevant to my readers?

2. Is it timely, newsworthy, part of an industry trend or broadly interesting?

Items that rate a solid "yes" to both of these questions stand a good chance of being used either as a news item (contingent upon reasonable compliance with the final three questions given below) or as part of a larger feature.

If the answer to the second question is "maybe" or "somewhat," then your chances of being used are greatly enhanced when it scores a "yes" on each of the final three considerations.

3. Does it fit into an existing column or department in my publication?

4. Is it written and delivered for easy use in my publication?

5. Is there an attractive and readily useable visual?

What all of this boils down to is knowing the characteristics of the publications you work with. Good PR people read and study the media and know what kinds of stories will sell and where.

"delete" key are weekly band schedules, "what's on tap" lists and brewmaster dinner announcements. But that doesn't mean that there aren't good PR opportunities in these day-to-day events. Does the band come back so often that the brewer has named a beer after them and they have inserted lyrics about your beer into their songs? Does your tap list include a favorite seasonal dedicated to a local hero with a colorful past or the debut of that quirky but popular cilantro beer? Is your brewmaster dinner featuring beers paired exclusively with Ethiopian cuisine? Any of these might make interesting copy—if not for an industry trade magazine, then for more consumer-oriented periodicals with similarly long deadlines and national audiences like *Zymurgy, All About Beer* or *Malt Advocate*.

PERFORMANCE RECOGNITION

When I sold public relations services, I used to tell clients that "PR" stood for "performance recognition" and I still believe that is true. The bottom line is that you can't make news out of nothing. You have to *do* something new, different or interesting to get coverage. The media just aren't going to get excited about your run-of-the mill fish-and-chips special on Fridays or the new batch of "John's Pale Ale" that you make 14 times every year. That said however, it doesn't take much to make little things into news.

When it comes to generating publicity, sending out the press release is just one step in the process. Long before that happens you have to see the potential for a story and nurture its development. One thing that public relations consultants do for clients is help them find or develop the media stories that already exist in the things that they do.

If your fish and chips are made from salmon, tuna or trout and dished up with Asian barbeque sauce made from your rye stout instead of the usual tarter sauce, then it might get the attention of food writers. When it comes to the pale ale, it may turn out to be the 100th batch your brewery has produced. Spice that up with a special event at the brewery, a charity donation on the sales of that batch or a new name honoring a local civic leader and you may be able to ring the bell.

The big key to making news stories out of routine events is having a "creative engine" on your team. The creative engine is someone who is always thinking about promotional ideas and media angles and who can create or augment activities to make them more interesting to the media.

One small brewpub chain that I know gets an inordinate amount of national attention when you consider the number of similar businesses in operation around the country. Why? Because one of the owners and day-to-day managers in the business is an astute creator of media stories. He is constantly pulling together unique combinations of elements to make interesting media content related to beer and brewing. At the GABF, his booth always stands out with some special gimmick or the appearance of an attention-getting personality. When he wins (another) GABF medal, there is often an interesting story behind the creation and brewing of the beer itself. And daily life at his pubs is full of interesting activities and events—some of which I am still discovering after nearly 10 years covering his business.

If you are lucky, you or someone already involved with your business may have the ability to be your creative engine. Likely as not however, you'll need to hire someone to help you out in this area. This may be a PR person, a designer, a homebrewer, an events promoter or meeting planner, etc. And unfortunately it isn't something you can send out an RFP for, you have to be on the look out for someone who thinks creatively and figure out a way to get them involved with your business when you find them.

Sometimes you can generate good media ideas through brainstorming with members of your own staff. Even within PR firms, good "idea" people may be brought in for a one-hour brainstorming session on a product or client they don't normally serve. Similarly, you may find that your day shift manager, two of your waitresses and one of your regular customers are full of ideas about how to promote your business. Try sitting them down—maybe with your PR consultant—for a brainstorming session about how to get attention for your business.

Of course PR folks succeed at generating ideas in part because they know what garners media attention generally. When I worked at a big PR firm, I found that nearly every program we developed fell into one of several frequently used tactics. Surveys are one example. The media love surveys and polls—even when somewhat less than scientific. Associations and institutes frequently use surveys to make news and commercial entities can use them effectively too.

A simple survey would be one where you ask consumers (at your facility or while visiting your website) about their favorite beer style—or maybe their favorite beer style for a specific upcoming

PROVEN PR TACTICS

Surveys and Competitions - People love to know what's on top and what other people think. Surveys can reveal interesting information about consumers that the media will publish while crediting you as the source. Competitions draw attention from consumers and media alike because they offer some credible assertion of what is best and everyone wants to check out the winner.

Something for Free - If you offer something for free, it will help you to get coverage. It might be a publication, a tour, a tasting or some sort of class. When media inform their readers or viewers about something of value, it enhances the relationship between the individual publication or program and its audience, so they love to offer freebies.

Community Service - Let's face it, "business" is a dirty word for many in the media, so one way to appear in their columns and airwaves is through charity. Supporting a good cause can get you noticed and taking the lead in creating a new program for a worthy charity will usually get you good press.

Seasonal Stories - Food and beer have lots of seasonal angles. Offer your local media ideas relevant to upcoming seasonal stories and be prepared to contribute. If you contact them regularly with helpful items, they will begin to include you and even feature you from time to time.

Local Connections - Most media strive for relevance by matching their audience's mind set, addressing the environs in which they live. Give the editor a story that matches the community they cover and they'll probably find a use for it.

occasion like Thanksgiving or Memorial Day. As long as the results are applicable to all beers and not specific to your own products, the media may find a use for such statistics and when they do, they'll mention that you are the source.

Depending on the level of detail in your sales records, you also might be able to issue some interesting statistics based on your own historical sales. How about a chart on beer types and when they are consumed? Pale ales are most popular on Wednesdays, porters sell mostly in January—that kind of thing. Depending on what you have and how the media respond, you might even issue monthly or quarterly advisories about consumption trends.

RINGING THE BELL

Many breweries got good coverage when they opened: just the fact that they were a brewery was enough to generate excitement and air play. But now that you have been open for awhile—or if you are the sixth or fifteenth brewery to open in your community, the novelty has worn off. Now more than ever frequency and creativity are key and the approaches mentioned above should be of use to you. In closing, I'll leave you with two other ideas with regard to media contacts that may be helpful.

First, mix it up. In many communities, just a handful of local media outlets serve the market. Unfortunately, no editor wants to cover anyone too much—it just doesn't look good to his bosses or colleagues. To get regular coverage in your local outlets, you'll have to work all the different editors or producers. Once you've hit the food page, start working on a business story or use your building or neighborhood to get a bit from the architecture writer. Other opportunities may include automotive section, a jobs column or the women's section.

Second, in competitive metro markets, just figuring out who to talk to and getting their ear can be a huge challenge. Here a PR professional with great contacts can be worth their weight in gold. Be cautious though: anyone can talk a great game. As with all things, the proof is in the performance.

Finally, I'll remind you to communicate with all media using their preferred medium rather than yours. Sending out a stack of paper press releases may make you feel like you are accomplishing something, but more and more, e-mail is a more effective way to get your message into print.

Cheers!

Section IV

Planning and Funding Your Brewery

SOONER OR LATER, EVERY GOOD BUSINESS IDEA must result in a business plan. In this section we put down our beers and pick up a sharp pencil to start considering how to take your brewery from dream to reality.

We start with a look at some strategies for raising money from friends, family, strangers and even the US Government. We'll also consider other financial issues for operating your brewery with a look at insurance, site selection and key business centers for your operation. Then we present survey data from current breweries to help you understand the costs and other key quantitative elements of a real operating brewery. All of this leads up to the sample business plan which can serve as an example of what you yourself will prepare in order to get your business rolling.

Through this section you can begin to pursue your dream. By tackling the tough questions posed by the planning process you take the first step in that long but rewarding journey to serving your first beer.

Chapter Twenty-Four

The Hot Pursuit of Capital

Convincing Other People to Invest in Your Business is Your First Challenge

By John Hickenlooper

RAISING MONEY IS WORSE THAN KISSING your sister through a screen door with storm windows. Still, we need to build brewpubs and craft breweries so money must be raised. Even in perilous times your quest can benefit from some basic guidelines for rounding up capital. This chapter talks about how to prepare and which groups and individuals to ask.

Before you start asking for money, you must prepare thoroughly. Proper preparation not only increases your chances with each source, it also protects you, the fundraiser, from suffering excess "rejection dejection." At best only a fraction of those initially interested will ultimately invest in your project. That means you will hear lots of people saying "no." Often the biggest obstacle becomes your own mood. You need the strength of mind to persevere.

THE PLAN

The first step in asking for money is to have a great business plan. You don't have to spend a lot of money on printing and graphics, but it should read well and look good. No matter how smooth your patter, a few days after your presentation the potential investor will likely remember only isolated fragments. A good business plan becomes your agent in cajoling the investor, by reminding him or her to consider your project more seriously.

You'll find whole books on the construction of business plans at your local bookstore. A good business plan must not only dramatize the wonderfulness of your intentions, but also convey your ability to realize the vision and make it a commercial success.

It will center around a simple and clear description of your business. With a brewpub, everything from the decor to the cuisine, from the service to the floor plan must be described in detail. Plans for packaging breweries obviously need less space to describe the environment but still must be very detailed. Estimates of capital costs, such as construction and purchase of equipment, should be as extensive as possible. You should include the terms of your lease if possible or at least what you anticipate those terms will be.

Your business plan should evaluate existing competition and show why your business will be superior. The marketing section should be extensive, explaining in detail how the public will learn of your superior product and how they will be enticed to purchase your goods or services. What will your marketing and advertising budget be, and how will it be used? Think of a variety of promotions and how you would implement them. A well-conceived marketing plan becomes a blueprint to refer back to once you are open and too crazed for much creative thinking.

A savvy investor will turn immediately to your pro forma financial statements (pro formas), the heart of any business plan. Making accurate financial projections is part business and part magic, with the emphasis on the latter. The food service aspect of brewpubs creates a whole different dimension. If you don't have a strong restaurant background yourself, you need to avail yourself of someone in your area who does. Even without a brewery, a restaurant is a complex business. You have to convey to investors a mastery of that complexity. With or without food service, most investors expect a minimum of three years of financial projections.

Finally, distill all this intellectual fermentation into an executive summary. Investor-types are busy and many will read no further than the summary. Make it good. Touch all your highlights but keep it to a page, a page-and-a-half at most. Abstract only the essentials from the pro formas.

TERMS OF INVESTMENT

So now you have a glorious business plan. Its value will be amplified by its versatility. Not just investors, but everyone from bankers to government officials to insurance agents will listen longer and closer if you have a solid business plan. Hopefully while writing it you have been deciding what kind of deal you are going to offer your investors.

A new business is usually some combination of debt and equity. Limited liability companies, limited partnerships, or "subchapter S" corporations seem to be the vehicles of choice, and each can be used to blend an individual investment into debt and equity. Consult a lawyer as to which structure would be best for your project.

Some of these structures are limited to thirty-five investors, so you need to make sure your "units" are large enough to raise all the capital you'll need, but not so large that people feel they're unaffordable. Obviously, the larger the unit of investment, the fewer investors, which equals fewer hassles.

Each deal will be different. If you're a brewpubber, you might find a large restaurant that is available in a good location—perhaps with an adjacent storefront empty and aching for a brewery—and you will need to raise far less capital than someone starting from scratch in an old warehouse. A space that is already finished could be equally important in starting a packaging brewery. You will most likely have a much higher rent each month, but the lesser capital requirement should allow you to keep more of the equity and still offer investors an attractive return for their risk.

To exactly define an acceptable return and be able to exactly measure risk is what allows certain pretentious windbags to refer to deal-making as an art. Most investors in speculative ventures (such as brewpubs and packaging breweries) expect to see at least a 30 to 50 percent annual return if everything works. This is why the pro formas in the business plan are so important. You must document as best you can that your projections are conservative enough to be achievable, but at the same time they must be optimistic enough to convince investors that the return is worth the risk.

You must document as best you can that your projections are conservative enough to be achievable, but at the same time they must be optimistic enough to convince investors that the return is worth the risk.

One simple structure that is aggressive but seems to work well is to divide profits 50/50 between the investors and yourself and your partners, but only after the investors have gotten all their initial investment back at a fair rate of interest. In a limited partnership, this would be done with a provision that would allocate all proceeds be distributed 90/10 in favor of the investors until they have gotten back their investment with, say, 10 percent interest. At that point, with their "risk" removed, the investors would receive only 50 percent of future profit distributions. You must let investors know how long it will be before you intend to begin paying them back and to express your priorities should there not be sufficient cash flow for everything. (There seldom is.)

In a "subchapter S" corporation, the money contributed by each investor could be split between shares of stock (equity) and some sort of loan or debt. Following this approach, 10 to 20 percent of each individual investment would purchase stock in your company. The other 80 to 90 percent of individual investment would purchase a debenture—a loan to your business with a fixed interest rate and payment schedule.

The stock shares purchased by all the investors might equal half the total issued by the company. You and your partners would purchase the other half of the shares at a greatly reduced rate. And the interest paid to investors on the loan or debenture, would be higher than market rates due to the risk they are taking. Typically, the debenture covers a fixed period of time, perhaps four to eight years. Like a home mortgage, each payment would contain principal and interest, until the whole amount was repaid.

Such a structure works better for a brewpub than a packaging brewery. A brewpub will more quickly generate the positive cash flow necessary to begin repaying the debt. In the case of a packaging brewery, most cash is reinvested to grow the business. Repayments of debt would have to be flexible so as not to cripple the new company's growth potential.

Clearly these options can become quite complex and a lawyer's assistance is necessary. Remember that lawyers charge by the hour and bill for every minute and every phone call. By planning out the essential structure of the deal you want to offer your investors ahead of time, you will likely save yourself vast sums in legal bills.

The project and the terms of the investment are generally described in a separate document, usually in a private offering circular or private placement memorandum. If your lawyer or a friend can provide you with a sample from another start-up business, you can adapt the basic structure to the particulars for your enterprise, and eventually present your lawyer with a rough draft ready for his or her revision. Your savings will be significant.

FINDING MULLETS

So now you are armed with a business plan and some explanation of the terms of investment. Ideally you believe that you are offering investors a good deal—an opportunity to help create something unique, have a lot of fun, and make a sound investment at the same time. Who do you ask?

Start by asking everyone you know. Spare no one. Ask old friends, family, even business acquaintances. If you feel awkward you can pose a request humorously or just talk about your plans without directly asking for an investment. Be enthusiastic, but don't make it difficult for them to say "no." You need allies. Those with insufficient means or cautious dispositions might have friends more affluent or speculatively inclined. Their friends will have friends of their own. This is why it is so important to keep your spirits up even after a long string of rejections. Being a homebrewer is a great help in this phase.

If you can consistently keep a positive attitude, you will find that today's rejection often leads to tomorrow's investment. Don't judge yourself by the frequency of success, but rather by how often you ask. Babe Ruth set the record for striking out the same year he hit sixty home runs.

PRIMARY INITIAL TARGET

Aside from yourself, one of your best potential supporters is your landlord or landlady, who has a lot to gain if you are successful and will still have a renovated building even if you fail. He or she is more likely to be motivated if you are lucky enough to find an underappreciated building considered a nuisance by its owner.

I recommend that you negotiate a low-base rental rate (now there's some sage advice), but often if you are willing to include a percentage of the gross sales in the equation, a landlord/lady will be willing to grant a longer lease or option terms to extend the initial lease. This allows him or her to participate to a limited extent if you prove to be wildly successful (especially deserved if you convince him or her to invest $100,000 or $200,000 into your tenant buildout).

Some landlords/ladies, if they really get involved emotionally in the project, become direct investors as well. This is usually a good idea, when possible, as it will increase the probability of cordial relations.

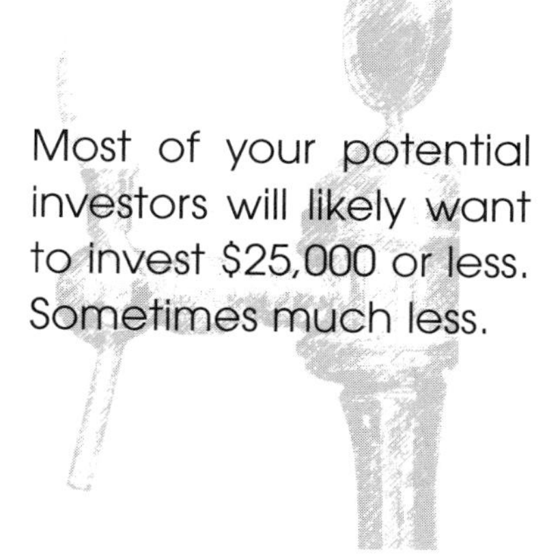

Most of your potential investors will likely want to invest $25,000 or less. Sometimes much less. Investors capable of making larger investments exist, but they are harder to find. Many cities have venture capital clubs—groups of investors and entrepreneurs who meet monthly or quarterly to discuss various projects. Often you can get yourself placed on their program and have five or ten minutes to present your proposal. Most larger-scale investors look skeptically at restaurant-related deals, unless the operating partners have extensive experience.

You should probably expect to raise at least 75 percent of your capital from private individuals. Endeavor to get commitments for 125 percent, because up to 40 percent of the people who tell you they are definitely going to invest will fail to do so. This is a law of nature.

Once you have gotten some firm commitments from private investors, you are ready to talk to banks. This phase is usually where the real frustration begins.

BANKS AND OTHER INSTITUTIONS

Bankers are generally a strange breed. Most of what you may have heard about them is true. They get paid a great deal of money to avoid any semblance of risk. Ironically this is almost the reverse of the typical brewpub entrepreneur, who takes on incredible risk, often with scant compensation.

A common truism is that bankers only like lending to people so wealthy they don't need to borrow. For the rest of us mortals, bankers are addicted to the term "collateral." You must own real property, such as cars, houses or retirement funds worth at least 25 to 50 percent more than the value of your loan. You pledge this real property, which usually is the core of your life, to the bank in case the business is unable to pay its loans. Welcome to the world of collateral. Banks also like to see that the individuals seeking loans personally invest in the project as much as possible, although this is not a necessity.

Even with ample collateral and significant personal investment, banks are unreliable participants in start-up ventures. Perhaps their best potential is for a small loan in a larger package that is centered around some other institutional financing.

Many cities have revolving loan funds set up to encourage development in certain designated parts of the city. Some of these loan funds are for "blighted" areas, others perhaps for historic districts. The latter are usually good places to look for a home for a brewing facility. Municipally controlled loan funds also require collateral, but are more willing to accept equipment to be owned by the business for that collateral.

Most Federal loan programs, such as the Small Business Administration, are impossible to secure for start-up restaurants and are equally difficult for start-up packaging breweries. Other local loans such as those mentioned above are not always so restrictive. Ask around to see if there is a pro-downtown development group which could provide information of such loan programs in your city.

Another source for capital, also very difficult for start-ups, is leasing companies. Even a modest full-grain brewing system runs well over $100,000. The right leasing company, if they have faith in the overall project, might be willing to lease back up to 75 percent of that cost. Certainly "point-of-sale" cash register systems are commonly leased throughout the restaurant business, as well as dishwashing machines and some other kitchen equipment. Packaging breweries might find a leasing company for bottling lines or distribution trucks. Leases commonly are two to three percent higher than bank loans, but they are willing to accept more risk.

A FINAL NOTE

Perhaps the easiest way to raise capital is to need less of it. If financing is a problem, try to do as many tasks yourself as you possibly can. Work on the design yourself long before you talk to an architect. Keep legal, accounting, and other consulting services to a minimum.

And shop wisely. Used brewing or bottling equipment can often be rehabilitated for a fraction of the cost of new equipment. Restaurant auctions are an excellent way to learn the business as well as affording the opportunity of saving tens of thousands of dollars. Local craftsmen and tradesmen can sometimes seem like small potatoes, but the total carpenter's bill on a large brewpub can easily get into the $50,000 range.

Raising capital is usually the hardest task in the entire process of starting a brewery or brewpub. But perhaps because of that, it is also one of the most satisfying once you have succeeded. Especially if you can enjoy that satisfaction while drinking one of your own beers.

Chapter Twenty-Five

The Ins and Outs of Brewery Finance

By surveying possible sources of funding you can focus on those most suitable for your venture.

By Rick Wehnert

WHAT'S THE MOST IMPORTANT FACTOR IN making your brewery or brewpub a success? Is it your gold medal-winning recipe that brings all sorts of craft beer enthusiasts (and their money) to your brewery? Or, is it that new bottling line that allows you to bottle twice the amount of beer in half the time? Could it be your location that funnels in all the foot traffic from the ballpark across the street?

All of the above considerations, along with a solid business and marketing plan, are among the prerequisites for success in the craft brewing industry. There's also another important element to consider for successfully running any type of business: cash flow.

How many pints, bottles, growlers and kegs do you have to sell to begin to realize a profit? It may be more than you think when you factor in all of your expenses. You need to pay for employees, insurance, landlords, equipment repairs, ingredients and marketing costs...all of which continue to rise. Even if you are blessed to have enough cash in the bank to purchase new equipment, is that really the best use of your capital?

"I can't tell you how many people we see that use short-term debt to finance long-term equipment," says David Peketz, director at GHP Horwath, P.C., one of Denver's largest CPA firms. In layman's terms, cash is king. You have better uses for your working capital than to sink it into a piece of equipment that will not begin to repay you for months or even years, which vastly increases your potential for becoming cash poor. Think of it in these terms: Do you make money by *owning* your brewing and restaurant equipment? Or do you make money by *using* your brewing and restaurant equipment?

The first thing to understand is that every brewery is different and has different financial needs. For one it may be important to get a quick approval for financing with a minimum of paperwork. For another, it may be getting the best deal in terms of the interest rate on a loan. For a third brewery, it may be more important that they do not have to come up with a down payment. Each of these needs, and many others, can be easily addressed by carefully choosing the kind of financing you use. Here are the ABCs of the financing options available.

BANKS

Banks are typically the first place a new or expanding business owner will look for financing. Banks often have the cheapest money to lend, not to mention that every business needs a place to deposit their money. Don't let the old axiom that "banks only lend money to businesses that don't need it" deter you. It may be difficult to get a loan out of a bank when you are just starting, but banks are a

> If possible, try to work with a community bank. They are smaller and understand the needs of a small business better than the larger banks do.

great source of money for established businesses and for businesses in low-risk industries.

Establishing a strong relationship with your banker will pay great dividends down the road. Banks are a great source of working capital, operating capital and short-term loans. However, banks are collateral lenders. That means that they will want to take a lien position on any pre-existing collateral that you have to offer, such as existing restaurant/brewery equipment, or, more likely, the equity in your home.

Banks will normally ask for a substantial down payment on the loan—one of the ways that they will judge your level of commitment to repaying the debt. When applying for a loan through your bank you will need to provide the following:

Two years of personal tax returns on all owners of the brewery (and the brewery itself once you are in business)

A signed and recently dated Personal Financial Statement for all owners.

A detailed copy of your business plan.

An explanation of how the money you will be borrowing will be spent, and more precisely a business plan that clearly shows loan repayment capacity.

If possible, try to work with a community bank. They are smaller and understand the needs of a small business better than the larger banks do. Make an appointment with your banker and dress appropriately. Try not to appear overeager. Banks only care about *if* and *when* you can pay them back.

SBA LOANS

The Small Business Administration, a government agency dedicated to the interests of small businesses, might be a better way to fund the growth of your business. Mike Spinelli, senior loan officer of Citywide Banks, says, "If you are a small brewpub and you want to go to a bank for a loan, you should probably consider an SBA loan." Loans that are guaranteed by the SBA can generally be used for just about any type of responsible business expense, although there are some restrictions.

Your bank will take your application to the SBA, and the loan process can take several weeks to a few months. However, after qualifying, you will be rewarded with a competitive interest rate on a business loan that can stretch out over many years.

The downside to SBA loans is the amount of paperwork required by the borrower and the SBA bank as well as the lengthy time before a deal is closed. Also, when you take out a loan that is guaranteed by the SBA, you need to prepare yourself for the fact that you have essentially just taken on a partner that will be very interested in your business and in some cases can restrict future borrowing. To read more about SBA loans or to find out how to apply for one, visit their Web site at www.sba.gov or do an Internet search under "preferred SBA lenders in (your city)" for a list of banks that can help you start the process.

LEASE FINANCING

When financing equipment, many brewers find leasing simpler than going through a bank and quicker than going through the SBA. For the most part, leasing companies have no interest in the equity in your home or in the balance sheet of your brewery. Most companies process applications quickly and with a minimum of paperwork. You will pay a slightly higher interest rate than if you were borrowing from a bank, but you will typically not be required to put anything more than the first and last payment down on the lease.

You may be able to structure your lease to accommodate seasonal cash flow and or with small initial "contact" payments. This allows your business to maintain a positive cash flow while purchasing your equipment and getting to the point where it generates revenue before regular monthly payments come due. In addition, your company will continue to establish business credit and the lease will not show up on your personal credit bureau (although as an owner of the company, you will be required to sign a personal guarantee). Lease benefits include quick approvals,

FINANCIAL TERMINOLOGY

Capital - The total money invested in a business from all sources.

Cash Flow - Money coming into and out of the business on a routine basis. When the amount going out exceeds the amount coming in, you have a "cash flow problem."

Collateral - Assets pledged to the bank through a lien or other source of funds to protect their investment. If you fail to pay off the loan, they own the collateral and can sell it to recoup their loss.

Debt - Any form of financing structured as a loan and obligating the business to repay the money in the future. Often secured by a lien on some asset that acts as collateral.

Equity - Business financing that participates in the ownership and risk of the venture. When the business succeeds, equity gets a share of the profits; when it fails, equity holders usually have the last claim to the business assets.

Lien - The legal claim of a bank or other loan provider the property (collateral) of a business or individual to secure the payment of a debt.

Working Capital - Defined as the business's current or short-term assets (cash, inventory, accounts receivable, etc.) minus current or short-term liabilities (short-term debt, accounts payable, etc.). As a business grows, the amount of money tied up in working capital grows.

quick funding and the potential for flexible repayment schedules. For these services you may pay a bit more in interest, but many businesses find the extra convenience well worth it.

CREDIT CARDS

Borrowing against your credit cards is perhaps the easiest way to get a quick boost for the company. If you already have the credit cards, then you don't have to apply and you don't have to explain yourself across the desk from a "suit."

Be very careful when using your credit cards as they have one of the few finance agreements that actually allows the credit card company to change the terms of the agreement at their will. Also, using a concept known as Universal Default, should you miss one payment on *any* of your other credit cards, they can raise the rate on *all* of your credit cards. Yikes!

Tim Cetto, president of Pinnacle Business Finance in Tacoma, Wash., states that as a commercial lender, one of their biggest hurdles to approving a lease or loan is "the huge amounts of revolving debt that some business owners carry." Although you may be using credit cards to finance business expenses, they do not help you establish business credit and will actually negatively affect your personal credit score. That score is like borrower's gold....protect it.

CASE STUDY: BUCKBEAN BREWING CO.

Doug Booth and Dan Kahn are working together to start a new brewery in Nevada. Booth and Kahn have all the intangibles that it takes to run a successful brewery and Buckbean Brewing Co. promises to have a bright future as soon as it gets off the ground. However, before Booth and Kahn can sell their first bottle of ale, they need to deal with the real challenges of raising nearly $1.5 million in capital to start the brewery. They plan on raising about $1 million through a network of friends and family and other interested parties.

"The great part about using a bunch of investors to raise capital is that it also works as a form of marketing. We're generating a buzz about our brewery months before it is even open," says Kahn.

However, "it has proven to be really difficult to get people to act as quickly as we'd like," Kahn admits. Thus, financing is going to play a critical role in the creation of the Buckbean Brewing Co. "Financing is what is driving this brewery," says Booth. Kahn and Booth plan on using a combination of SBA loans as well as lease financing for the equipment. This will allow what other capital they raise to be used for building improvements, marketing and other startup costs.

GO WITH THE FLOW

Now that you have the ABCs of brewery financing under your belt, remember to keep a few things in mind. Like Buckbean Brewing Co., keep your options open as to what kind of financing works best for your business. What works for other brewers may not be in your best interests. Many growing businesses find the best solution in combining several types of financing. Using a variety of lenders helps you establish relationships that will make it much easier to get financing down the road.

Lastly, remember that time is money. The goal should be for you to make an educated financial decision while still getting the equipment you need into your brewery as quickly as possible. The sooner you are using it, the sooner you will be making money with it. Think of it this way: if you could start your brewery soon enough to sell an extra 1000 kegs in your first year do your really want to wait another six months hoping for rates to come down? Personally, I'd rather sell more beer! ◗

Chapter Twenty-Six

Covering Your Assets

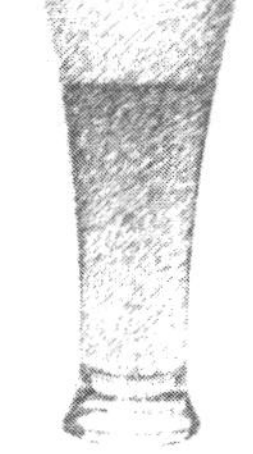

A Primer on Property and Liability Insurance for Breweries

By Peter J. Whalen

LIKE ANY OTHER BUSINESS DECISION YOU make, when purchasing insurance, it's best to know what you need before you buy into a plan so you can make an informed decision. This chapter looks at property and liability insurance issues specific to a brewing business. The coverages discussed here would supplement the basic property and liability coverage that any business would carry. While this information will not make you an insurance expert, it will prepare you to obtain an adequate property and liability insurance program for your brewery business.

PROPERTY INSURANCE

This section includes coverages for hard assets as well as cash and lost income opportunities. Two general rules to follow are to always purchase *replacement cost coverage* and to always *insure to value*.

Replacement cost coverage insures that at the time of a loss you will be paid enough to replace the damaged property. Other contracts deduct for depreciation, which can leave you short of the cash you need to get back in business quickly.

Insuring to value means you have chosen an amount of coverage (limit) which accurately reflects the total figure needed to replace all of your property, including building, contents, and loss of income. If insurance costs get too expensive, you should look to save money by increasing your deductible rather than scrimping on the upper limit of coverage.

Another reason to insure to value is that most insurance policies require you to do so in order to receive full compensation. If they determine that you have underinsured, they will apply a significant penalty when paying a partial loss. This will also jeopardize their interest in renewing your policy.

The following are short definitions and discussions on certain property and liability coverages you need as a business, and particularly as a craft brewer.

Loss of income (also known as business interruption). This is probably the most "important but ignored" coverage available. It provides funds to pay bills during the period you are closed after a loss. After the fire, bills do not stop, particularly debt service and key salaries. In addition, you still need an income to maintain your lifestyle while you are rebuilding. Loss of income coverage is there for you to pay any ongoing bills and profits that would have been earned if you were open. You should definitely purchase a sufficient amount of this coverage.

Utility Interruption. A business can be shut down because they cannot receive a utility (electricity, gas or water) due to an incident occurring far away from their premises such as a car accident or storm. This presents a significant exposure, one that is usually excluded from basic business interruption insurance. Inquire about adding this coverage onto your policy.

Boiler and Machinery. Brewers use boiler and machinery coverage to protect against losses due to machinery breakdown, including your equipment and your HVAC systems. If you cannot produce or distribute your beer because your equipment malfunctions, the consequences could be severe, especially if it triggers a spoilage problem. Make sure when you purchase this type of insurance policy that it includes off-premise power failure and loss of income.

Employee Dishonesty and Money and Securities. Both of these coverages protect you against the loss of cash or its equivalent. Unless you write (and sign) all checks yourself, and no other employee handles cash, you need employee dishonesty. Money and securities covers you if someone else other than an employee steals money. Since it is often difficult to determine just who did the crime, it is preferable to have both coverages so as to avoid any possibility of denial of the claim.

Selling price endorsement. This addition to your policy can make a big difference to craft brewers. It simply changes the language of the policy so that you receive the full selling price, rather than just your investment, for your finished product on-site at the time of a claim. This is another way of protecting your profit.

LIABILITY INSURANCE

Because your products are in the public eye, you should be sure to carry enough liability insurance. I suggest a minimum of $1 million for smaller operations with additional layers of coverage for larger breweries. Specific coverages discussed below include non-owned automobile, product recall, liquor liability, employment practices liability and an umbrella coverage.

Non-owned automobile. Most businesses occasionally ask an employee to run an errand, whether it be on their way to or from work or during normal working hours. If the employee is driving their personal automobile at the time of an accident, you as the employer, could be sued. Although your employee's personal auto policy would pay, they may be carrying very low liability limits and any lawyer would be swift to include you in the suit upon discovery that the employee was doing something on your behalf. Unless you have a non-owned auto policy, you would have no coverage for this exposure. The good news is that obtaining this type of policy is usually uncomplicated and quite inexpensive.

Product recall. This coverage is appropriate to a craft brewery with any outside sales. If you were to find out that there was something wrong with the beer you provided to either retail liquor stores or restaurants, you would have to react immediately. The craft brewing industry is known for having a very high standard of quality control. However, there is a chance that your product could leave your premises providing some threat to the public. For instance, a contaminant could infiltrate your beer or perhaps your bottling machine malfunctioned leaving tiny pieces of glass in the bottles. The cost of recalling your product could be severe, but you would have no choice. Product recall would reimburse you for the expense related to such an operation.

Manufacturers often are named in lawsuits as a matter of routine. If someone is in an accident after consuming your product, there is little question that you would be involved in any subsequent legal preceding.

Liquor Liability. This presents a separate and distinct exposure from general liability. The need for this coverage is obvious to brewpubs who are serving alcohol daily, but packaging breweries need it as well. Manufacturers often are named in lawsuits as a matter of routine. If someone is in an accident after consuming your product, there is little question that you would be involved in any subsequent legal preceding. Additionally, most craft brewers participate in beer festivals and/or occasionally donate beer to charitable or promotional causes. Regardless of how ridiculous the circumstances may be, thousands of dollars in legal fees could easily be spent proving just that point. Of course, make sure legal expenses would be covered by your liquor liability policy.

Employment Practices Liability (EPL). This coverage protects you from employment related issues such as discrimination, wrongful termination and sexual harassment. These are all sensitive problems which we could all face at some point. I believe brewpubs are particularly vulnerable to these challenges due to their workforces being younger and transient in nature.

Umbrella. This term refers to additional liability coverage being added to all your underlying policies such as general liability, liquor liability, workers' compensation and auto. It usually comes in increments of $1,000,000. This coverage is very important to consider once your business starts to build net worth.

OTHER ISSUES

I have omitted automobile and workers' compensation insurance from this article because these coverages, although usually less complex than property and liability policies, can vary dramatically depending on the state in which the brewery is located. When choosing an insurance company, consider the company's financial strength. Unless nothing else is available, never elect to do business with a company less than an A.M. Best rating of A-minus. You buy insurance to feel secure. The last thing you need to worry about is the inability of the insurance company to pay your claim should one arise.

The information above is in no way intended to be complete. Every business is unique and deserves individual analysis to determine all that is required to accomplish comprehensive insurance protection. However, this information will allow you to approach the insurance marketplace from a more educated position. ◗

Chapter Twenty-Seven

There's No Such Thing as a Bad Site, Just Bad Site Selection Decisions

By James F. McDaniel

TAKE A RISK. GAMBLE, PLAY THE LOTTERY, roller blade the Andes. But remember this: site selection risks are far less when science replaces assumptions, presumptions, and conventional wisdom applied in the guise of 'inside information.'

Sun Tzu was a Chinese general and the author of the oldest military treatise in the world. The Sun Tzu approach to winning wars provides us with fundamentals that can lead to the combination of a site and a brewpub concept that add up to success. The first point is to understand what is being brought to the site. Brewpubs are retail businesses. That has much less of the lore and intrigue of beer brewing, but that mindset is essential in grasping what needs to be present at a potential site. It also provides for a standard of measuring the worth of all the decisions that are to come.

ESTABLISHING WHAT'S TO COME

As a retail business your brewpub must have a well defined concept. While the key product is the beer, that must be supported with consistent and complimentary surroundings and supporting products and services. Trying to have those elements evolve after choosing a site goes right to Sun Tzu's description of a loser. That is some one who engages in battle (or builds a brewpub) before knowing how and why they're going to succeed. With a planned and detailed description of the concept and how it is to be executed, site characteristics that support, or restrict the concept are much more easily identified and addressed. This is a brick and mortar decision that requires a well laid foundation spelled out by the retail concept.

KNOWING WHAT'S UNKNOWN

Before a site visit you should gather and examine certain resources. Start by mapping the site on MapQuest.com or a similar site. In addition to telling you how to get there, it provides a clear picture of the site and the traffic arteries that serve it. By adding local restaurants, you can see what else is in the area that may compliment or compete with your offering. You can also make printouts so that the location is clear to all concerned. This is very effective when decision makers are geographically separated, or when site visit schedules cannot be coordinated.

Next, order demographic data that will tell you the makeup of the resident and daytime populations around the site. There are several sources for this service. The best of them are rational demographers that understand the strengths and weaknesses of U.S. Census data. What you are ordering is data that is attached to a geographic map. That data is adjusted to the 10-year national Census. The key points are that the demographer is applying solid forecasting methodology and careful placement of the center of the report— your exact site location.

As simple as this might seem, there are numerous cases of data reports that come from sloppy statistical applications centered on points well distant from the actual site location.

You'll commonly be able to get demographic reports using radii of one, three and five miles from your proposed site. From the brewpub's perspective these are the residents and daytime workers who typically make up the majority of the most frequent customers. Brewpubs that serve lunch can expect its most frequent customers from inside a three mile area. The most frequent dinner customers typically come from within five miles. A full service, casual style dining operation can typically expect 65 percent of its sales to come from within five miles of its location. "Typical" is used in this description because there can be site differences that allow it to attract, or be in a location where, customers are drawn from a much wider geographic region. Examples of these differences would be a site that has a view of shorelines or mountains, Others would be where there are retail or recreational draws, i.e., regional shopping malls and sports stadiums.

Based on the craft beer consumer profiles, the characteristics to look for in demographic reports are: white males, ages 25 to 45 with emphasis on the lower end of this range, college educated.

An income level that corresponds to the area's cost of living such that these target consumers would be expected to have sufficient discretionary funds to be actively buying food and beverages away from home. Since college degree holders typically have higher incomes than the general population, it is reasonable to expect that Median Household Incomes above $40,000 would be a desirable base. Caution is needed if incomes in the one, three or five mile rings go above $150,000. We see consumption patterns that are very much different than most full service, casual-style consumers when these higher levels are present. It is most often a negative to building sales.

GATHERING ON-SITE INTELLIGENCE

Armed with a good, detailed street map and demographic data, an on-site visit becomes far more valuable. Now you can compare actual conditions around the site to the data. You can expect that some on-site elements will not appear to be present in the amount or kind reported while others would seem to be greater than expected. The known data needs to be examined with what appears to be unknown. Here's a list of things you'll want to do:

- Identify all restaurants within two miles.
- Identify significant 'retail generators' within two miles.
- Go to the areas with the target population and drive to the site from each.
- Identify relative traffic flow rates.
- Determine what customers must do for ingress and egress.
- Be a customer at the direct, or near-direct competitors within two miles.

The objective is to have a consistent, repeatable method of examining any potential site so that all candidates can be described and measured with the same basic information. Feelings will come into the decision making process soon enough. Before they do, data and facts need to be at the forefront.

As these measurements are made its also necessary to envision the concept and site as they compare to the state of restaurant operations around the site:

1. Identify its strengths and weaknesses as compared to the other restaurants within 2 miles.
2. Identify its strengths and weaknesses with all other direct, or near-direct competitors within 2 miles.
3. Identify its strengths and weaknesses with all other direct, or near-direct competitors in the entire market.
4. Get traffic counts for this site and measure them against the two mile and market area competitors.

USEFUL RESOURCES

Concept Management
Gerry Hornbeck
1164 Safety Harbor Cove
Old Hickory, TN 37138
615-847-5775
www.gahornbeck.com

Claritas
Site analysis and market demographics.
5375 Mira Sorrento Place, Suite 400
San Diego, CA 92121
800-234-5973

Experience has shown that this phase of the process can be the most enlightening. There will be restaurants that seem to have little to offer but have long waiting lists. There will be restaurants which seem to be a solid match to the population, that are attractive, and convenient, but have no business. There will be newly built office parks that clearly exceed the daytime population data. There will be sizeable amounts of unoccupied retail, or office space in what initially seemed be a growing community. These are the kinds of inconsistencies that need to be answered as fully as possible. In the process, the strengths and weaknesses of the concept and the site will become much more understandable. Sun Tzu is at his best during this phase. Adjustments and changes can be enacted before moving onto the site. This can be the time when it is clear that this is not the place to take on the market and its competition.

LOCATION LOGIC

The emotion of making a 'deal' can be overwhelming. It can be balanced with a foundation that is crafted from the tools of mapping, demographic data, on-site counts and observations. This foundation, in combination with a defined concept and expectations, allows for a realistic, logical discussion of the merits of the site. The importance of loose ends is better understood. An example would be whether or not the city will allow an additional curb cut into the parking lot. On its face that may seem of small consequence in light of the property owner's very attractive financing package. However, lack of that curb cut would make this site's ingress/egress one of the most difficult of all restaurants within two miles. All that passing traffic would have to make several turns and go through an adjoining parking lot to get to the building. Because there is hard data and onsite intelligence to apply, the logic and greater significance of that curb cut is moved forward in the negotiations. There is a clearer understanding of how this restaurant can, indeed, go on this site and succeed.

What's left is the skill and talent of decision makers. Before them is location logic to be applied. As that skill and talent is wrapped together with logic and data, the decision makers are demonstrating management science. They know why they come to the decision they do. They know why they will proceed, they know why they would move on to another potential site. Indeed, there is a "Science of Site Selection."™

Chapter Twenty-Eight

Brewpub Feasibility Planning: Market Analysis Studies

A close look at one tool you can use in selecting a site

By Mark Admire

DEVELOPING A BREWPUB? YOU'D BETTER do your homework.

In today's "survival of the fittest" business environment, a new brewpub operation will need to compete head-to-head with the restaurant industry's top concepts. The developer of a brewpub concept needs to be certain the operation he or she envisions has legitimate potential for success. To evaluate the concept's potential, a detailed feasibility study is in order.

More than a marketing or site location review, a brewpub feasibility study gathers and analyzes a great deal more data than the typical restaurant feasibility study. The information must be gleaned from several sources and applied to the unique characteristics of the brewpub concept.

The evaluation process consists of a step-by-step progression using multiple research techniques to determine whether a market area is suitable for a brewpub. This process will provide valuable clues to which concept characteristics might offer the best chance of success.

Given the current penetration of brewpubs in the US, developers must closely analyze the consequences of adding a brewpub concept within a specific market area. The consulting firm you choose should be well versed in the unique qualities of the brewpub concept (i.e. restaurant/brewery/bar). It would be a prudent move for the developer to solicit a consulting firm that knows and understands how the "brewery component" will compare to other restaurants, bars and brewpubs in the market area.

The developer and consultant must communicate closely throughout the research stage of the study. For instance, how will local zoning laws, alcohol regulation or licensing issues affect the project's potential? The developer will need to provide important information to the consultant about the project as a whole, with emphasis on the type of brewpub concept planned, its size and why the developer thinks a brewpub is needed.

Brewpub start-ups can purchase several different feasibility studies. Economic feasibility studies include both market and economic studies. The economic study will usually include some form of rate-of-return analysis. An economic feasibility study should give the investor or lender sufficient information as to whether the project is feasible or not.

Another type of study, the one this discussion will focus on, is the market study. This study concentrates on supply-demand issues and includes financial projections down to the earnings before interest, taxes, depreciation and amortization (EBITDA). Since this study does not include a full rate-of-return analysis, it would be up to the developer to furnish the missing financial structure of the deal.

A market study with operating projections usually contains the following sections:

- Market Area Analysis
- Project Site and Area Analysis
- Competition Analysis
- Demand Analysis
- Facilities Review
- Operating Budget Summary

Let's look at each of these elements.

MARKET AREA ANALYSIS

This section analyzes demographic, economic and other market characteristics of the area surrounding the proposed site. Data reported should include per capita food and beverage consumption, census figures, income averages, employment statistics, retail sales, tourism and transportation. The report should present figures on consumer demand for food, beverage (with emphasis on craft beer), lodging, entertainment, etc. The research data is then summarized into a positive or negative impact report for the proposed brewpub concept; the developer will use this initial result to modify his project proposal.

For instance, population growth is often a key ingredient for the success of most business developments. The developer of a new brewpub will need to know where this growth is occurring, and whether the growth is in the socio-economic groups that make up the brewpub demographic. Another important statistic to be closely examined is the growth of retail sales in the area. Is there a correlation between a geographic shift in area retail sales and traffic patterns around the proposed site? The answer to this question and others like it can tell a developer where the consumer dollar is moving.

If tourism is a major consideration for the brewpub developer, then the report should give attention to the potential for growth in this area. Since "tourism" is defined rather loosely by many governmental units, the developer should pay close attention to the data used by the consultant. Also, the tourism information provided by the consultant should include the travelers' income statistics, places of origin, spending patterns, socioeconomic status and age.

This is by no means an exhaustive list of what should be contained in the market area analysis. For example, information about theme parks, hotels, convention centers, sporting facilities, historical sites and resorts should be included if they are located in the area being studied.

PROJECT SITE AND AREA ANALYSIS

Once a market area has been defined, the consultant should prepare a detailed site analysis of the proposed property. He will begin by describing where the site is located. A map is usually included, pinpointing the exact location. This map is useful in showing the relation of the site to demand-generators and attractions within the area. There should be a general description of the surrounding area and how the brewpub concept will compete.

The report must consider transportation options available in the area. The site's distance from main traffic arteries, airports, and its ingress and egress should be discussed. Any known future changes to the roadways and streets that provide access to the site should be noted. Whether the consultant investigates local zoning, licensing and building codes should be decided at the time of the initial engagement agreement.

This section normally concludes with the consultant's evaluation of the strengths and weaknesses of the project site. Once modifications have been made to the project outline, the consultant will analytically "test" the concept's viability with the competition.

The alternatives for craft beer consumption in the market directly affect the success or failure of a brewpub concept.

COMPETITION ANALYSIS

Here the consultant pays close attention to the number of brewpubs, restaurants and bars currently in the market area, as well as any planned properties scheduled to be built or likely to be built in the near future. The alternatives for craft beer consumption in the market directly affect the success or failure of a brewpub concept.

The competition is typically analyzed by segment, such as similar-size (concept) properties, location and similar class. The consultant may personally inspect competing properties, review travel-rating guides and interview local managers. He should consider the following factors when analyzing a competing property: location, menu prices (food and beverage), market segments, customer demographics, facilities and services, physical condition, chain affiliation and how the property is perceived by guests and the surrounding community.

DEMAND ANALYSIS

The demand analysis is used to determine whether the consumer demand for the concept is sufficient to successfully develop and operate a brewpub. Following are some questions that a demand analysis attempts to answer:

- Is the present craft beer demand greater than the current retail supply?
- Is the present supply inferior in quality to the needs of the consumer market?
- Is the existing retail supply capable of accommodating a new market segment?

The sections previously discussed are often conceived as an introduction to this section of the feasibility report. There is no hard-and-fast rule on how detailed the demand analysis should be, or how many market segments should be reviewed. Generally the following markets are analyzed by the consultant:

- Individual and small groups (business professionals, office workers)
- Large organized groups and convention attendees
- Tourist and transient (business travelers)

The developer must closely examine the data assumptions used by the consultant. Data sources for demand analysis are obtained from the U.S. Department of Commerce, chamber of commerce statistics, lodging reports, visitor and convention bureaus, local brewpub managers, charge-card statistics and sales tax figures. The developer should make sure that the data used is timely and applicable to the area being studied.

The more logical the consultant is in presenting the data, the easier it will be for the developer to interpret the information and the underlying assumptions. The developer should conclude —by his independent judgment—whether the consultant's assumptions appear reasonable. The risk of the project is more easily analyzed when the consultant's assumptions are known.

> The developer should make sure that the projected seat turnover levels are reasonable and not based solely on the consultant's most optimistic projections.

Usually the consultant projects the estimated annual growth rate over a two- to five-year period for the different market segments studied. Developers should realize that the further the estimates are made into the future, the less accurate they are likely to be. It is also very important for the developer to understand that the estimates presented by the consultant are based on factors that may not materialize in the future.

FACILITIES REVIEW

The consultant may comment on the type of brewpub that would best fit the proposed location, given the study's overall results. The first step in fashioning such a recommendation is to review the design characteristic of the proposed brewpub concept. Unless it is absolutely necessary to recommend a totally different design, the feasibility report should recommend modifications to the existing plan based on market demand.

Often the developer will have a specific theme for which a certain design is required. The developer should inform the consultant of the primary design characteristics so that time and money will not be wasted redesigning a static plan.

Generally the consultant will recommend an overall design concept that he feels is most suitable for the specific market and will be well received. The recommended design should fit the community, and the decor should be planned with the guest in mind.

This section of the report should also discuss guest seats, with the number of seats closely matching demand. The developer should make sure that the projected seat turnover levels are reasonable and not based solely on the consultant's most optimistic projections. The mix of single and multiple guests should also correspond to projected demand. Finally, the consultant should address any special event considerations such as banquets, catering and festivals.

OPERATING BUDGET SUMMARY

The final section of a study will focus on a projected operating budget. The projections will be based on the results of the demand analysis, site selection, competition and concept characteristics, and will be presented as estimates of revenue and expenses and/or earnings before interest, taxes, depreciation and amortization (EBITDA).

The developer must carefully review the operating expenses. The consultant should state in the report the assumptions that were used in obtaining the project's various operating expenses. For example, marketing expense may be stated as a percent of gross-brewpub revenue. The marketing expenses should be computed with a fixed and variable cost relationship. The consultant should also include a breakdown specifying the marketing activities that underlie the expenses incurred.

As with other sections of the feasibility report, the consultant must make major and material assumptions concerning the proposed operation of the project. Especially important are the labor costs expected and average brewpub costs for food and beverage projected. If overly optimistic projections are used, then the chances for a successful project dim significantly. The developer should look for estimates that are reasonable, rather than estimates that will hold up only if everything goes exactly as planned.

Today's brewpub developer is under great pressure to succeed. By taking the time to closely analyze a project's feasibility report, he will be less likely to make a major error. For help in making a good decision, developers should choose a consultant who has a proven record in the brewpub industry, and who is respected by those who requested the study. The need for close communication between the developer and the consultant has never been more important than in today's environment.

Once it is complete, the developer must read the feasibility report carefully and question the underlying assumptions made by the consultant. In the same light, the financial estimates should tie into the data developed in other areas of the report.

A feasibility study cannot tell a developer with certainty whether a brewpub concept will succeed or not. However, when properly used, it can alert the developer to potential problems and to the conditions that will need to occur to give the planned property its greatest chance for success. ◗

ADDITIONAL RESOURCES

Katz, Jeff B. "Restaurant planning, design, and construction: a survival manual for owners, operators, and developers." John Wiley & Sons, Inc.: 1997.

Lawson, Fred. "Restaurants, Clubs and Bars: Planning, Design and Investment for Food Service Facilities." 1987, 1994

National Restaurant Association. "Conducting a Feasibility Study for a New Restaurant." 1998.

National Restaurant Association. "Restaurant Industry Report." 2003.

Chapter Twenty-Nine

Performance Pro Formas

Creating the Income Statement for a Brewpub Startup

By Kevin Finn

AN ESSENTIAL PART OF ANY BREWPUB business plan will be the *pro forma* (or projected) financial statements. Prospective investors and bankers often look only at the executive summary and the *pro formas*. To present a credible plan, you must develop realistic financial statements based on real data.

Three different financial statements often appear in business plans: the income statement (or profit and loss statement), balance sheet and statement of cash flows.

An income statement should tell how your business is performing over a period of time. That period may be a week, a month or a year. The balance sheet indicates what the business has and what it owes at any one point in time. Theoretically, by counting everything in the brewpub at any given moment these assets would be reflected on our balance statement. Those assets would be offset by what is contributed to the business and what is borrowed to start the business. Finally, the statement of cash flows tells us where cash is coming from and where it is going. For the purposes of this article we will focus on the income statement.

To develop *pro forma* financial statements, you must make some assumptions. For purposes of this article, we'll imagine a hypothetical brewpub with 7,500 sq. feet and 200 seats. We will use a food-to-beverage ratio of 65/35. Bank or debt financing will be $600,000 with an interest rate of 10 percent for a term of seven years. As an upper limit reference point we will use information on restaurants with annual sales that exceed $2 million.

The following financials were developed using information from the National Restaurant Association "1998 Restaurant Industry Operations Report" figures for Full Service Restaurants with average check per person of $10 and over.

FORECASTING SALES

Probably the most difficult part of generating an income statement is estimating sales. The first step would be to establish the food-to-beverage mix. Factors that will effect that mix include 1) the overall menu and concept (bar food, casual or upscale), 2) whether wine and liquor will be served in addition to beer, 3) and the availability (if any) of guest beers.

As a general rule of thumb, bars and taverns selling bar food will see lower food sales than upscale restaurants. At the low end, taverns may have 50 percent of their revenues from food and an upscale brewery/restaurant may have 80 percent from food. At Iron Hill, food sales account for approximately 70 percent of our total sales. As a comparison, the industry average for full service restaurants is about 79 percent, thus brewpubs sell more drinks than the average full service restaurant.

To estimate sales, I suggest you use three methods: sales per seat, sales per square foot and table turns. While other methods are available, I believe they are cumbersome to use for a small, independent restaurateur.

Before proceeding further you should know the approximate annual sales of your competition. You should be able to find this out from your real estate agent or vendors. This data keeps you from making the mistake of thinking that you can do twice the annual sales as your competition.

The median total sales per seat for a profitable full service restaurant (check average over $10) is $7,554 per seat[1]. The median total sales per square foot are $237[2]. Therefore, our hypothetical brewpub will have the following range of estimated sales:

- 200 seats x $7,554 per seat = $1,511,000 annual sales
- 7,500 square feet x $237 per square foot = $1,778,000 annual sales

As you can see, the two methods are close but are off by about 17 percent. The difference may be attributed to the fact that a 7,500 square foot brewpub will use about 1,000 square feet for a brewery.

To establish an upper limit or "Best Case" Income Statements we will use figures for a restaurant that does over $2 million dollars per year in revenues. For $2-million-plus restaurants the median amount per seat[3] and the amount per foot[4] increases significantly to $11,649 and $834 respectively:

- 200 seats x $11,649 per seat = $2,330,000 annual sales
- 7,500 square feet x $383 per square foot = $2,873,000 annual sales

A third method involves using "average daily seat turnover." I personally like this method because it allows you to separate the dining room sales versus the bar sales, but I do not recommend it for a new brewpub. The advantage is that it also allows comparisons from day to day and brewpub to brewpub. Using the hypothetical brewpub above, and average check of $15.00 per person and the median average daily seat turnover[5] of 1.0:

200 seats x 1.0 person per seat per day x $15.00 per person x 365 days = $1,095,000 annual sales

Based on sales of over $2 million dollars per year, the seat turnover increases to 1.8, resulting in estimated annual sales of $1.97 million.

THE EXPENSES

The next challenge is to estimate cost of sales. One of the strategic advantages of brewpubs is that we manufacture and sell beer directly to the consumer, creating higher gross margins compared to other restaurants. But often poor menu and kitchen design create high costs for food products that can offset the margins generated by beer. At Iron Hill, our goal is 30 percent cost of sales on our food products. For our purposes, cost of sales on food will be 34.6 percent and cost of sales on liquor and wine will be 30.0 percent.[6]

At Iron Hill, our beer cost of sales varies from 12 percent to about 16 percent, including labor. Of that amount, roughly half of the cost is in labor. A good estimate for a new brewpub would be 15 percent cost of sales. Again, using our fictional numbers we obtain the expense profile shown in Exhibit 1.

EXHIBIT 1: REVENUES BY CATEGORY AND COST OF SALES

Revenues		
Food Sales	1,300,000	65.0%
Beverage Sales		
Beer	500,000	25.0%
Liquor & Wine	180,000	9.0%
Misc.	20,000	1.0%
Total Sales	**2,000,000**	**100.0%**

Cost of Sales		
Food Cost of Sales	449,800	34.6% of food sales
Beverage Cost of Sales		
Beer	75,000	15.0% of beer sales
Liquor & Wine	54,000	30.0% of other sales
Total Cost of Sales	578,800	28.9% of total sales
Gross Profit	**1,421,200**	**1.1%**

Miscellaneous sales represent revenues from billiards tables. Once obtained, the ratios are entered into the sales and cost of sales forecast as shown in Exhibit 5.

BREAK EVEN ANALYSIS AND FIXED COSTS

Once you have established a range of sales based on one or more of the above models it is important to establish a break-even sales level. Break-even analysis tells you the level of sales you must achieve to cover all your fixed and variable costs. First, you must determine your fixed costs—things like rent, salaries and interest on your debt. Exhibit 2 gives a set of assumed fixed costs for our hypothetical brewpub.

To estimate variable costs we are going to use data obtained from the Restaurant Industry Operations Report[7] "Statement of Income and Expenses". This report estimates various operational expenses as a ratio to total sales. This will allow us to develop a variable cost ratio that we can use to estimate our breakeven sales and income statement.

We have already estimated the cost of sales for our hypothetical brewpub to be 29.9%. In comparison, the operations report shows the average cost of sales for restaurant industry is 33.5%. Therefore we are saying that because we are operating a brewpub we are realizing an increase in our gross margin of 4.6% over the restaurant industry average.

The next step is to develop operating expenses using the operations report. The operations report indicates the following percentages in Exhibit 3:

* Adjustment reflected in lower cost of sales for brewpubs as reflected in Exhibit 1.

We now have the information we need to estimate our Breakeven Sales. From Exhibit 2 we estimated our Annual Fixed Cost to be $372,500 and from Exhibit 3 our variable cost ratio to be 73.2%. To obtain Break Even Sales we divide our fixed cost by one minus our variable cost

(1 - 0.732 = 0.268) (Exhibit 4):

EXHIBIT 2: ANNUAL FIXED COST	
Rent: $15/ ft x 7,500 ft =	112,500
Taxes and Insurance	10,000
Bank Payment:	120,000
Salaries and Benefits:	
Head Chef	40,000
General Manager	50,000
Floor Manager	40,000
Total Fixed Cost per Year	**372,500**

EXHIBIT 3: VARIABLE COSTS	
Cost of Sales	
Cost of Sales	33.5%
Adjust for Brewpub*	(4.6%)
Gross Margin	71.1%
Operating Expenses	
Salaries & Wages	28.3%
Employee Benefits	4.3%
Direct Operating Expenses	5.6%
Music & Entertainment	0.1%
Marketing	2.1%
Utility Service	2.8%
Repairs & Maintenance	1.7%
General & Administrative	3.9%
Adjust Fixed Wages	(4.5%)
Total Variable Cost	**73.2%**

* Adjustment reflected in lower cost of sales for brewpubs as reflected in Exhibit 1.

EXHIBIT 4: BREAKEVEN SALES		
Fixed Cost (FC)	=	372,500
Variable Cost (VC)		73.2%
Break Even = FC / (1-VC)		
Break Even Sales	=	**1,400,000**

PUTTING IT ALL TOGETHER

We now have established a range of sales that you can expect at your location. The breakeven sales are $1.4 million and best-case sales are $2.9 million. In preparing a business plan, you usually provide three sets of financial statements, "best case," "worst case" and "expected" or "most likely" case. We are going to assume that most likely annual sales for our example brewpub are going to be somewhere between the breakeven and best case numbers that we generated earlier. We will use $2.0 million in annual sales for the first year of our "most likely case" financial statements.

As an illustration we will develop a *pro forma* income statement for the first five years of operations using the "most likely" case sales of $2 million per year. We will then compare it to the sales and net profits of the best and breakeven case.

First, your total sales and fixed costs should be converted to months and entered into each month you plan on operating during your first year. To simplify our statements, we are assuming a January 1 Year 1 start date and equal monthly sales.

Second, adjustments to each month's sales should be made. For instance, if you are planning for a soft opening, lower your first few months' sales. If you believe that there will be a drop in sales during the summer or winter or an increase in sales during the holidays, make adjustments in the appropriate months. Also consider factors that may affect your particular market like sports seasons if you are near a ballpark or arena, school schedules if you are near a university, and so forth.

For subsequent years, you should anticipate revenue growth. For our example, a five percent yearly growth rate was used for Year 2 through Year 5, based on the National Restaurant Association's predicted year 2000 growth rate.[8] The result is shown in

EXHIBIT 5 - MID-CASE SALES & COST OF SALES FORECAST

SALES	Variable Rate	Month 1	Year 1	Year 2	Year 3	Year 4	Year 5
Food	65.0%	108,333	1,300,000	1,365,000	1,433,250	1,504,913	1,580,158
Beer	25.0%	41,667	500,000	525,000	551,250	578,813	607,753
Liquor & Wine	9.0%	15,000	180,000	189,000	198,450	208,373	218,791
Misc.	1.0%	1,667	20,000	21,000	22,050	23,153	24,310
Total Sales	**100.0%**	**166,667**	**2,000,000**	**2,100,000**	**2,205,000**	**2,315,250**	**2,431,013**
Increase % over previous year				5%	5%	5%	5%
TOTAL COST OF SALES							
Food	34.6%	37,483	449,800	472,290	495,905	520,700	546,735
Beer	15.0%	6,250	75,000	78,750	82,688	86,822	91,163
Liquor & Wine	30.0%	4,500	54,000	56,700	59,535	62,512	65,637
Misc.	0.0%	-	-	-	-	-	-
Total Cost of Sales	**28.9%**	**48,233**	**578,800**	**607,740**	**638,127**	**670,033**	**703,535**
Cost of Sales/Total Sales			**28.9%**	**28.9%**	**28.9%**	**28.9%**	**28.9%**

EXHIBIT 6 - MID-CASE INCOME STATEMENT

	Variable Rate	Month 1	Year 1	Year 2	Year 3	Year 4	Year 5
VARIABLE COSTS							
Total Sales	100.0%	166,667	2,000,000	2,100,000	2,205,000	2,315,250	2,431,013
Cost of Sales	28.9%	48,233	578,800	607,740	638,127	670,033	703,535
Gross Margin	71.1%	118,433	1,421,200	1,492,260	1,566,873	1,645,217	1,727,477
Operating Expenses							
Total Payroll							
Fixed	10,833	130,000	130,000	130,000	130,000	130,000	
Variable	23.8%	39,667	476,000	499,800	524,790	551,030	578,581
Payroll Burden	4.3%	7,167	86,000	90,300	94,815	99,556	104,534
Direct Operating Exp.	5.6%	9,333	112,000	117,600	123,480	129,654	136,137
Advertising/Promotion	0.1%	167	2,000	2,100	2,205	2,315	2,431
Music & Entertainment	2.1%	3,500	42,000	44,100	46,305	48,620	51,051
Utilities	2.8%	4,667	56,000	58,800	61,740	64,827	68,068
Repairs & Maintenance	1.7%	2,833	34,000	35,700	37,485	39,359	41,327
Admin. and General	3.9%	6,500	78,000	81,900	85,995	90,295	94,809
Total Operating Expenses	**73.2%**	**132,900**	**1,594,800**	**1,668,040**	**1,744,942**	**1,825,689**	**1,910,474**
FIXED COSTS							
Occupancy Costs							
Rent	9,375	112,500	115,875	119,351	122,932	126,620	
Taxes & Insurance	833	10,000	10,000	10,000	10,000	10,000	
Total Occupancy Cost		**10,208**	**122,500**	**125,875**	**129,351**	**132,932**	**136,620**
Net Operating Profit		23,559	282,700	306,085	330,707	356,629	383,919
Other Expenses							
Interest	5,000	60,000	60,000	53,676	46,719	39,066	
Depreciation	5.0%	8,333	100,000	100,000	100,000	100,000	100,000
Total Other Expenses		**13,333**	**160,000**	**160,000**	**153,676**	**146,719**	**139,066**
Income Before Taxes		10,226	122,700	146,085	177,031	209,910	244,853
Taxes Incurred		3,579	42,945	51,130	61,961	73,469	85,698
Net Profit		6,647	79,755	94,955	115,070	136,442	159,154
Net Profit/Sales			4.0%	4.5%	5.2%	5.9%	6.5%

EXHIBIT 7 - BEST-CASE SALES AND PROFITS

	Month 1	Year 1	Year 2	Year 3	Year 4	Year 5
Total Sales	241,667	2,900,000	3,045,000	2,274,220	2,486,109	2,722,119
Net Profit	26,545	207,051	230,079	258,412	288,413	320,187
Net Profit/Sales		7.1%	7.6%	11.4%	11.6%	11.8%

EXHIBIT 8 BREAK EVEN SALES AND PROFITS

	Month 1	Year 1	Year 2	Year 3	Year 4	Year 5
Total Sales	116,667	1,400,000	1,470,000	1,483,711	1,442,314	1,409,936
Net Profit	(655)	(7,860)	4,873	19,509	35,127	51,799
Net Profit/Sales		-0.6%	0.3%	1.3%	2.4%	3.7%

Exhibit 5, "Mid-Case Sales & Cost of Sales Forecast." The forecast has only one month shown for the sake of brevity but you should develop a forecast that indicates your first twelve months of operations.

OPERATING EXPENSES AND VARIABLE COSTS

The variable costs are the operating costs associated with running a restaurant. It is important to note that not all of these costs are technically variable costs. For instance, utilities are fairly fixed based on factors like architectural design and the efficiency of your HVAC systems. Additionally, you may be under contract for leased equipment. But for our purposes we will consider them variable costs.

Payroll: Payroll has a fixed and a variable component. As defined in this example, fixed labor costs are management and chef's wages. These costs are not truly fixed but "step" up as you add more personnel. At Iron Hill, we add one manager for every $1 million in total sales and one chef for every $750,000 in food sales.

Payroll Burden: Payroll burden varies based on the number of employees employed and the benefits provided to those employees.

Direct Operating Expenses: These are expenses needed in the operation of a restaurant and include supplies, cleaning, uniforms, etc.

Advertising and Promotions: At Iron Hill, we include advertising, in-house promotions, complimentary gift certificates and customer comps in this category.

Music and Entertainment: This category will vary, based on your concept. It includes cable and satellite television or music, live entertainment, juke boxes, etc. Because we have live entertainment, we spend about one percent of sales in this category at Iron Hill.

Repairs and Maintenance: Includes all non-capital repairs, maintenance contracts, etc.

Administrative and General: Includes all expenses that any business would incur during the course of doing business. Includes credit card fees, insurance, business taxes, etc.

Once you have established variable costs, they can be used to develop operating expenses on your income statement as illustrated in Exhibit 6. Variable costs ratios developed in Exhibits 1 and 3 have been entered into the variable rate column in Exhibit 6.

NET OPERATING INCOME AND NET PROFIT

The next step is determining your net operating income (NOI). At Iron Hill, we define NOI as the profit generated at the unit, which includes occupancy costs (rent, taxes, insurance and common area maintenance charges), and any other miscellaneous operating expenses or income. For the most part, occupancy costs are all fixed costs excluding fixed labor costs. For our illustration occupancy costs are $10,208 per month in Year 1 ($112,500 + 10,000 / 12). We are assuming a rent increase of three percent per year for Years 1 through 5.

The final step is to determine net profit. For this illustration a very rough estimate of five percent of sales was used for depreciation. Your accountant will run a depreciation schedule to determine the exact amount. The interest payments can be calculated based on your actual financing. You can create an amortization schedule to determine the exact amounts. Income taxes will depend on your business structure. For this example, I used a blended rate of 35 percent for federal and state income taxes.

REFERENCES

National Restaurant Association & Deloitte & Touche LLP (1998), 1998 Restaurant Industry Operations Report.

"Restaurant Industry Forecast," National Restaurant Association, Available: www.restaurant.org/research/forecast.html

The final income statement would be a compilation of Exhibit 5 and Exhibit 6. Based on the fictional brewpub with $2 million dollars in sales, the first year profit would be approximately $80,000 (4.0 percent of sales). By Year 5 the net profit rises to almost 6.5 percent. This compares to an industry average of about 5.8 percent for a full service restaurant doing sales volume above $2 million.[9]

By increasing sales to $2.8 million we create the best case income statements. Fixed costs will remain the same, increasing your profit margins. To create a best case, just plug in the best case sales numbers into the income statement. Based on this illustration, the best case net profits would range from 7.1% to 9.1%. The break even case uses sales of $1.4 million with a net profit range of –0.6% to 3.0%.

In all of the above cases I have been fairly conservative. The idea is to give yourself a set of *pro forma* financial statements that you can take to your banker or investors that are credible. They are all based on industry standards that your banker and investors can understand.

[1] National Restaurant Association & Deloitte & Touche LLP (1998), 1998 Restaurant Industry Operations Report, page 46.

[2] Ibid, page 56-57.

[3] Ibid, page 62-63..

[4] Ibid, page 56-57.

[5] Ibid, page 49.

[6] Ibid.

[7] National Restaurant Association & Deloitte & Touche LLP (1998), 1998 Restaurant Industry Operations Report, page 55.

[8] "2000 Restaurant Industry Forecast," National Restaurant Association, Available: http://www.restaurant.org/research/forecast.html

[9] National Restaurant Association & Deloitte & Touche LLP (1998), 1998 Restaurant Industry Operations Report, page 64-65.

Chapter Thirty

The Four Corners of a Brewpub: Building for Success

Each component must contribute to the overall effort in order to succeed.

By Jack Streich

A BREWPUB CONSISTS OF FOUR COMponents: brewery, kitchen, dining area and office. This chapter looks at each to discuss factors you should consider in planning for each to be an effective part of your business strategy.

THE BREWERY

You build a brewpub around the brewery. Since your primary focus is on excellent beer, great care must be taken to create a brewery to be proud of.

Your company must have an experienced brewer on board from the outset. They will help you in site selection, brewery design and specification, vendor relations and brewery installation.

During the planning stage, make some fundamental decisions. In order for your brewer/consultant to properly solicit bids for brewing equipment, you must determine the styles of beer to be produced (different styles require different equipment), and how much beer of each kind is to be produced. These are critical decisions, and an experienced brewer should address them. Solicit as many bids from as many manufacturers as possible. Obviously, the size of the restaurant will determine the volume and style of beer to be produced, but there are other considerations to take into account as well.

Based on the size and layout of the building, projections can be made of approximate gross beer sales. However, other factors to look at, depending upon local and state laws, are:

1. Can you sell beer for takeout?
2. Can you sell kegs of beer to other retailers?
3. Can you sell bottles of beer to other retailers?
4. Can your dining room/bar area expand?

These factors will affect your annual production. Even if you don't plan to exploit these options initially, consider being able to do so if you want to or need to in the future. Leave room for additional vessels if possible. Consider having a small bottling line in the building eventually. Build in flexibility. The market may change over time, and you should be prepared to adapt to changes.

THE KITCHEN

Brewpubs have succeeded with a range of food formats from self-service pizza to higher-end steak and seafood. You should go with your strengths, but don't stray from your central focus of quality beer. The selected menu should complement your beer, not overshadow it. A friend recently dined at a brewpub with a high-priced fine dining room. "They brought me a twenty-dollar salmon steak with a Christmas tree of tarragon growing out of it and suggested a wine to go with it!" he blurted. "I forgot I was in a brewpub!"

The brewpubs most successful at connecting the kitchen and brewery are the ones with a healthy relationship between the chef and the head brewer. Without a relationship of mutual respect and open lines of communication, the customer will be slighted. A good brewer can develop a beer to complement a seasonal dish, just as a good chef can develop a dish to complement a seasonal beer.

Furthermore, a brewpub kitchen should not be an afterthought. A professional should plan the menu and purchase the equipment. Even if the restaurant will serve sandwiches and chips, consult a professional. Just as the brewery was sized and designed with the style of beer and the projected volume to be sold, so should the kitchen be planned.

The chef/restaurant consultant's agenda should be to:

1. Develop a menu which complements the types of beer to be served with assistance from the president and the brewmaster.
2. Maximize the use of space in the designated kitchen area.
3. Set up efficient, manageable work stations which will minimize labor costs and preparation time.
4. Purchase equipment which matches the selected menu and size it according to the projected number of meals to be served per day.
5. Establish regularly scheduled meetings with the brewmaster to further the complementary relationship between the food and the beer.

The dining and bar areas are where your customers spend virtually all of their time. These areas are the sales floor, and every effort should be put forth to enhance your company's ability to sell products.

THE DINING ROOM/BAR

The dining room and bar of your brewpub are the face of your company. Customers do not judge their visit to the brewpub based simply on how good the beer or food was, but on their entire experience. Their experience generally doesn't include a tour of the kitchen or the brewery. (While I highly recommend offering tours, you'll find that a minute percentage of customers participate.) The dining and bar areas are where your customers spend virtually all of their time. These areas are the sales floor, and every effort should be put forth to enhance your company's ability to sell products.

Designing and operating a successful bar and dining room are crucial components of your business. Again, do not take these tasks lightly and have a professional handle them. A restaurant and bar manager needs to work with the brewer and chef to bring the carefully prepared products to the customer in a tasteful, efficient presentation. This requires careful planning of the layout, training of service staff, and diligent focus on the customers' needs.

While a tastefully decorated dining room is an important facet of your business, the decor is only part of what makes a well-run dining room and bar. When planning the layout, your restaurant manager or consultant should have four considerations in mind.

Customer comfort: Adequately space the tables so servers can move around them without disrupting the diners' enjoyable experience. Have the music system set up so that the manager can readily adjust it to suit the time of day and number of customers in the restaurant. Lay out the bar area so that servers do not disrupt drinkers when picking up and delivering drinks. Have the temperature of the dining area readily adjustable by the manager.

Flow of products: As foods and beverages move from kitchen and bar to your patrons, do not have the servers travel through congested bar or waiting areas. Carefully place the beer taps. Bartenders should not be queued up waiting for access to taps. Do not have bartenders travel back and forth to deliver large orders of drinks to wait staff. Situate service stations so that servers can quickly bring customers condiments, utensils, water, etc.

Cleanliness: The restaurant should remain spotless at all times; your staff should never be too busy to clean up a spill. Design the dining area so that it can be cleaned easily and thoroughly. Place mop and sponge stations where staff can readily access them in emergencies. Restrooms, restrooms, restrooms! Monitor, clean, and restock them at least hourly.

Server training: Your host staff, wait staff, and bar staff are probably the only people who will come in contact with most customers. You count on these people to represent you and your products. Therefore you must train your staff to treat each customer as you would treat them yourself. The server is a salesperson. Virtually all of the company's revenue derives from their efforts to encourage the customer to spend money in a pleasant, positive manner. In reading good training texts, you'll find that all of them reiterate the same theme: constantly train and retrain your staff.

In the highly competitive restaurant industry, a knowledgeable staff is crucial. They should enthusiastically convey your positive message to the customer and have learned responses to commonly asked questions. A good server knows the components of each dish on the menu and can give a thorough description of each beer using several key words determined by the owner and brewer to convey information to the customer.

Last, constantly remind the server that his or her job is to bring in virtually all of the revenue to the company. His or her appearance, disposition, preparedness to educate and serve the customer, and his or her drive to sell your products are what make the company successful.

THE OFFICE

A well-planned, well-run brewpub cannot be successful without an organized office. I regard the staff accountant as the anchor of a well-run office. The staff accountant is a watchdog for all of the department heads. The brewer, chef, restaurant manager, and maintenance director should look to the staff accountant as an ally, helping to cut costs and losses, and not as a censor.

Expedience is extremely important in the operation of a brewpub office. Department heads should inspect and sign off on invoices and then submit them to the staff accountant for processing (accounts payable, receivable, etc.). A good staff accountant will carefully inspect incoming bills, identify irregularities, and query department heads for explanations. Late payment penalties, interest, and overpayment of bills can undermine all of a company's cost-cutting measures. Closely monitor payroll, employee benefits, tax payments, and account balances.

Like any other area of the brewpub, set up the office with efficiency in mind. Wherever possible, minimize paperwork. When selecting a computer system for restaurant operations, try to choose one that interfaces with your accounting software.

Keep organized files of each vendor. Meticulously document tax payments and data, and file for audits by the company's accounting firm and government agencies.

A professional should operate the office, just like any other area of the brewpub. A good staff accountant will save you enough money to justify a good salary.

> Examples of useful data for a proposed site are the number of cars passing the site, average income of the residents, and breakdown of ages and races of constituents.

THE FEASIBILITY STUDY/ APPROPRIATE FINANCING

Will this work? Can this venture generate enough money to pay your vendors, your taxes, your payroll, your insurance, your bank, your investors, and yourself? In short, is it feasible? There is no foolproof formula for opening a successful brewpub, but you can predict costs, market trends in the area and tendencies of potential customers.

The feasibility study is your way of showing investors that you have planned to use their money wisely and will show them a return on their investment. The sample business plan included in chapter 22 of this book will help you address the major points necessary to secure financing and will help you to create a budget for your project.

Banks and investors will want you to answer a number of questions. You must ask yourself these questions and come up with responses which will assure success to financiers. The ultimate question is, "Will this work?"

Demographic studies are an excellent tool for determining this. Your local chamber of commerce and real estate broker have a tool they use called a demographic study. These studies are readily available at little or no charge. A demographic study is a listing of a specific area and some data about its population. Examples of useful data for a proposed site are the number of cars passing the site, average income of the residents, and breakdown of ages and races of constituents. The number of restaurants in the area, the degree of success they enjoy, the types of popular food, and the average cost of meals and drinks are also determining factors. You need to convince the investor that you know what the customers want and that you are prepared to supply it to them.

Another issue to address is the actual building in which you will build your brewpub. If it was a restaurant, why is it available and was it closed because of poor management, poor location, or other factors? Your business plan must reflect your response to this question.

While you compile information for the business plan, prepare a spreadsheet with projected costs of goods and services necessary to open the brewpub. This is your start-up budget. A certain amount of capital must be set aside for paying salaries, vendors, insurance, and rent before there is cash coming in and in the event of a slow start to your venture. This is working capital. The reason why so much importance has been placed on hiring experienced professionals during the planning stage of the start-up is that they can project costs accurately and can save money by avoiding expensive mistakes. In the planning stage of your business, develop a strong relationship with an accountant. A good accounting firm can take the information you have compiled with the help of your departmental experts and see to it that the numbers work to make the venture profitable.

Another necessary ally is a good lawyer. Set up a corporation complete with a partnership agreement. You will sign a number of contracts which your attorney needs to inspect.

A brewpub is a multifaceted business. Several different departments need to be set up properly and operate efficiently. Crafting a strategy for opening and developing your business requires the cooperation of all the professionals from these departments. The benefits provided by their expertise will offset the cost of consultants in the short run. ◗

Chapter Thirty-One

Roadmap to Success

Key Success Factors for New Breweries

By Will Kemper

A GREAT DEAL OF WORK GOES INTO each and every brewery before any beer ever reaches the consumer. To get rolling, you'll need to work on planning, financing, and feasibility studies. Be aware that this work can require thousands of hours of work. The magnitude of this commitment as well as the implications for success or failure make these preoperational activities extremely important.

PLANNING

Louis Pasteur said, "Chance favors the prepared mind." Whether through chance, luck, or sheer persistence, a brewery's success depends greatly on the quality and thoroughness of the planning. Insufficient planning can lead to your business's premature demise.

A successful brewery, like all successful manufacturing entities, combines three critical components into a powerful and effective force. These components include a product desired by some identifiable group of consumers, a sales effort that reaches those consumers and brings in revenues and finally the business savvy needed to manage the business. The overall strength of any business depends on the strength of these components. Like a chain, it is only as strong as the weakest link. Certainly the best scenario is when all three entities are strong and working in a cooperative fashion.

In planning these key functions, you'll also need to look at the market for your product, consider financing needs, and construct a timeline of activities that details all aspects of build-out and start-up. Finally, you'll need to have a very good idea of how operations will run in the first year: who you'll employ, what you'll buy and how much money will come into your account.

FINANCING

Breweries exist within a wide range of start-up structures. There are multimillion-dollar, state-of-the-art breweries as well as scavenged, bare-bone-budgeted facilities. Success and failure can come with either extreme as well as every possibility in between. The key is to have the proper financing for the project that you are undertaking. The lack of adequate funding is what undermines the success of many businesses.

The financing necessary to accomplish the intended goals can also be very different. Besides the basic operational philosophies addressed above, issues such as sizing, return on investment, and feasibility have to be addressed in order to determine the appropriate financing.

How funds are spent or misspent go a long way in determining the quality of the end result. As with worker performance, there is an extremely wide range of efficiency in how brewery expenditures work. The cliché "You get what you pay for" has been proven valid time and again. A cheap approach will likely lead to a cheap product. There are also many cases whereby moneys were lavishly spent on inadequate equipment or extravagantly wasted within other areas. Inappropriate usage of funds goes with a lack of knowledge of how money can be effectively used within a given area.

For example, a key funding element is site identification. When this gets out of control, there's usually no going back. This can impact whether or not the venture is underfinanced or if significant changes have to be made in other areas. Significant changes or compromises to offset excessive site spending may affect efficiency or product quality.

For a base funding level the amount should be such that the venture is not underfinanced. This is the reason most businesses, including breweries, fail. Therefore, a fundamental question for anyone trying to establish a brewery is, what is that amount? Because of the many ways in which funds are used or misused, it is easy to see how a minimum funding level for one venture might be twice as much as a similar venture even though there is a comparable scale and scope of operations.

The funding needed is ultimately determined by the adequacy or know-how of the individuals involved in the project. Competent people can do a lot more with fewer resources than less competent people. Normally, people have varying degrees of capability regarding business, sales, and production. Highly competent individuals in one area can be useless or even counterproductive in other areas.

The craft brewing industry has evolved into a much more sophisticated industry than what it was in its early years. If a company does not have a professional level of understanding for the various aspects of business, sales, and production, this will result in added costs stemming from mistakes. Knowledge costs, either by acquisition or the lack thereof.

FEASIBILITY

Feasibility in planning addresses the likelihood of a proposed project being successful. Proper planning should ultimately lead to a conclusion that success is both realistic and likely. A feasible business plan should thus be realistic and likely to succeed.

In the planning stages it can be difficult to correctly gauge feasibility. Most feasibility assessments are based on information which is assumed to be pertinent or valid. If the base information is false, misleading, or not applicable to the project or the issues at hand, feasibility is affected. The key here is for your actual business to resemble, as closely as possible, the one detailed in your plan. And while it is impossible to forecast all the circumstances and conditions your business will face, it is foolhardy to waste time and money establishing a business plan that is not workable.

While it is impossible to forecast all the circumstances and conditions your business will face, it is foolhardy to waste time and money establishing a business plan that is not workable.

A feasible plan cannot be created without adequately addressing the three main areas necessary for the success of the operating microbrewery — business, sales, and brewing expertise. When operations commence, if any one of these main areas is not ultimately conducted in a professional and competent manner, the venture is quite likely doomed. It is far better to realize shortcomings during planning instead of afterwards.

Business. The business planning side of the operation will work to establish the initial financial structure of the business and later to maintain the necessary ongoing financial needs. A business plan also serves as the coordinating influence for sales and production.

The sales side of the microbrewery has to work to find and maintain accounts. A brewery is established to sell its products to others (distributors) for them to sell on from there to retailers. Assuming adequate sales without a competent sales strategy is one of the quickest ways to grind to a sudden halt.

The production side has to work to supply a consistently good commercial product for the consumer. Without this, the business and sales sides will not be able to thrive due to the obvious limitations.

Sales. The sales projections originate from market research. By talking with retailers and distributors as well as other brewers, you can gain a wealth of information on pricing, promotion needs and costs and the likelihood of achieving certain levels of sales. This research can also initiate the development of relationships that will be essential to the early months and years of your brewery's success.

Getting your first distributor can be an exciting development. After all, the distributor already serves the accounts, and your brands, it seems, will be easy for them to add to the existing accounts. From this perspective, it hardly seems necessary to hire sales people or spend a lot of money on point-of-sale promotional materials.

But this thinking has hurt many breweries. They signed the distributor and went home to wait for orders that never came. In truth the distributor's key job is to store and deliver beer. While they will add some accounts for you, especially at the beginning of the relationship, you will not see sustained growth without a focused sales and marketing effort. The survival of your business depends on the sales generated by the brewery.

Brewing expertise. Errors in equipment purchases and production approaches can also affect the ultimate success of your brewery. Improper sizing, inefficient operating requirements and a lack of essential capabilities can all ruin your ability to make quality beer in a cost effective manner.

Shortcomings of the production system will result in inefficiencies and/or a less marketable product by creating a technically flawed product.

When designing equipment, performance should address engineering as well as specific technical brewing considerations. These are not necessarily compatible. Oftentimes an engineer's focus does not take into account desired technical specifications. However, a brewer's perspective might also be insufficient. Many capable brewers can work within a given brewery setting, but they are lost when it comes to engineering. Efficient production of high-quality product requires inputs from both the engineer and the experienced brewer. There is no other way.

A well-engineered system is both efficient and capable of the necessary production levels required. Efficiency translates into ease of production. There is a cohesiveness of the manufacturing program. Additionally, worker input levels should not be too cumbersome. If workers are too involved with having to constantly deal with incidental tasks, or if the brewery is too physically demanding, areas such as quality control and laboratory support tend to decline. Plant capacity is reduced, and operating expenses are increased with an inefficient operation. For aggressive projections it is imperative to have a highly efficient brewing system.

Feasibility assumes a product which is competitive within the market. Can the brewery supply the product that is correct for the market? Does the brewing system satisfy the technical issues? Shortcomings of the production system will result in inefficiencies and/or a less marketable product by creating a technically flawed product.

Technical issues include thermodynamics, material handling, process monitoring, reproducibility, raw materials, laboratory support, fermentation, fluid dynamics, filtration, packaging, and chemistry. Undesirable results within any one of these areas will adversely affect production efficiency and product quality. A few of the many common shortcomings that may seem insignificant but adversely affect beer quality include:

1. Failure of the brewhouse to achieve correct temperatures and heat exchange
2. Excessive oxygen pickup in the brewhouse, conditioning, and packaging areas
3. Extended hot wort manufacturing and handling times
4. Insufficient cold wort aeration or oxygenation
5. Excessive trub carry-over during vessel transfers
6. Incorrect read out of monitoring instruments
7. Fermentation and aging temperatures not properly controlled
8. Insufficient refrigeration (especially during the summer)
9. Chemical make-up of brewing liquor not properly addressed
10. Yeast deficiencies (viability, concentration, handling, storage, nutrients, etc.)
11. Reoccurring equipment failure

Some of these problems may ultimately lead to more serious situations whereby the product is not marketable. Such product is not salvageable if this point is reached. The problem is compounded much further if the flawed product reaches the consumer. Besides the obvious loss of revenue, the future of the microbrewery is severely cast in doubt when these instances arise. There are examples of large well-established breweries going out of business when this occurred.

CONCLUSION

To be a strong and successful microbrewery the three main areas of business, sales, and production all need to be working in harmony. All weak links related to those operations need to be recognized and remedied. With the increasing number of micros, it is even more important that planning be done with foresight, adequate financing secured, and reasonable feasibility studies conducted. ◗

Chapter Thirty-Two

Brewpub Operational Survey Results

Key Operating Parameters from American Brewpubs

By Brewers Association Staff

IN EARLY 2006, THE BREWERS ASSOCIATION conducted operational surveys with brewpubs, asking them to anonymously share some of their most sensitive operational data. The results are presented here, providing a basic guide to many of the key decisions that go into starting a brewery. Keep in mind that this is a small sample and that any new business may exhibit quite different attributes suited to their own location and circumstances.

For this survey, we grouped results by four barrelage classes:

Group 1: 0-500 barrels
Group 2: 501-1000 barrels
Group 3: 1001- 1999 barrels
Group 4: 2000 + barrels

BREWPUB DEMOGRAPHICS

Collectively, the 81 brewpubs answering our survey have been in business an average of 8.5 years, with Group 3 enjoying the longest average longevity with almost 10.5 years. Not too surprisingly, the smaller the brewery (in terms of production) the greater the chance it will be a stand-alone operation. Group 3 once again stood out in the statistics as being home to most of the large multi-unit brewery groups. In terms of location, again the smaller the brewery, the better chance it was located in a small town/rural setting, while suburban settings seem to favor larger production facilities. The mid-range barrelages represented in Groups 2 and 3 populated urban settings more often than either their smaller or larger brethren.

IN THE BREWHOUSE

Within Group 1, we find that those brewing an average of just over 350 barrels a year produce slightly under 1.5 brews per week. When it comes to brewers, the average number employed for both full- and part-time is below one (a full 33 percent of respondents don't employ *any* full-time brewers). System sizes ranged from a low of 1 barrel up to 15, with the average just under 8 barrels. Sales were overwhelmingly on-site, with combined to-go and outside account sales coming in under 10 percent.

With average annual production in Group 2 at 751 barrels, weekly brews clock in at two per week on systems averaging 11.5-barrel capacity. Twenty-seven percent of this group brews on 15 barrel or greater systems, with two of the 30 respondents using 20 barrel and one on a 30-barrel system. All 30 brewpubs in the group employ at least one full-time brewer, but none employed more than two. Like Group 1, the vast majority of sales were on-site, but with outside account-packaged sales alone doubling the previous group's sales to 10 percent.

The number of brews per week for Group 3 jumps to over 5.5, more than doubling the output of the previous two groups, but on systems that on

HOW MANY YEARS HAVE YOU BEEN IN BUSINESS?

	0-500 bbl	501-1000 bbl	1,001-1,999 bbl	2,000 bbl and over
Average years	6	8.8	10.4	8.7
Number of responses	18	30	22	11

ARE YOU A SINGLE UNIT PUB OR PART OF A GROUP?

	0-500 bbl	501-1000 bbl	1,001-1,999 bbl	2,000 bbl and over
Single	89%	83%	77%	73%
Multi-unit	11%	17%	23%	27%
Number of responses	18	30	22	11

IF PART OF A GROUP, HOW MANY UNITS ARE IN THE GROUP?

	0-500 bbl	501-1000 bbl	1,001-1,999 bbl	2,000 bbl and over
Units	2,18	5,2,2,2,2	2,3,27,32,19	2,2,6,3
Number of responses	2	5	5	4

HOW WOULD YOU CLASSIFY YOUR LOCATION?

	0-500 bbl	501-1000 bbl	1,001-1,999 bbl	2,000 bbl and over
Small town	67%	46%	41%	40%
Suburban	22%	27%	27%	40%
Urban	11%	27%	32%	20%
Number of responses	18	30	22	10

WHAT IS YOUR ANNUAL PRODUCTION?

	0-500 bbl	501-1000 bbl	1,001-1,999 bbl	2,000 bbl and over
Average bbls	374	751	1,380	3,583
Number of responses	18	30	22	11

ON AVERAGE, HOW MANY BREWS DO YOU PRODUCE PER WEEK?

	0-500 bbl	501-1000 bbl	1,001-1,999 bbl	2,000 bbl and over
Brews per week	1.33	1.96	5.62	7.5
Number of responses	17	30	22	11

WHAT SIZE IS YOUR BREW SYSTEM?

	0-500 bbl	501-1000 bbl	1,001-1,999 bbl	2,000 bbl and over
Average size	7.86	11.4	11.16	16.41
Number of responses	18	30	22	11

WHAT PERCENTAGE OF YOUR BEER IS SOLD:

	0-500 bbl	501-1000 bbl	1,001-1,999 bbl	2,000 bbl and over
On-site	91%	85%	79%	54%
Packaged to outside accounts	5%	10%	11%	38%
To go	4%	5%	10%	8%
Number of responses	18	30	20	10

average are similar to Group 2 in size. In fact, the largest individual system among the 22 respondents was 20 barrels, with 68 percent brewing on 15-barrel or smaller systems. Again, the large majority of these brewpubs employed up to two full-time brewers, with only 14 percent employing three or more. Once again, on-site dominated the sales data, but this time the to-go numbers doubled over the previous group while the packaged account numbers remained statistically the same.

Group 4, at 2,000 barrels and above, averages over 3,500 barrels annual production with an average of 7.5 brews a week. Fifty-five percent of this group brews on 20-barrel systems and employs on average just over two full-time brewers, similar to Group 3. Within this group, on-site sales notch just over 50 percent and represent a 25-percent decline from the previous group's sales. However, the percentage of sales to outside accounts is up 27 percent coming in at 38 percent of sales for Group 4.

Generally speaking, when we look at year-round and seasonal brands, the average numbers pretty clearly settle out into two distinct sets. Those brewing 1,000 barrels and fewer produce six to seven year-rounds and 13 seasonals. Those above 1,000 barrels brew an average 5.5 year-round brands and 16 seasonals (although the Group 3 seasonal numbers come in at 23, they're a bit skewed due to one respondent brewing 100+ seasonals).

It will come as no surprise that the dominant style in terms of sales across all four of our groups is IPA/Pale Ale, notching 30+ percent of responses across all barrelage groups. On the lowest sales side, the Stout/Porter group blew away its competition—it was tagged for least popular by 50 percent of Group 1, 74 percent of Group 2 and 73 percent of Group 3. Only Group 4 came in under 50 percent of respondents (36 percent).

SALES AND PRICING

As we look at the breakout of sales within brewpubs, some interesting trends appear. While food accounts for the majority of sales by a large margin in all categories, the percentage of sales of in-house brewed beers increases as the brewing capacity of the pub increases. At the high end is Group 4 with in-house beers representing 37.4 percent of total sales, and it's interesting to note that wine and spirits sales in this group are the lowest of any category as a percentage of overall sales.

Turning to product variety, our smallest barrelage group consistently has the highest percentage of types of beer available across all categories (see chart on page 164).

Pint pricing is amazingly consistent across the board, with a mere 23-cent difference between the high (Group 3) and low (Group 1) prices. The range for beers not brewed in-house is even smaller at 7 cents, except that this is taking into account only three of the four groups—Group 3's mean price of $4.20 is a clear anomaly, coming in 55 cents higher than the next highest priced pint at $3.65 (Group 2).

Worthy of note is the more than doubling of average annual revenue from Group 1 to Group 2...double your barrelage and double your revenue?

COSTS AND WAGES

Not nearly as exciting as revenue and sales, expenditures and costs are necessary evils. As in packaging breweries, labor costs are just about the highest single expenditure for a brewpub operation. Food cost was actually incrementally higher than labor for Groups 1 and 4, but the numbers were only a couple of percentage points different. And, as with production breweries, the smaller operations end up paying more for insurance by a healthy margin.

As we look at payroll and benefits, the general rule of "as the operation gets bigger, wages get higher" certainly applies. Average salaries for head brewers in Groups 3 and 4 were about 12 percent higher than Group 2, which in turn was about 13 percent higher than the 500-and-under barrel brewpubs. Likewise, average chef salaries topped out at $47,000 for the 2,000+ barrel operations, diminishing by 15 percent for Group 3, 19 percent for Group 2 and 21 percent for Group 1. Only in the general manager position was there close parity, with the larger three groups having identical average salaries. Hourly wages tell a very similar story, highlighted by the fact that all four categories have the same average wage for cooks.

The vast majority of salaried staff receives medical benefits. As with salary, the larger operations consistently offered more benefits beyond this, including dental, vision and retirement. However, the numbers for profit sharing and ownership share were much more closely in line across the four groupings. The availability of comparable health and retirement benefits for hourly employees was evidenced in the responses, but there was a clear divergence in the offering of profit sharing and ownership share for this group of employees.

HOW MANY BREWERS DO YOU EMPLOY?

	0–500 bbl	501-1000 bbl	1,001-1,999 bbl	2,000 bbl and over
Full Time	0.72	1.2	2.1	2.2
Part Time	0.88	0.5	0.82	0.91
Number of responses	18	30	22	11

HOW MANY YEAR-ROUND BRANDS DO YOU BREW?

	0–500 bbl	501-1000 bbl	1,001-1,999 bbl	2,000 bbl and over
Average	6.6	6.8	5.2	5.7
Number of responses	18	30	22	11

HOW MANY SEASONAL BRANDS DO YOU BREW EACH YEAR?

	0–500 bbl	501-1000 bbl	1,001-1,999 bbl	2,000 bbl and over
Average	13.1	13	23.1	16.5
Number of responses	18	30	22	11

DO YOU ALSO SELL:

	0–500 bbl	501-1,000 bbl	1,001-1,999 bbl	2,000+ bbl
Other craft brewers' beer on tap	28%	21%	14%	20%
Other craft brewers' beer in bottles	28%	7%	10%	20%
Major domestic brands on tap	33%	11%	19%	10%
Major domestic brands in bottles	66%	54%	24%	40%
Imported beer on tap	28%	7%	14%	0%
Imported beer in bottles	55%	29%	29%	10%
Other fermented beverages (mead, cider) on draft	28%	21%	29%	30%
Other fermented beverages (mead, cider) in bottles	22%	25%	38%	10%
Wine	94%	93%	100%	100%
Spirits	89%	71%	95%	70%
Number of responses	18	28	21	10

WHAT IS THE MEAN PRICE FOR A 16-OUNCE PINT OF YOUR BEER?

	0–500 bbl	501-1000 bbl	1,001-1,999 bbl	2,000 bbl and over
Mean price	$3.45	$3.47	$3.68	$3.52
Number of responses	18	29	22	10

WHAT IS THE MEAN PRICE FOR A 16-OUNCE PINT OF BEER NOT BREWED IN-HOUSE?

	0–500 bbl	501-1000 bbl	1,001-1,999 bbl	2,000 bbl and over
Mean price	$3.61	$3.65	$4.20	$3.58
Number of responses	10	16	9	3

WHAT IS YOUR BREWPUB'S ANNUAL GROSS REVENUE?

	0–500 bbl	501-1000 bbl	1,001-1,999 bbl	2,000 bbl and over
Annual gross revenue	$1,200,000	$2,500,000	$2,700,000	$2,950,000
Number of responses	16	25	17	9

WHAT PERCENTAGE OF YOUR SALES COMES FROM:

	0-500 bbl	501-1,000 bbl	1,001-1,999 bbl	2,000+ bbl
Your Beer	19.6%	30%	30%	37.4%
Food	60%	53.1%	58.2%	49.6%
Beer not brewed in-house	7.7%	2.2%	1.6%	2.8%
Wine	4.7%	3.2%	3.8%	3.2%
Spirits	7%	5.8%	6.1%	4.3%
Merchandise	1.2%	2.4%	1.3%	2.3%
Other	0.5%	0%	0.7%	0.5%
Number of responses	16	27	19	11

WHAT PERCENTAGE OF YOUR ANNUAL GROSS REVENUE IS SPENT ON:

	0-500 bbl	501-1,000 bbl	1,001-1,999 bbl	2,000+ bbl
Raw brewing material cost	5.3%	3.8%	5.7%	9.4%
Food cost	30.1%	22.1%	26.0%	28.6%
Wine and liquor cost	15.0%	4.0%	9.7%	16.9%
Labor costs (including benefits)	28.0%	29.7%	31.0%	28.1%
Insurance cost	4.7%	3.3%	1.6%	3.2%
Utilities cost	6.0%	4.8%	3.1%	3.7%
Excise tax cost	2.3%	0.7%	1.1%	1.7%
Other tax cost (income, payroll, ales etc.)	6.6%	5.0%	7.6%	5.1%
Number of responses	10	17	14	7

WHAT IS THE ANNUAL SALARY FOR YOUR...

	0-500 bbl	501-1000 bbl	1,001-1,999 bbl	2,000 bbl and over
Head brewer	$33,000	$38,000	$43,000	$43,000
General manager	$41,000	$49,000	$49,000	$49,000
Chef	$37,000	$38,000	$40,000	$47,000
Number of responses	14	27	21	11

WHAT IS THE AVERAGE HOURLY WAGE FOR YOUR...

	0-500 bbl	501-1000 bbl	1,001-1,999 bbl	2,000 bbl and over
Assistant brewer	$8.00	$10.00	$12.00	$12.00
Other cooks	$10.00	$10.00	$10.00	$10.00
Servers and bartenders	$5.00	$6.00	$5.00	$4.00
Number of responses	16	26	19	11

WHAT BENEFITS DO YOU OFFER YOUR HOURLY STAFF?

	0-500 bbl	501-1,000 bbl	1,001-1,999 bbl	2,000+ bbl
Medical	100%	88%	100%	100%
Dental	50%	40%	59%	67%
Vision	17%	32%	36%	33%
Retirement	17%	40%	55%	44%
Profit sharing	17%	20%	32%	56%
Ownership share	8%	4%	5%	11%
Number of responses	12	25	22	9

WHAT BENEFITS DO YOU OFFER YOUR SALARIED STAFF?				
	0–500 bbl	**501-1,000 bbl**	**1,001-1,999 bbl**	**2,000+ bbl**
Medical	90%	91%	80%	100%
Dental	40%	45%	60%	57%
Vision	20%	45%	40%	29%
Retirement	20%	64%	70%	57%
Profit sharing	0%	9%	10%	29%
Ownership share	0%	9%	0%	14%
Number of responses	10	11	10	7

DO YOU HOLD REGULAR BEER DINNERS?				
	0–500 bbl	**501-1000 bbl**	**1,001-1,999 bbl**	**2,000 bbl and over**
% Yes	44%	17%	59%	64%
Average #/year	4	5.4	5.2	5.1
Number of responses	18	29	22	11

WHAT TYPES OF PACKAGES DO YOU OFFER FOR OFF-SITE AND TO-GO SALES?				
	0–500 bbl	**501-1,000 bbl**	**1,001-1,999 bbl**	**2,000+ bbl**
22-ounce bottles	12%	14%	27%	45%
Six packs	12%	11%	23%	55%
64-ounce "growlers"	88%	96%	100%	91%
1/6-barrel kegs	53%	64%	59%	64%
1/4-barrel kegs	18%	36%	50%	64%
1/2-barrel kegs	77%	82%	82%	73%
Number of responses	17	28	22	11

BEER EDUCATION AND CULTURE

The final three questions dealt with craft beer consumer education and appreciation. Information was gathered on beer dinners, food pairing suggestions and the ability of patrons to conveniently remove beer from the brewpub to continue their education and appreciation at an off-site location.

The numbers for regular beer dinners, while generally solid, lagged in Group 2 with a scant 17 percent on average offering such events. The cross-category average for number of dinners per year clocked in at a healthy 4.9 (call it 5). The use of menu pairings also registered a good rate of positive responses, with Group 4 checking in with an impressive 73-percent use rate.

The 64-ounce growler (and other similar packages) clearly dominate the six most common package varieties used in brewpubs for to-go sales. A close second was the availability of the 1/6-barrel (three out of four establishments in all four barrelage groups offer this option), with the 1/6-barrel keg available in at least 50 percent of brewpubs across all categories. A significantly higher percentage of the bigger operations (Groups 3 and 4) offered the full range of package options compared to smaller pub restaurants.

These represent just some of the highlights that emerged from the data. There are undoubtedly many more insights to be gleaned from these numbers for brewpub operators and owners who take the time to run comparisons with their own data. ◗

DO YOU OFFER BEER AND FOOD PAIRING SUGGESTIONS ON YOUR MENU?

	0-500 bbl	501-1000 bbl	1,001-1,999 bbl	2,000 bbl and over
% Yes	39%	52%	43%	73%
Number of responses	18	29	21	11

WHAT STYLE OF BEER ACCOUNTS FOR YOUR LOWEST SALES VOLUME?

0-500 bbl	501-1,000 bbl	1,001-1,999 bbl	2,000+ bbl
Barley wine Bitter Brown porter Cask Cream ale Foreign style stout IPA Pils Porter Seasonals Stout Stout Stout Stout Stout Wheat	American light Gruit Light ale Peach ale Seasonals Porter Porter Porter Porter Porter Porter Porter Robust porter Scotch ale Scottish 60 Shilling Stout Stout Stout Stout Stout Stout Stout Stout Stout Stout Stout Stout	Anything on beer engines Dark wheat & Rauchbier Foreign-style stout Fruit stout Lagers Mild Oatmeal stout Oatmeal stout Porter Porter Porter Rauchbier - Milds -- Unusual Herb Beers Smoked beer Stout Stout Stout Stout Stout Stout Stout Stout Stouts/porters	Barleywine Golden Neo-lambic Oatmeal stout Oatmeal stout Rauchbier Rice beer Scotch ale Specialty Stout Stout

WHAT STYLE OF BEER ACCOUNTS FOR YOUR HIGHEST SALES VOLUME?

0-500 bbl	501-1,000 bbl	1,001-1,999 bbl	2,000+ bbl
Amber ale American lager & Pale ale American light lager American wheat ale American wheat ale Blonde ale Blonde ale & Pale ale Cream ale Golden ale Hefeweizen Honey ale IPA IPA IPA Lager Oatmeal stout Pale ale	Amber ale American (filtered) wheat American amber/red American brown and Pale American Golden ale American pale ale American style hefeweizen Bavarian helles Cream ale Cream ale Cream ale English ale Hefeweizen Helles Honey wheat IPA IPA IPA IPA IPA IPA Kolsch Kolsch & IPA Pale ale Pale ale Pale ale Pale ale Pilsner Vienna lager Wheat ale	Amber Amber ale Amber lager American IPA Bavarian dunkel Blonde Golden ale Golden ale Golden ale Honey ale Honey wheat IPA IPA IPA IPA IPA Light lager Light lager Munich helles Pale ale Pilsener Red or IPA	Alt Amber ale Amber ale Brown ale IPA IPA IPA Pale ale Pale ale & Scotch ale Scottish-style ale Wheat ale & Amber ale

Chapter Thirty-Three

Packaging Brewery Operations Survey

Essential Data on Costs at Various Brewery Volumes

By Brewers Association Staff

IN 2006, THE BREWERS ASSOCIATION began a series of anonymous surveys, focusing on key operational questions that many brewers share. The goal was to collect useful benchmarking information for brewers on a regular basis. The chapter presents data from 2006 and periodic updates will be conducted and published in *The New Brewer* magazine for all members of the Brewers Association to read.

We received a total of 49 responses to the survey from packaging brewers. We split the results into six size categories: 0-5,000 barrels, 5,001-10,000 barrels, 10,001-15,000 barrels, 15,001-30,000 barrels, 30,001-60,000 barrels and 60,001 barrels and above.

The largest number of responses came from the smallest barrelage category with 21 respondents. Next came the 5,001-10,000 group with 10 responses. We received only two responses from breweries with 10,001-15,000 barrels. The next three groups logged in with seven, four and five respondents, respectively.

The charts show the mean (average) results of the responses to each question. With the small number of responses in many categories, the results should not be seen as true industry averages, but rather as snapshots of where the responding breweries stand.

WHAT'S BREWING?

Among the greater than 60,000 barrel crowd, ales represent an average of 97 percent of total production, with 60 percent of respondents (three out of five) listing pale ale/IPA as their highest volume style. Interestingly, the number of brands brewed year-round and seasonally is about equal for 80 percent (four out of five) of respondents in this barrelage category. When we look at the breakout between sales of draft and bottles/cans, it is about equal at 49 percent draft and 51 percent bottles/cans.

In the 31,001-60,000-barrel range, ales again predominate with 86 percent of production and pale ale/IPA representing half of the best-selling style responses. The difference in numbers of year-round brews and seasonals is only slightly greater here than in the largest barrelage category, but the difference between draft and bottle/can sales opens up to 38 percent draft and 62 percent bottles/cans.

Looking at the 15,001-30,000 barrel group, we find that ales continue their predominance at 92 percent of total production. The previous grip that pales and IPAs had among styles begins to slip and comes in at 43 percent of the best-selling style for these breweries. The ratio of year rounds to seasonals clocks in at 3:2, while it's 2:1 bottles/cans to draft.

With only two responses for the 10,001-15,000 barrel category, take these results with a healthy grain of salt! Ales make up a dominating 95 percent of production, while bottle/cans make up 67 percent of sales.

The 5,001-10,000 barrel responses show a 85-15 percent ales-to-lagers split, and with 10 responses we also saw a much greater variety of styles making up the best sellers (only 30 percent are represented by the pale/IPA styles). There is relative parity in the next cut, with an average of eight year-rounds and seven seasonals, while the 2:1 package to draft ratio holds.

Among the smallest category of brewers, 0-5,000 barrels, we find the highest percentage of lagers being brewed at 28 percent of production, with 3 of the 21 respondents exclusively brewing lagers. Forty-five percent answered that a pale ale or IPA was the best-selling style, while Kölsch and amber tied for second place with 10 percent of responses to this question. A comparison of year-rounds to seasonals yielded a 3:4 ratio. Interestingly, the smallest had something in common with the biggest: draft sales were right around the 50-percent mark, while all other categories came in at 2:1 package to draft.

MAKING THE SALE

It comes as no surprise that the larger the brewery, the more states they ship beer to. The 60,000-plus group sent beer to an average of 27 states, while the smallest group ventured to an average of three states.

Likewise, larger breweries tend to have larger sales staffs, with the largest breweries averaging 13.6 full-time equivalent salespeople to only 1.09 average for breweries producing less than 5,000 barrels.

One interesting result, which the small sample prevents us from drawing definitive conclusions from, appears in the question about dollars spent on marketing and advertising. The highest dollars-per-barrel spending average appears in the mid-size breweries. The largest and smallest groups spend the least, according to our respondents.

Likewise, the price for kegs of beer is lowest in those mid-tier brewers—from 5,001 barrels to 30,000 barrels, where the draft-to-package sales ratio is tilted steeper toward bottles and cans. Case prices seem to increase as the breweries get larger.

PAYING FOR IT

Labor is the largest cost for most brewers, making up from 12 to 38.5 percent of a brewery's total expenses. As expected, raw materials costs decline as a percentage of expenses as a brewery grows, as do packaging costs as breweries take advantage of economies of scale. Insurance costs are most onerous for small brewers.

And it should come as no surprise that as breweries get larger they are able to pay their employees more and offer more benefits. Among the breweries producing more than 60,000 barrels, the average salary for a brewery manager or head brewer was $91,666 with other salaried brew staff averaging $48,500. Hourly wages for brewer staff in the largest breweries average $18.45.

In this group, 100 percent of salaried workers receive medical, dental, vision and profit sharing benefits. Eighty percent receive retirement benefits and 20 percent are offered ownership shares in the company. The same benefits hold true for hourly staff.

In the 30,001-60,000 group, brewery managers average $76,250, other salaried brewers $40,750 and hourly brew staff $13.38 per hour. All salaried staff receive medical benefits, but dental, vision and other benefits are less common for salaried workers. About half of the respondents offer benefits to hourly workers.

Head brewers at breweries producing 15,001-30,000 barrels make an average of $58,844, while other salaried brewers earn $34,838 and hourly workers get $13.38 per hour. Benefits are a mixed bag at this tier.

With only two responses in the 10,001 to 15,000 barrel group, the numbers are not statistically relevant. But the average was $81,000 for the brewery manager, $42,000 for other salaried brew staff and $11.13 per hour for hourly.

The 5,001-10,000 barrel group pays an average of $41,200 for head brewers, $29,555 for other salaried brewers and $11 per hour for hourly staff. Benefits are available for about half the workers.

In the smallest tier, head brewer salaries average $34,800, other salaried staff earns $28,033 and hourly brewers make $10.32 an hour. Benefits are not very common at this level.

HOW MANY YEARS HAVE YOU BEEN IN BUSINESS?

	Brewery size in barrels					
	0-5,000	**5001-10,000**	**10,001-15,000**	**15,001-30,000**	**30,001-60,000**	**More than 60,000**
Years	5.4	10.8	10.5	16.1	10.3	18.2
Responses	21	10	2	7	4	5

WHAT SIZE BREW SYSTEM DO YOU BREW ON?

	Brewery size in barrels					
	0-5,000	**5001-10,000**	**10,001-15,000**	**15,001-30,000**	**30,001-60,000**	**More than 60,000**
Avg Size in bbls	20	31	35	53	56	164
Responses	21	10	2	7	4	5

WHAT PERCENTAGE OF YOUR BEERS ARE...

	Brewery size in barrels					
	0-5,000	**5001-10,000**	**10,001-15,000**	**15,001-30,000**	**30,001-60,000**	**More than 60,000**
ales?	72	84.9	95	92	86.22	97.2
lagers?	28	15.1	5	8	13.78	2.8
Responses	19	10	2	7	4	5

HOW MANY BRANDS DO YOU BREW...

	Brewery size in barrels					
	0-5,000	**5001-10,000**	**10,001-15,000**	**15,001-30,000**	**30,001-60,000**	**More than 60,000**
year-round?	4	8	5	6	7	6
seasonally?	5	7	7	4	9	4
Responses	21	10	2	7	4	5

WHAT STYLE OF BEER ACCOUNTS FOR THE HIGHEST SALES VOLUME?

Brewery size in barrels					
0-5,000	**5001-10,000**	**10,001-15,000**	**15,001-30,000**	**30,001-60,000**	**More than 60,000**
Pale ale	Amber lager	India Pale Ale	Pale ale	India Pale Ale	Hefeweizen
India Pale Ale	Amber ale	Fruit Beer	Amber ale	Pale ale	American pale ale
India Pale Ale	Amber ale		American wheat	American strong ale	India Pale Ale
India Pale Ale	India Pale Ale		India Pale Ale	Light ale	Amber ale
Pale ale	India Pale Ale		Pale ale		Pale ale
Mexican light lager	Brown ale		Scottish ale		
Pale ale	Scottish ale		Alt		
Kolsch	Pale ale				
Kolsch	Blonde ale				
Amber ale	Belgian-style wit				
Irish red ale					
Pils					
Vienna					
American pale ale					
Double IPA					
Pale ale					
Amber ale					

WHAT STYLE OF BEER ACCOUNTS FOR THE LOWEST SALES VOLUME?

Brewery size in barrels

0-5,000	5001-10,000	10,001-15,000	15,001-30,000	30,001-60,000	More than 60,000
Golden ale	Coffee stout	Lager	Porter	Stout	Fruit beer
Hefeweizen	Brown ale	Porter	Porter	Stout	Fresh hop ale
Porter	Bock		Porter	Smoked porter	Munich dark lager
Pilsener	Experimental		Mild	Esoteric styles	Stout
Stout	Oktoberfest lager		Barleywine		Golden
Dark lager	Fruit beer		Wit		
Brown ale	Oatmeal stout				
Hefeweizen	Porter				
Stout	Amber ale				
Kolsch					
Brown ale					
Pale ale					
Stout					
Helles					
Stout					
Light lager					
Hefeweizen					

WHAT PERCENTAGE OF YOUR SALES IS....

	Brewery size in barrels					
	0-5,000	5001-10,000	10,001-15,000	15,001-30,000	30,001-60,000	More than 60,000
draft?	51.9	33.5	32.5	33.1	38.3	47.8
bottles/cans?	38.9	56.2	67.5	63.5	61.7	39.5
in-house?	9.2	10.3	0	1.4	0.7	0.7
Responses	19	10	2	7	4	5

HOW MANY STATES DO YOU DISTRIBUTE IN?

	Brewery size in barrels					
	0-5,000	5001-10,000	10,001-15,000	15,001-30,000	30,001-60,000	More than 60,000
States	3	11	7.5	15	15	27
Responses	21	10	2	7	4	5

HOW MANY SALES PEOPLE DO YOU EMPLOY (IN FULL-TIME EQUIVALENTS)?

	Brewery size in barrels					
	0-5,000	5001-10,000	10,001-15,000	15,001-30,000	30,001-60,000	More than 60,000
employees	1.09	1.65	9	4	8.5	13.6
Responses	21	10	2	7	4	5

WHAT IS THE MEAN PRICE, FOB YOUR LOADING DOCK, OF A...

	Brewery size in barrels					
	0-5,000	5001-10,000	10,001-15,000	15,001-30,000	30,001-60,000	More than 60,000
case?	$16.60	$16.88	$16.47	$16.78	$21.15	$19.06
keg?	$78.23	$69.71	$73.00	$70.57	$82.48	$81.00
Responses	21	10	2	7	4	5

HOW MANY DOLLARS PER BARREL ARE SPENT ON...

	Brewery size in barrels					
	0-5,000	**5001-10,000**	**10,001-15,000**	**15,001-30,000**	**30,001-60,000**	**More than 60,000**
advertising?	0.67	3.2	3.67	3.1	2.2	1.5
marketing?	2.5	3.9	6	7.4	7.5	5
Responses	17	8	2	7	4	5

WHAT PERCENTAGE OF YOUR ANNUAL EXPENSES IS YOUR....

	Brewery size in barrels					
	0-5,000	**5001-10,000**	**10,001-15,000**	**15,001-30,000**	**30,001-60,000**	**More than 60,000**
raw material cost?	19.1	15.56	17	15.93	14.75	7
labor cost? (including benefits)	22.12	19.39	38.5	21.15	12.58	29
insurance cost?	5.43	2.04	2.9	1.4	1.35	1
excise tax cost?	6.37	5.22	6	4.8	4	5
other tax cost?	4.64	3.87	5	5	21	3
utilities cost?	7	3.43	3.9	3.68	2.85	4
packaging materials cost?	7.6	23.13	29	25.22	17.5	18
beer freight cost?	1.05	1.49	1.5	2.1	2.5	3
Responses	8	8	2	6	3	1

WHAT BENEFITS DO YOU OFFER YOUR SALARIED STAFF?

	Brewery size in barrels					
	0-5,000	**5001-10,000**	**10,001-15,000**	**15,001-30,000**	**30,001-60,000**	**More than 60,000**
Medical	47%	100%	100%	100%	100%	100%
Dental	10%	60%	50%	29%	75%	100%
Vision	10%	40%	50%	29%	75%	100%
Retirement	5%	60%	100%	86%	75%	80%
Profit sharing	0	30%	0	57%	75%	100%
Ownership share	10%	10%	50%	0	0	20%
Responses	21	10	2	7	4	5

WHAT BENEFITS DO YOU OFFER YOUR HOURLY STAFF?

	Brewery size in barrels					
	0-5,000	**5001-10,000**	**10,001-15,000**	**15,001-30,000**	**30,001-60,000**	**More than 60,000**
Medical	29%	70%	0	86%	50%	100%
Dental	10%	40%	0	14%	50%	100%
Vision	5%	30%	0	14%	50%	100%
Retirement	5%	40%	0	71%	25%	80%
Profit sharing	0	30%	0	57%	50%	100%
Ownership share	0	10%	0	0	0	20%
Responses	17	10	2	7	4	5

WHAT IS THE ANNUAL SALARY OF YOUR BREWERY MANAGER?

	Brewery size in barrels					
	0-5,000	**5001-10,000**	**10,001-15,000**	**15,001-30,000**	**30,001-60,000**	**More than 60,000**
salary	$34,800	$41,200	$81,000	$58,844	$76,250	$91,666
Responses	21	10	2	7	4	4

WHAT IS THE AVERAGE SALARY OF OTHER SALARIED BREWING STAFF?

	Brewery size in barrels					
	0-5,000	**5001-10,000**	**10,001-15,000**	**15,001-30,000**	**30,001-60,000**	**More than 60,000**
salary	$28,033	$29,555	$42,000	$34,838	$40,750	$48,500
Responses	17	10	2	7	4	4

WHAT IS THE AVERAGE HOURLY WAGE OF YOUR OTHER BREWING STAFF?

	Brewery size in barrels					
	0-5,000	**5001-10,000**	**10,001-15,000**	**15,001-30,000**	**30,001-60,000**	**More than 60,000**
salary	$10.32	$11.00	$11.13	$13.38	$13.38	$18.48
Responses	16	10	2	7	4	4

WHAT IS THE AVERAGE ANNUAL SALARY OF YOUR SALES STAFF?

	Brewery size in barrels					
	0-5,000	**5001-10,000**	**10,001-15,000**	**15,001-30,000**	**30,001-60,000**	**More than 60,000**
salary	$34,571	$45,900	$50,000	$45,000	$58,950	$52,100
Responses	14	10	2	7	4	4

WHAT PERCENTAGE OF SALES STAFF SALARY IS COMMISSION BASED?

	Brewery size in barrels					
	0-5,000	**5001-10,000**	**10,001-15,000**	**15,001-30,000**	**30,001-60,000**	**More than 60,000**
salary	27.5%	14.6%	25%	15.4%	10.1%	7.5%
Responses	14	10	2	7	4	5

WHAT PERCENTAGE OF YOUR BEER DO YOU SELF DISTRIBUTE?

	Brewery size in barrels					
	0-5,000	5001-10,000	10,001-15,000	15,001-30,000	30,001-60,000	More than 60,000
self	28.8%	8.1%	1%	10.4%	15.5%	6.6%
Responses	20	10	2	7	4	4

Chapter Thirty-Four

Creating a Business Plan

Key Success Factors for New Breweries

THROUGHOUT THIS BOOK, WE HAVE presented information about and approaches to planning and starting your own brewery. If you've gotten this far, you are no doubt serious about starting your own business and you've begun to ask, "What's next?" The answer is, "a business plan."

Even if you are independently wealthy, the business plan plays an essential role in helping you to think through the details of what you are about to undertake. But in most cases, the business plan also plays another essential role: that of demonstrating to potential investors that you have a sound plan for making money in the brewing business.

This chapter was once an actual business plan used to successfully raise money. As such, it provides an example of what your brewery business plan will need to look like and a model for you to reference as you research and develop your own plan. Of course the actual figures used and indeed, much of the narrative are now quite dated. In truth, this doesn't matter much. No single business plan can reflect the myriad variations in local conditions and costs, the vast range of opportunities and market demand likely to be present for a new brewery. The only way to create a useful business plan for your new venture is to carefully research actual costs in your community and thoughtfully consider the market opportunity you have available. Only in this way can you create a business plan that will attract funding and guide you through the successful creation of your business.

As sources of up-to-date information, you will find other chapters of this book useful as a first reference. In addition, you'll need to do research in your own local community to find out about utility, labor and real estate prices. Check with state officials about taxes on beer production and income taxes for small businesses and employment. Current industry trends can be acquired from the Brewers Association which has a special membership class for breweries-in-planning. If you will pursue a brewpub, you'll want to contact the National Restaurant Association to find out about the planning resources they offer as well. Beyond that, there are many other resources mentioned throughout this book that will be useful to you.

Finally, heed these words from the originator of this plan: "We got lucky. If we did this over, we would aim to raise 40 percent *more money* in the beginning." The single most common mistake of new businesses is under-estimating the amount of capital it will take to get started. You'll do yourself a big favor it you don't make that mistake at the outset.

Changes to this business plan are to the company's name (we're calling it the Craft Brewing Company), years and certain figures and names, which we've changed to "XX."

SAMPLE BUSINESS PLAN

Business Plan for
The Craft Brewing Company Inc
Prepared on Month Day, Year
For further information, contact:

TABLE OF CONTENTS

TEXT OF THE SAMPLE BUSINESS PLAN

Executive Summary

Description of the Business: The Craft Brewing Company Inc. is a privately held corporation owned and managed by the president and vice president. The business of the company is the production of high quality, fresh beer for the local and regional markets. The Craft Brewing Company will be located at XX, which is a warehouse less than a five minute walk from the center of XX. A five year lease, renewable for an additional five years at the same rate is being negotiated. The Craft Brewing Company will initially produce three different styles of beer: a dark ale, an amber ale, and a golden ale. These products will be distributed in kegs to licensed retail outlets. The products of the Craft Brewing Company will be wholesaled to premium pubs, taverns and restaurants in the city of XX, throughout XX County, and then to the broader regional market. In addition, the Craft Brewing Company will have its own tap room where retail customers may come to view the operation of the brewery, while purchasing beer by the glass, beer to go, snacks, and retail items such as T-shirts and glassware with our logo printed on them.

The Craft Brewing Company will produce beer with a 14-barrel, stainless-steel brewing plant. Production capacity of our 14-barrel brewing plant with five fermenters is approximately 700 barrels a year (1 barrel equals 31 gallons, which equals two standard 15.5-gallon kegs). The addition of more fermentation tanks at regular intervals will increase capacity to approximately 2,800 barrels annually, which is the estimated limit imposed by the size of the space being leased. The management team intends to produce and sell approximately 670 barrels in the first year and then double production and sales in the second year. Thereafter, the management team will increase production and sales by approximately 500 to 600 barrels annually, until the approximately 2,800-barrel limit imposed by the space we are initially renting has been reached.

Management Responsibility: As president, XX is responsible for the overall implementation of the Plan of Action and the daily operation of the business. The president will oversee the tenant improvements and installation of the brewery. The president will carry out the licensing process, secure financing of operational expenses, acquire and service retail accounts, and direct the daily start-up operations. The president will also be head brewer, and will be responsible for all tasks related to daily beer production.

As vice president and general manager, XX will assist the president in all areas related to the business start-up and the daily operation of the brewery. The vice president/general manager will specifically be responsible for advertising, promotions, purchasing, inventory control, and the management of the tap room and its retail sales.

Marketing and Distribution: The Craft Brewing Company produces beer in kegs for wholesale to the licensed liquor retail market. Kegs will be self distributed by the Craft Brewing Company to its local clients. In the first year, the president will market the company's products and be personally responsible for acquiring local retail accounts and distributing kegs to those accounts. The president is the individual most familiar with the company's products and with the local market for these products. The president is therefore the best qualified person to represent the company to its customers. The marketing strategy will consist of direct person to person sales calls by the president to local premium retail outlets. Craft Brewing Company products will also be advertised in the local print media.

The Craft Brewing Company will also have a tap room on the site where customers may come to purchase our products at retail prices. This retail outlet will allow us to receive pint price on the sale of beer, which will make an important contribution to our profit margin. Snacks and promotional merchandise such as glassware and T-shirts will also be sold to increase our public exposure and profit margin.

Professional Support: The following personnel will be used as needed. See Attachments for professional references and resumes.

Brewing Consultant: XX
Business Consultant: XX
Master Brewer: XX
Accountant: XX
Finance: XX
Attorney: XX

Estimated Production, Sales, and Income: The following numbers are our projections of production levels, gross sales, and net income for the Craft Brewing Company, during the first three years of operation.

Year	Production	Gross Sales	Net Income
One	671 bbl.	$181,508	$46,121
Two	1,077 bbl.	$256,741	$70,534
Three	1,558 bbl.	$329,387	$88,508

BUSINESS PLAN INTRODUCTION

Craft breweries are a historic means for satisfying the public's demand for a greater variety of fresh quality beer. In the late nineteenth and early twentieth centuries, the United States supported nearly four thousand breweries, the majority being independent local and regional operations producing a vast array of Old World beer styles. Without question, Prohibition nearly destroyed this brewing tradition.

Today America is experiencing a revival of its brewing tradition. Craft breweries are defined by the industry as small breweries which produce less than 15,000 barrels of beer annually and distribute their beer for off-premise consumption. As of January 2006 there were more than 1300 craft breweries and brewpubs operating in the United States and Canada. In 2005 the craft brewery and brewpub industry in the United States experienced a 9 percent annual increase in barrels of beer produced, when compared to production for 2004.

The current demand for a greater variety of more flavorful beers originated with the import beer market. As the imported beer market grew, beer drinkers had an opportunity to further educate their tastes to the great variety of world beer styles. As a result the craft brewing industry in the United States has benefited from the public's increased awareness of and demand for more flavorful beers. Imported beers account for more than 10 percent of beer sales in the United States, which represents a significant market share. However, the craft brewery industry demonstrated significant growth in recent years.

Beer drinkers are clearly demonstrating their demand for a greater variety of full-flavored beers. Unfortunately, beer does not transport well, and most styles of beer begin to deteriorate in quality if they are not consumed within a few weeks of having been brewed. While this is clearly a disadvantage for imported beers, craft breweries are at a clear advantage in being able to deliver the freshest product to the consumer.

Advantages of Craft breweries: One of the advantages of a craft brewery is its ability to supply its product to the consumer when it is at its peak of freshness. Craft breweries are brewing a handcrafted product on a more limited scale where quality is the most important concern. For this reason, using the highest quality traditional ingredients — malted barley, hops, yeast, and water — is justified, rather than the chemicals and cheaper adjuncts such as corn and rice which are used by large scale brewers to cut costs. Fresh quality beer produced locally, without chemicals in processing or for preservation is the key note of the craft brewing industry.

The craft brewery has the additional advantage of bringing the beer drinking public into immediate contact with the equipment and operation associated with beer production. A well designed craft brewery with a tap room allows the public to witness firsthand the creation of the handcrafted beer they are drinking.

The Market: Our city has a growing population which supports a variety of restaurants and pubs. Many of these restaurants and pubs are carrying craft brewed beer on several taps and enjoying significant sales of these products. These currently operating licensed retail outlets are our primary targets as customers. Our craft brewery will be identified with the local community and will appeal to the city resident who, with friends, family members, and business associates, is eager to support a locally produced beer. Having once tasted our fresh ale, these consumers will be sure to ask for our product at their favorite local restaurant or pub.

Specialty beers can be produced for seasonal holidays, community events, and local bars which desire to offer a unique, specially contracted beer to their customers. To increase our market exposure, table tents, beer menus, T-shirts, decorative keg tap handles, and other promotional materials will be utilized at the brewery and distributed to our licensed liquor retail clients.

Since our product will be sold to licensed retail outlets, promotions will be handled at the point-of-sale using these low cost promotional items, which will be provided free of charge to our accounts. Direct advertising to the general public will be on a regular but limited scale in the local print media. We will earn the confidence of our retail licensees and their beer drinking customers by providing a consistent quality product and supporting that product with point-of-sale promotional items.

Production Process: The Craft Brewing Company will initially produce three styles of traditional British ale. Brewing begins by cracking the highest quality malted barley with a roller mill. This grist is then mixed with hot water in the mash tun, producing mash. A sweet liquid called wort is filtered out of the mash and transferred to the brew kettle. The wort is then brought to a rolling boil and hops are added to contribute bitterness, flavor, and aroma. After boiling, the wort is transferred through a heat exchanger, cooling the liquid down to fermentation temperature. The wort is then pumped into the primary fermenter where yeast is added. After one week of fermentation the fresh ale is transferred to a cold conditioning tank where it is clarified and carbonated for a second week. Now at the height of freshness, the ale is racked to kegs where it is ready to be distributed to the market and served. (See attached designs for the specifications on the major brewing equipment.)

Management Team: Craft Brewing Company is a privately held corporation managed by the president and vice president. All decisions will be made by the management team, officers, and shareholders, in compliance with the Company's articles of incorporation and bylaws.

President: XX is an accomplished homebrewer with seven years of experience. XX has been researching and preparing for this project for more than six years and has a solid understanding of the brewing process and the market for craft brewed beer.

Vice President: XX is likewise an experienced homebrewer who is capable of managing the brewing plant unassisted. The vice president has ten years of experience in the retail sales and restaurant industries, working as a cashier, hostess, bartender, and waitress in many fine establishments.

Consultant: The management team will be assisted by XX, a highly qualified professional brewing consultant. Mr. XX is the managing consultant on several successful brewing projects.

The management team is committed to the success of this plan. All decisions will be made with the best interest of the business and other investors in mind. Whenever necessary, the management team will rely on the assistance of professionals on a contractual basis.

Plan of Action: Having signed the Letter of Intent on the building lease and opened the corporate general account with an initial capital contribution of $75,000, as discussed in the Executive Summary above, the following tasks in order of priority will be completed. First, the management team will pursue the required equity capital by means of this business proposal and a share offering circular form which will be delivered to prospective investors.

Once the share offering has been delivered to prospective investors, the president and his brewery consultant, XX, will complete the final building utility and brewery layout designs. Once these plans have been finalized, the president and brewery consultant will place an order for the capital brewing equipment. The capital equipment for the brewery will be delivered ten to twelve weeks from time of order. The brewery consultant will personally supervise the installation of the brewery once the equipment has been delivered.

While the capital equipment is being fabricated, the president will complete the process of acquiring all permits necessary to begin capital improvements to the space being leased. Once a building occupancy permit has been issued, and while waiting for the main brewing plant to be fabricated and delivered, the management team will carry out the building improvements which have been designated as their responsibility in the lease Letter of Intent. At this time, the management team will also complete the process of filing for liquor and business license from the relevant federal, state, county, and city authorities.

The management team is seeking financing from private investors to contribute toward the costs of the capital equipment, improvements to the building, and the first several months operating capital. See the Use of Proceeds section in the Share Offering Circular for a more detailed discussion of these expenses.

Approximate Expenses — Start-Up:

$XX,000	Brewery Equipment, Delivered, Installed, and Operational
$XX,000	Building Improvements
$XXX,000	Total Capital Improvements
$XX,000	Start-up Professional Fees
$XX,000	Operating Capital
$XXX,000	Total Capital Investment

PRODUCTS

Initial Products: The Craft Brewing Company will initially produce three flagship beers; a dark ale, an amber ale, and a pale ale. The dark ale, brewed within the general porter style parameters which have proven so popular on the West Coast, will have a distinct roasted-chocolate flavor, nicely balanced with the mild-spicy hop nose characteristic of premium hops. This ale will be fairly dry, medium bodied, and quite dark with ruby-red tints around the edges. Our experience with the many different porters and dark ales being produced throughout the United States, leads us to anticipate that this ale will be very popular with beer drinkers who enjoy traditional, dark British porters, stouts, and brown ales.

Our second flagship product will be an amber ale brewed within the style parameters commonly known as pale ale, which includes amber-colored ales. This amber ale will have a lightly sweet, malty flavor, balanced by the aroma hops. This ale will have a fruity-hop flavor in the finish and the hop nose, which is so characteristic of amber ales. It will be light to medium bodied and amber-red in color. Pale ales are one of the most popular of traditional British beer styles being produced by craft breweries in the United States. It is a beer which is both satisfying to the experienced ale drinker and yet not too overpowering as to frighten off the neophyte.

Our third flagship product will be a golden ale, a light bodied, only slightly sweet and lightly hopped ale, with a rich golden color. This golden ale is a style of beer which is designed to be light and thirst quenching, with a more moderate alcohol content than our other beers. It will be an excellent accompaniment to an afternoon lunch or the evening meal when the beer drinker chooses to have two or three beers without becoming filled up or intoxicated. This beer is intended to appeal to experienced ale drinkers, as well as novice beer drinkers who have not yet experienced the ale revolution.

Future Products: In addition to these three flagship beers, other styles are being planned as limited, seasonal offerings. For example, barley wine, raspberry stout, brown, special bitter, and India pale ale. All of these are popular specialty styles enjoying steady seasonal demand.

The production of specialty beers will depend on local demand as expressed in customer surveys conducted by the management. They will be produced on a limited rotating basis, depending on the availability of fermenters. The management will actively pursue contract brewing accounts with local licensed retailers who are interested in having a special beer produced solely for sale to their own customers. In addition, our tap room will allow us to offer new products on our own taps to test the public's response to these new products before offering them for wholesale to other retailers.

Although our beer recipes will be designed to meet certain style parameters which have been proven to be popular by other brewers in the industry, our beer recipes will be adjusted so that the final products have their own unique quality. We are not attempting to imitate the products of other brewers. On the contrary, we will produce our own unique ales within style parameters which have a demonstrated track record of success.

Suppliers: One important element of our beers which will help to ensure their popularity will be the use of the highest quality, traditional ingredients. All of our ingredients will be purchased from the most reputable local suppliers. Our malted barley will be supplied by XX. They carry the finest domestic and imported specialty malts which are needed for making traditional British ales. Our hops will be supplied by XX. They carry all of the premier hops produced in the Pacific Northwest, and many of the noble hop varieties of Europe which are essential for producing original versions of traditional ales. Finally, our yeast will be supplied by XX. They specialize in storing and shipping yeast cultures in such a variety that brewers have the opportunity to craft beers to their own particular flavor profile.

As the growth of the industry indicates, there is an increasing variety of handcrafted beers being made available to the American public. The advantage our beers enjoy in this market will stem from using the finest ingredients provided by the most reliable local suppliers. In addition, our beers will have their own unique flavor profile and be the freshest available to our local customers. Finally, our products will benefit from the additional demand which is generated by the customers knowledge that these beers have been produced within the community with local pride.

Bottling and Export: When starting a craft brewery, it is necessary to consider all available options. This is especially true when it comes to the issue of how the product will be packaged for sale. The issue of packaging is largely dependent on the amount of capital available and the nature of the local market. While there are some benefits to bottling a portion of the brewery's capacity for local retail sales, a top-quality bottling line entails a large initial capital investment and a much larger input of labor.

After having carefully researched the local market, we have determined that our best option is to initially concentrate solely on draft sales. We have concluded that a sufficient demand exists to support our business with draft sales alone. Our strategy is based on the belief that the most important task is to first concentrate on developing a sound local base of satisfied retail accounts and loyal draft beer drinkers, before diversifying our product line.

Despite our decision to initially concentrate on local draft sales, we recognize that a bottled product on local grocers' shelves would help to raise our public profile and increase our profit margin. For this reason, the management team of Craft Brewing Company is carefully examining the option of hiring another brewery to produce for us sometime after the second year of operation. Many small scale brewing companies in the United States have enjoyed tremendous success by contracting with a different brewery to produce a bottled product which the contracting company then distributes to its own customers. By contracting a bottled product from another brewery we will be able to service our own draft accounts without reducing our draft capacity. In addition, contracting would allow us to increase both market exposure and profit margins, without the great expense associated with owning and operating a bottling line.

Finally, we would like to raise the issue of exporting a contracted bottled product. We have carefully researched the beer market and developed several important relationships with beer importers and retailers. It is our firm belief that a specially designed product, contracted from a local brewery and then wholesaled by the Craft Brewing Company, would receive shelf space and enjoy steadily growing sales.

THE INDUSTRY

Industry History: Within the brewing industry, the Craft Brewing Company is considered to be a production craft brewery and brewpub combination. A brewpub is a restaurant or tavern which produces its own beer. A production craft brewery is a small brewery that sells beer in bottles or kegs to other retailers. Today these small breweries are proliferating rapidly, but they are a relatively new phenomenon which can be considered revolutionary.

The craft brewing revolution began in 1977 with the birth of the New Albion Brewing company in Sonoma, California. The primary characteristics, which distinguished New Albion and other new craft breweries from the established industrial breweries, were their small size, limited financing, and concentration on producing premium, specialty lagers and ales rather than the standard pale lagers. The most significant difference was the fact that most new craft breweries were built from the grassroots by homebrewers with more enthusiasm than formal training.

Today there are about 1300 craft breweries and brewpubs operating in the United States (2005). Industry statistics demonstrate that while the major brewing companies are flat-to-declining in sales, the market for premium specialty products is expanding. Tastes are changing, and quality, variety, flavor, and freshness are what the beer drinking public is coming to demand. It has become evident that every city, even small communities, have the potential to support at least one local brewery, and larger cities such as Portland and Seattle are already supporting many more.

As the craft brewing industry has grown and prospered, a whole host of associated industries has sprung up to meet the needs of craft brewers. Brewing consultants, equipment fabricators, ingredient suppliers, publicists, distributors, and even educational programs are now catering to the special needs of craft brewers and, as a result, making the business of small-scale craft brewing much easier today than it was just ten years ago. These enterprises are now devoting large sales staffs and significant resources to servicing the craft brewing industry, because they are confident that this is a growth industry for the future.

Institutional Support: As the craft brewing industry has grown and prospered, a variety of new professional organizations, trade associations, and educational programs have been established to assist craft brewers and educate the public.

Professional and trade associations include: the Brewers Association, and the XX Small Brewers Association.

These professional organizations perform many essential tasks for the craft brewing industry including: publishing industry statistics and information; representing the industry in legislative lobbying efforts; conducting trade shows and conferences; undertaking public relations with the media; and developing programs for brewery insurance, quality control, and continuing education for brewers.

Some important examples of the quality publications provided by these organizations include: *Zymurgy®* (American Homebrewers Association®), *The New Brewer* (Brewers Association), the *North American Brewers Resource Directory* (Brewers Publications). These and other publications are an invaluable resource for starting and successfully operating a craft brewery.

The ever-increasing number of trade conferences and craft brewing festivals which help to improve the quality of our product and educate the beer drinking public about our products includes: the Brewers Association's annual Craft Brewers Conference, the American Homebrewers Association National Conference, the Great American Beer Festival®, and a rich range of local and regional beer festivals.

Finally, in any discussion of institutional support we can not neglect the educational programs which recently have been designed specifically to further educate craft brewers. These programs include: the Beer Judge Certification Program; courses on quality control and brewing technology at the Siebel Institute of Technology in Chicago; and a variety of programs on sanitation, microbiology, brewing business management, etc., at the University of California at Davis.

The sources above represent only a portion of the proliferating number of institutional resources available to craft brewers today.

Industry Prospects: Well into the second decade of the craft brewing revolution, a variety of statistical evidence clearly demonstrates that this industry is much more than a temporary fad. We are at this time witnessing a proliferation of craft brewing enterprises, trade associations, institutional support, and beer festivals, organized specifically to celebrate craft brewing. Likewise, the great number of associated industries which view the craft brewing industry as an important market for their products and services is a strong indication that the craft brewing phenomenon has matured into a stable industry.

Industry statistics on annual production levels, malt beverage sales, tax assessments, and contemporary trends in the sales and consumption of various alcoholic beverages, indicate a growing consumer preference for craft brewed beers. In both the United States and Canada, beer is the alcoholic beverage of choice. However, while the production of major domestic brewers and the volume of imported beers has declined recently, the specialty beer market shows no signs of losing momentum. In one interesting recent development, a number of craft breweries have even begun to export their products to Europe and Asia, with Japan being a particularly promising market.

Two potentially negative trends which may affect the industry are neo-Prohibitionism and tax increases. Neo-Prohibitionist legislation which cuts into the profit of brewers or restricts their market (i.e., alcohol warning label requirements and restrictions on the sale and consumption of alcoholic beverages) will always remain a threat in a pluralistic society. However, lately a greater amount of information has become available proving the healthful aspects of moderate drinking. In addition, the craft brewing industry and support institutions such as the Institute for Brewing Studies are working to protect small brewers' interests.

Unfortunately, in times of economic instability, many governing bodies may look at the success of today's and tomorrow's brewers as a way to increase revenues by raising taxes on beer. One answer to this threat are the lobbying associations which have been organized to protect the interests of small brewers. One important example of these lobbying efforts is the exemption won by small brewers (less than 60,000 barrels production) from the new Federal Excise Tax on beer, imposed in 1991. In our region, the XX Beer and Wine Wholesalers Association is actively lobbying the State government.

Growth in Adversity: Despite the important efforts of these groups, the potential for new taxes will continue to be the greatest threat to the craft brewing industry. Although small brewers have been exempted from the latest Federal Excise Tax increase, this exemption could be lifted, or other state and local taxes could be imposed. It is important for this reason to consider the potential impact of higher taxes on our industry.

Recent statistical analysis of beer sales have reached the conclusion that beer sales are relatively price inelastic and respond more slowly to increases in the price of beer. These studies would seem to indicate that a not unreasonable rise in taxation on beer would only result in a minor drop in beer sales. Although the determination of who bears the cost of a given price increase is complicated, these studies indicate that with a product as price inelastic as beer, the increase will probably be paid by the retail customer.

One additional set of conclusions from these studies concerns price increases and product substitution. The evidence indicates that there is probably little substitutability, among consumers between beer, wine, and distilled spirits. This means that (all other factors remaining constant) an increase in the price of one category, should not result in the substitution of another category of alcoholic beverage. Consequently, we may conclude that the growth in sales of specialty beers, which are priced as a premium product, is the result of changing consumer tastes, not changes in the price structure of beer.

Studies of income elasticity also demonstrate that beer sales are relatively inelastic with respect to the consumer's income. Recent industry reviews, which consider the impact of the recession and the business cycle on beer sales, have reached the conclusion that the business cycle has little discernible influence on the craft brewing industry. Finally, industry statistics clearly show that throughout the last recession, the craft brewing industry continued to grow at an impressive rate.

Clearly there are threats to our industry, but statistics demonstrate that consumer tastes and preferences are changing. In such a market, the best strategy is to provide the consumer with the highest quality product. Beer drinkers are also voters who will go to great lengths to reject unreasonable attacks on their favorite beverage.

THE MARKET AND COMPETITION

Potential Customers: The most important customers of the Craft Brewing Company are the owners and managers of local licensed liquor retail outlets. These local outlets consist of pubs, taverns, and restaurants in the cities of XX, XX, and XX. However, since it is our marketing strategy to concentrate on satisfying the demand of a core group of customers in the first year, a select number of retail outlets in these cities will receive priority.

All of the establishments listed above are located in our core local market. Most of these establishments have at least four taps allocated to specialty and craft brewed beers, several have more than six craft beer taps. The president has spoken with the owners of all of these establishments, and they have all expressed strong interest in featuring a quality local product once it is available.

An important part of our marketing strategy is to concentrate on providing our customers with the best possible, most responsive service they have ever received when purchasing beer. Consequently, it will be necessary to take on new accounts carefully, so as to have enough beer in stock to meet the demand of our core accounts. One potential mistake would be to try to provide beer for more customers than our initial capacity allows. For this reason we will prioritize our accounts according to certain criteria which we would like to see our retail customers meet. The fact is that we do not want to sell our product to simply any retailer that expresses an interest. We want our products in the right places, along side other quality beers, and receiving the proper attention necessary for serving craft brewed beer at its peak of quality. For this reason we will initially concentrate our sales efforts on establishments which are already serving craft brewed beers, before offering our products to bars which are not yet carrying craft brewed beers.

There are additional licensed retail outlets in XX, which would be satisfactory retailers of our products. The fact is that there has been a very positive response from licensed retailers in our local market. Our only problem will be to decide which outlets may carry our products in the early months when production is still limited, and which will have to wait. We will make this decision carefully so as to develop a core group of satisfied, loyal clients, while planning for a much broader distribution in the future. Eventually we intend to introduce our products in local restaurants and taverns which have not yet begun to offer their customers craft brewed beer.

Competition: Our competitors in the local market are primarily those craft breweries in XX and XX who distribute their products to this region, in addition to the super-premium draft imports being offered. The local breweries include: XX

All of these breweries distribute their products to licensed retail outlets in our local market, through licensed liquor distributors. These local distributors include: XX

First let us begin this evaluation of our competition with a brief discussion of the super-premium imported draft beers which we consider to be our competitors because many of them are similar in style and price to domestic craft brewed beers. Although these beers are by and large excellent products, the fact remains that they find it difficult to compete with domestic craft brewed beers. The imports do have strong name recognition in many cases, but they can not compete in the areas of freshness, direct and personal service to local retailers, or local brand loyalty. Furthermore, shipping costs and advertising for these products usually place them several dollars above craft brewed beers in price, and these beers are subject to the new, higher Federal Excise Tax rate. Statistics demonstrate that while craft brewed beers are enjoying steady annual growth in sales, the market share of super-premium imports has recently begun to decline.

By and large, the domestic craft breweries listed above, all consistently produce quality products. For this reason, it is the responsibility of the individual brewing company to make some effort to help consumers distinguish their beers from those of their competitors. Some brewing companies rely on the excellent quality of their products and word of mouth as their strongest marketing point. This strategy is often used by new brewing companies which in the early years have less capital available for advertising. Other pioneer craft breweries benefit from greater brand recognition, due to their longer operating history and easily recognizable logos.

Another way to win loyal consumer support is to develop a distinctive flavor profile, such as a characteristically assertive hop flavor. In contrast to these methods, some brewers spend thousands of dollars on a strong advertising campaign through the local and national media to increase their market share. Others with smaller advertising budgets may choose to rely on less expensive, but often equally effective, point-of-sale promotional materials.

Finally, the most fundamental marketing strategy which may be employed is through pricing. Some brewers choose to underprice their competition to gain market share. Others, choose to price their products above the market average, in order to capture an image as the brewer with the most premium products. Still others may price their products near the industry average. This strategy helps them to avoid being seen as a discount brewer, while at the same time avoids driving off potential customers who refuse to buy beer which is priced significantly above that of the competition.

All of the brewers competing in our market rely on some mix of the above marketing strategies to acquire a base of loyal local support and then increase their market share. The Craft Brewing Company will likewise pursue a marketing strategy appropriate to its production goals, financial means, and the particular characteristics of our local market. Our marketing strategy will be carefully discussed in the next section of this business plan. However, it should be emphasized here that the demand for craft brewed products is growing and as the statistics demonstrate, the craft brewing industry's share of the beer market is also growing.

Most craft brewers are in agreement that competition is healthy. The great variety of craft brewed products available to consumers has only served to further educate the beer drinking public to the quality of our products, creating ever greater demand. Although we are in competition with other craft brewers, our share of the market will not come so much at their expense, as it will at the expense of imported beers and domestic industrial brewers whose customers are gradually shifting to fresher and more flavorful craft brewed products.

Market Size and Trends: The size of our local craft brewed and specialty ale market in XX is sufficiently large to provide us with a market share which will ensure the initial success of the Craft Brewing Company. Likewise, this market has been steadily growing at a rate which is more than adequate to achieve our projected growth in sales. Our market research and conclusions are based on statistical analyses of beer sales volumes by individual breweries, which are reported to the State Liquor Control Board each month. These sales reports have also been analyzed and reprinted in a more comparative form published monthly by the State Wholesalers Association. In addition to these reports, we have carefully questioned brewers, local licensed retailers, and local licensed beer distributors to determine the average monthly level of craft brewed beer sales and the growth in sales which have occurred over the last several years.

Using the above sources, we have determined that for last year, average sales of craft brewed beers in our local market was approximately XX kegs each month. In addition, approximately another XX kegs of imported ales and other specialty beers were sold in this market each month. We consider specialty imported beers such as Guinness Stout, Bass Ale, Heineken, etc., to be our competitors because these are also considered to be super-premium, specialty products which are priced in a similar range as craft brewed beers. It is these imports, as well as other craft brewed beers, which we will be competing with for taphandle space at the businesses of local licensed retailers. Consequently, a careful analysis of our local market leads us to the conservative estimate that the size of the local market for our products last year was approximately XX kegs of specialty beers each month, on average. At the average super-premium keg price of $XX, the total dollar-unit market for our products last year was approximately $XX each month on average, or $XX for the year.

The same sources, which we relied on to determine the size of our local market, have also helped us to determine that for the last several years this market has been growing by approximately X percent annually. When questioned on their expectations for future growth, local beer distributors expressed the opinion that they anticipate that our local market will continue to grow at or near the present level of X percent annually. If we trust the experts who are most familiar with our market, we can anticipate that with X percent growth this year, sales of beers in our market should reach approximately XX kegs of specialty beers each month on average. Given the demographic and economic growth trends of our local region, we believe this estimate to be on the conservative side.

Regional Demographic Growth: In a national study of population changes, XX County was projected to be the fifth fastest growing county in the United States between now and the end of the decade. In XX County, employment has increased XX percent since 1980, which compares favorably with the State's employment growth rate of XX percent during the same period. During the recession years, although the unemployment rate in XX County rose, it remained below the state and national averages. XX County may not be impervious to recession, but the large number of government officials who are employed and live in this area make our local market less vulnerable to business fluctuations.

One consequence of having government as the largest employer in our local market is reflected in the volume of retail sales. When we examine retail sales levels, it becomes apparent that XX County has developed into a regional consumer market. While retail sales have increased by XX percent since 1970, the population has increased by XX percent. These two figures indicate that a large nonresident population is making purchases in XX County. XX County's retail sales are clearly being augmented by the large number of persons who daily visit the State's center of government. Regardless of who these persons may be, many of them stop to do a little shopping, have some lunch, and even drink a beer, while they are in XX. Of the XX billion in retail sales that occurred in XX County last year, XX percent occurred in XX, and XX percent occurred in the city of XX.

We are still a relatively small urban area, but it is our smallness and the quality of our environment and living which continue to attract new residents. Retail sales can be expected to grow along with XX County's population. More and more restaurants and pubs will be opened to serve the needs of our growing community. Consequently, local restaurant and bar sales of specialty beers can also be expected to grow with the State, its government, and the city.

Regional Market Growth: XX and XX States are considered to be our broader regional market, which is an important sales region once our local market demand has been satisfied. The following are sales reports posted with the Liquor Control Board and XX Beer and Wine Wholesalers Association for last year that provide the following annual percentage growth rates in beer sales.

Brewery % Change During a One-Year Period

(List primary craft brewing competitors in your market.)

This annual growth in sales figures is a good indication of the overall health of the industry that we propose to enter and compete in. Clearly, the XX craft beer market and our local market have sufficient growth potential to accommodate many new craft breweries.

Estimated Local Market Share and Sales: Sales, distribution, and tax records can help us to determine the relative market share and popularity of our competitors and their products. Our research, counting taps and questioning licensed retailers as to their levels of sales, also gives us a good picture of which craft breweries have the largest shares of our local market. For example, the craft breweries with the most popular products and largest market shares in our local market are the XX, XX, and XX.

XX is perhaps the most successful craft brewer in our local market, selling approximately XX kegs a month on average. As a percentage of the approximately XX kegs of super-premium, specialty beers sold each month in this market last year, XX currently controls a little more than XX percent of the local market we intend to compete in. The other market leaders each control from XX percent to XX percent of the specialty beer market.

The management team of the Craft Brewing Company is determined to produce approximately XX kegs (XX barrels), during the first twelve months of production. Of these XX kegs, approximately XX kegs of beer will be marketed and sold in our local market in this first year of production. These approximately XX kegs will be sold in our local market through the following three marketing channels:

1. Wholesale distribution to local licensed retailers: $XX per keg
2. Retail keg sales to the public from our warehouse: $XX per keg
3. Retail pint sales to the public in our tap room: $XX per pint

The following is the estimated breakdown of sales in our local market through these three channels in the first year of production:

1. Wholesale distribution to local licensed retailers: XX kegs
2. Retail keg sales to the public from our facility: XX kegs
3. Retail pint sales to the public in our tap room: XX kegs

If we include the XX kegs being sold through our own tap room, this means we will be marketing approximately XX kegs or approximately XX kegs each month on average during the first year. If we assume a total local market of approximately XX kegs each month on average for this year and next year, then the Craft Brewing Company intends to capture from 12 to 14 percent of the local market during this time.

Clearly we intend to be a very competitive market-share leader in our local market. Therefore, let us examine what we believe to be the important advantages which we have over our competitors in the local market which will help us to win a 12 to 14 percent market share.

First, the Craft Brewing Company intends to price its products slightly below the level of our strongest competitors. Specialty draft imports and other craft breweries must absorb the additional costs associated with delivering their products to the XX area, often over great distances. The Craft Brewing Company, on the other hand, will handle its own distribution and save on delivery and storage costs in its local market. In addition, it is simply part of our strategy to always price our products slightly below those of other market leaders, since this is what our local licensed retailers have told us would be of particular importance when they are making decisions on trying a new beer on their taps.

Second, the Craft Brewing Company will be a local entity in which the community can take special pride. Our brewery and tap room will create jobs and enhance the atmosphere of the downtown area. It is common sense to assume that given everything is nearly equal in the areas of price, style, and quality, people will choose to patronize local producers rooted in their community.

Third, the Craft Brewing Company will be able to provide the very freshest beers to our local market. Other craft breweries must rely on beer distributors to deliver their products to the XX market, and these beers may spend some time sitting in local warehouses before being distributed to licensed retailers. Our products, on the other hand, will be distributed directly from our own cold room in our own delivery van. Consequently, kegs of our ales will never reach the market beyond their peak level of maturity, nor before they are perfectly matured either.

Fourth, we are committed to making the best beers possible, using the highest quality ingredients available. We are serious when we make this commitment. We would not be entering this market if we were not certain that we could make excellent ales which will be highly competitive. Brewing beer is what we do and we believe that a commitment to quality will go a long way toward assuring our long term success. Consistently high quality beer can sell itself without much promotion, but a poor quality beer will not succeed for long, no matter how actively it is promoted.

Fifth, the Craft Brewing Company will be able to serve its products on its own taps in a tap room which will be named XX. Our own retail outlet will permit us to try new products before offering them for distribution to the wholesale market. In addition, a tap room will allow us to receive the full retail pint price on a significant percentage of our barrel production. Every keg sold at retail pint price rather than wholesale keg price, will significantly increase our profit margin, while at the same time helping us to reach our 12 to 14 percent market-share target. XX will be a casual drinking room separated from the brewery by a large glass window which will allow customers to view the activities on the production floor while enjoying their favorite beverage. XX will also be the display and sales center for retail promotional items which will bear our corporate and product logos. Although the cash profit on these items is only 50 percent, they represent a much greater value as free advertising by increasing our exposure in the community.

By bringing the management team into direct contact with the customers in our local community, our own retail outlet will help us to increase our market share as well as compete more effectively with outside craft brewers. Two-way communication between the management team and our customers will provide us with invaluable feedback on our products. Furthermore, as beer drinkers make themselves comfortable at our establishment, the Craft Brewing Company's image as a local community enterprise will be enhanced.

Finally, and most importantly, we believe that our commitment to service will assure that we earn a leading share of our local market and increase that share into the future. No other brewer has the potential to provide the level of prompt service to the licensed retailers in our local market that the Craft Brewing Company has. We have already begun to develop close relationships with the licensed retailers in our local market. We know them by name, we have visited them and purchased beers in their establishments, we have questioned them as to their priorities when deciding which beers to put on their taps, and we have carefully observed the preferences of their customers. We at the Craft Brewing Company are committed to the relationships we have begun to develop with our future customers and their customers. By using consumer surveys, delivering our own beer, serving our beer in their establishments, working closely with their employees, and carefully listening to licensed retailers and beer drinkers in XX, we are sure to earn a leading share in our local market and keep it.

As the local market and demand for draft specialty beers continues to grow, the Craft Brewing Company will expand its production to satisfy that demand and increase our market share. The following is a graphic representation of our market-share projections based on the previously stated assumptions concerning our industry's prospects for growth, our estimated monthly sales, and the marketing strategy which we will discuss in the next section.

ASSUMPTIONS

- Total local market for craft brewed and specialty draft beer last year equaled XX kegs a month or XX kegs a year.
- Annual growth rate in local market of X percent for next three years.
- Total local market for specialty draft beer from summer of last year through summer this year equals XX kegs a month or XX kegs a year.
- Craft Brewing Company's market share of XX to XX percent.
- Average wholesale keg price of $XX a unit.
- Average retail keg price of $XX a unit.
- Average retail pint price of $XX a unit, at 120 pints per keg.

LOCAL MARKET-SHARE PROJECTIONS

Production Year	**Year 1**	**Year 2**	**Year 3**
Estimated Total Annual Sales in Local Market (Kegs)	XX	XX	XX
Craft Brewing Company Estimated Share of and Annual Sales in Local Market	13.5%	13.5%	12%
(Kegs)	XX	XX	XX

The following is the dollar value breakdown in local beer sales through our three marketing channels for the first three years:

LOCAL SALES PROJECTIONS BY DOLLAR VALUE

Production Year	**Year 1**	**Year 2**	**Year 3**
Local Sales Wholesale Kegs	756	926	1,108
Dollars ($85)	$64,260	$78,710	$94,180
Local Sales Retail Kegs	40	140	160
Dollars ($110)	$4,400	$15,400	$17,600
Local Sales Retail Kegs by the Pint	294	336	336
Dollars ($300 per keg)	$88,200	$100,800	$100,800

Estimated Regional Sales: Thus far, this discussion of market share has only concerned the local market for which the management team will be personally responsible for promotions, sales, distribution, and service. In the fifth month of operation, the demand from our local market will no longer be sufficient to absorb all of the barrels being produced by the Craft Brewing Company. At that point, we will begin to market our products through a distributor to the broader regional market. For this purpose we will rely on XX to distribute our beer in the XX market. In the seventh, eighth, and twelfth months of operation we will purchase additional fermentation tanks and kegs in order to increase our production capacity to approximately 1,200 barrels a year. Further equipment purchases will be made in the second and third years of operation in order to increase our production capacity to approximately 1,800 barrels a year as the demand for our products in the local and regional markets continues to expand. All barrels produced above the level which our local market can absorb will be sold in the regional market through licensed wholesale distributors at an average price of $XX a keg.

The following chart indicates the estimated number of kegs which will be sold in the regional market after satisfying the local demand.

REGIONAL SALES PROJECTIONS

Production Year	**Year 1**	**Year 2**	**Year 3**
Estimated Total Regional Sales Kegs	252	752	1,512
Dollars ($68)	$17,136	$51,136	$102,816

Total Sales Projections: The following chart indicates the estimated combined total of local and regional sales for the first three years of operation.

TOTAL SALES PROJECTIONS

Production Year	Year 1	Year 2	Year 3
Local Sales			
Wholesale Kegs	756	926	1,108
Dollars ($85)	$64,260	$78,710	$94,180
Local Sales			
Retail Kegs	40	140	160
Dollars ($110)	$4,400	$15,400	$17,600
Local Sales			
Retail Kegs			
by the Pint	294	336	336
Dollars			
($300 per keg)	$88,200	$100,800	$100,800
Regional Sales			
Wholesale Kegs	252	752	1,512
Dollars ($68)	$17,136	$51,136	$102,816
Total Sales			
Kegs	1,342	2,154	3,116
Gross Beer			
Revenue	$173,996	$246,046	$315,396

These figures are based on the previously stated assumptions and represent our projections of sales targets to be achieved by the management team of Craft Brewing Company. In the fourth and fifth years we will continue to expand production by the amount of 500 to 600 barrels a year. By the fifth year of operation the Craft Brewing Company will be producing at near the 2,800-barrels-a-year capacity which the space in our brewing facility can accommodate.

MARKETING PLAN

The Fundamentals: It is the intention of the management team to establish the long term profitability and success of the Craft Brewing Company by carefully concentrating on building a core group of satisfied local customers. This core group consists of the licensed liquor retailers operating pubs, taverns, and restaurants in the cities of XX, XX, and XX. While it is these licensed retailers who are our direct customers, we recognize that ultimately our customers are the beer drinkers within our local market who patronize the establishments of our licensed retail customers and our own tap room. Consequently, the key to our marketing strategy is to make the highest possible quality beers which will satisfy the tastes and demands of beer drinkers in our market, while providing our licensed retail customers with the best service possible.

Our effort to make the best beer possible will be achieved by the following means. First, all beer profiles and recipes have been selected after careful market research to determine exactly what is popular among beer and ale drinkers in our market. The most important part of our research consisted of many long conversations with local licensed retailers, who were eager to tell us what their customers preferred when ordering a craft brewed beer and what they were looking for when buying beer to stock their bar taps. In addition, interviews with local beer distributors have been particularly helpful in pointing out which beers sell well in our local market, why they sell well, and what styles will compete well in this market. Having made the decision as to what flavor profiles we would like to reproduce in our beers, the president as head brewer will rely on his brewing consultant, XX, to determine the exact balance of ingredients and specific brewing techniques necessary to achieve those flavor profiles.

Our three initial products have been designed specifically to satisfy local tastes and demands, as they have been identified by our market research. However, we believe that ale drinkers in our local market have similar preferences to ale drinkers throughout the XX beer market, and we expect our products to be competitive throughout that broader market. As a final note regarding the design of our recipes, we intend to carefully monitor the responses of beer drinkers to our products when they first reach the local market and long after. Consumer feedback will be the means by which we gauge the reactions of beer drinkers to our products, so that we may make any necessary adjustments.

Another key aspect of our marketing strategy, which is intended to ensure we make the best beer possible and then sell that beer, is our determination to use the finest brewing ingredients available. Only premium ingredients will be used, without exception. We have made certain that our suppliers all have excellent reputations among the craft brewing community in our region. Nevertheless, as our operations progress, XX as head brewer, and XX as general manager, will continue to demand the highest quality from our suppliers and will be prepared to find new sources of brewing materials whenever our current suppliers fail to meet the exacting standards of the Craft Brewing Company.

Brewing the best beer possible is our motto, and we will not cut corners to save a few dollars at the expense of beer quality. We will use the finest ingredients, top quality brewing equipment, and well-proven brewing methods to establish our market share. Only a quality product will create consumer loyalty in our core local market and ensure regular growth in sales as that market expands.

Distribution: In the first year of operation, it is our strategy to concentrate on winning the loyalty of licensed retailers in our local market. In this effort, the president as head brewer, will have primary responsibility for local sales and for distributing beer from our cold room by delivery van when our customers place an order. We believe that only through close personal contact with our local customers can lines of communication and a long term business relationship be established. Once this relationship has been firmly established, a properly trained employee of the company will assist in making daily deliveries so that the president can concentrate on acquiring new accounts and increasing sales in the local market.

In the fifth month of operation, while the president maintains the accounts in our local market, the Craft Brewing Company will seek the help of a professional beer distributor to reach out beyond the local XX market. Of the three major liquor distribution companies operating in our region, XX carries XX percent of the craft brewed beers being distributed to licensed retailers in the city of XX. In XX County, XX is represented by import and craft breweries manager, XX. Mr. XX and the company he represents are spoken of highly by local licensed retailers and by the local brewers whose products they distribute. In a meeting with Mr. XX, the president and XX reached a verbal understanding that XX would represent and distribute Craft Brewing Company products at selected retail outlets in XX County and the city of XX. XX is clearly the distributor of choice in our region and will be relied on to distribute our products outside of the city of XX when capacity is being expanded in the second year.

Once full capacity with our five initial fermenters has been achieved, additional fermenters will be added to increase capacity. At this time, with increased capacity, we will more intensively promote sales of specialty and contract beers in our local market while arranging for XX to begin to distribute our flagship products to the XX, XX, market.

Once we are satisfied that we have achieved a competitive market share in XX and that our accounts in that market are being serviced properly by XX, we will then consider a further stage of expansion. While adding additional fermenters and kegs to our production line, we will begin to offer our products to the broader regional market, including the XX area. At this stage we will carefully consider which distributor we want to represent us and which accounts we would like to see our products in.

On-Premise Retail Sales: The tap room is another important distribution and sales outlet for our products. Our tap room has been designed to accommodate a maximum occupancy of fifty persons. The space will contain a serving bar, a display cabinet for retail promotional items, and seating for approximately thirty to forty persons, with some additional standing room available. The XX is designed to be an extension of the brewery where patrons can witness the brewing operation first hand and talk to the brewery staff, while enjoying some of our quality ales.

Our tap room is intended to enhance the experience of drinking a quality ale, when all of one's senses are brought into play. There will be no smoking in the XX because tobacco smoke would interfere with the beer drinkers ability to fully appreciate the flavor and aroma of the beers being served. Furthermore, we believe that a no smoking environment will be greatly appreciated since there are no other nonsmoking drinking establishments in town. The dimensions of our tap room are not large, so we have chosen to light the space well and to paint the walls in light colors in order to avoid the impression of being closed in, and so that customers may appreciate the clarity and rich colors of our products. Decorations will be limited to a few plants, one large fish tank behind the serving bar, wall displays of our corporate and product logos, and a few tasteful posters with aquatic themes. A variety of comfortable chairs and tables will be provided for casual seating. In addition, game boards will be available for those who wish to play a little chess, backgammon, etc., while they visit with friends. A small sound system will provide music whenever appropriate.

In our tap room, customers will be able to make a variety of retail purchases. Initially we will have a small selection of T-shirts for sale. But as cash flow permits, we will include other promotional items to increase our merchandise sales. A small selection of snacks, such as nuts, chips, and locally baked pretzels, will also be available to our customers. In regard to beer sales, customers will be able to purchase beer in a variety of volumes. Besides pints and 10-ounce schooners, a sampler of beer which includes a small glass of each of our products will be offered for sale. In addition, customers will also be able to have the take-out vessel of their choice filled for off-premise consumption. Finally, customers in the XX may also purchase a keg of beer at retail price from our cooler, for off-premise consumption.

Pricing: As mentioned previously, our pricing strategy is designed to make our beers competitive and to achieve a profit, while at the same time positioning our products amongst the best beers being produced by our competitors. A keg price of approximately $XX is the median price now being asked by competitors in our local market. Consequently, we intend to ask $XX for our kegs, in order to make our products just slightly less expensive than those of our competitors. When questioned as to their views on pricing, local licensed retailers indicated that this price for a quality product would be one incentive for carrying Craft Brewing Company products.

A further aspect of our pricing strategy is our determination to maintain stable prices over a substantial period of time. Although we can not be certain that significant changes to our cost structure will not occur, it is our plan to maintain prices at the $XX a keg level for at least two years. In this way we will provide our customers with a degree of predictability when purchasing our products. Changes in price will only take place when our own costs rise appreciably and thereby threaten the minimum profit margin we require to meet our operating costs and achieve our projected growth targets. Price changes will also be considered whenever our products fall significantly out of alignment with the median price being asked by our major competitors.

Our discussions with local licensed retailers and with other brewers have also made us aware that when a new brewery is starting up, it is necessary to offer the kegs from the first production runs at a price which is just below the standard price for those products. The first several production runs of any new brewery can be expected to produce excellent beers, but not necessarily the exact style of beer which is being aimed at. It may take two or three adjustments to the start-up recipe before the desired flavor profile is achieved. It may also take several production runs before consistency of flavor for a particular recipe is achieved.

Local retailers have told us that they would be willing to try these early beers, understanding that the recipe may still need some adjustment before we are all satisfied with the finished product. However, they have also expressed the opinion that these early beers should be offered at a discount, below the level that they will be priced at when the desired flavor profile is achieved. This pricing practice is typical of start-up breweries in our market, and we cannot ignore the expressed views of our customers. Consequently, our first kegs to be produced in the recipe adjustment phase will be offered to our customers at a price of $XX a keg, which is near the bottom of the price range which our products will compete in. In the effort to achieve the desired flavor profiles with the smallest number of test production runs necessary, the president will be assisted by brewing consultant, XX, and former head brewer of the XX Brewery, XX. Between these three experienced brewers, it is expected that it will require two test runs for each recipe, before the desired flavor profile is achieved with the third production run. At that time we will be justified in pricing our kegs at their full market rate of $XX.

The following is the projected price breakdown of the wholesale and retail items to be sold by the Craft Brewing Company.

ITEM	PRICE
Beer:	
Wholesale Kegs	
(1/2 bbl.) — Self Distributed	$85.00
Wholesale Kegs	
(1/4 bbl.) — Self Distributed	$50.00
Wholesale Kegs	
(1/2 bbl.) — Distributor	$68.00
Wholesale Kegs	
(1/4 bbl.) — Distributor	$38.00
Retail Kegs	
(1/2 bbl.) —	$110.00
Retail Kegs	
(1/4 bbl.) —	$60.00
Pint	$2.50
Schooner	$1.50
Sampler	$2.50

Pint and schooner glasses will be of the standard size prevailing in our industry. The "Sampler" will consist of several small glasses, each containing one of the various products available on our taps.

Promotional Merchandise and Snacks: Promotional merchandise, such as T-shirts, glassware, lapel pins, etc., and snacks, such as fresh baked goods, nuts, chips, etc., will be priced at twice our cost in order to realize a consistent and reasonable profit.

Advertising and Promotions: As general manager, XX is responsible for point-of-sale promotions and advertising. Initially, point-of-sale promotions will consist of table tents, coasters, and tap handles, provided free of charge to our customers. When cash flow permits, other items such as neon signs, bar towels, and mirrors, all displaying our logo will be given to local retailers who have demonstrated a strong sales record with our products. All promotional items are considered to be an advertising tool since they will display the corporate logo and logos of individual products.

The vice president's experience working in the restaurant and bar industry has taught her that the owners of these establishments and their service employees are especially grateful when promotional materials are maintained by the company distributing them. Consequently, we will take full responsibility for the display of our point-of-sale promotional items, placing them on tables, and replacing the supply at regular intervals.

Our research of the food and beverage service industry has also led us to conclude that only a knowledgeable bar and wait staff can properly represent our products to the consumer. Consequently, both the president and vice president will provide brief, yet informative, introductions to our products for the wait staff of our licensed retail customers. These product introductions are intended to familiarize these important representatives of our products with the brewing methods used by Craft Brewing Company. In addition, our licensed retail customers and their wait staffs will be invited to visit the brewery and witness first hand the production of the beer they will later be selling. These brewery tours are intended to help develop a special relationship between the Craft Brewing Company and those who serve our products to beer drinkers in our core market.

The vice president is also responsible for carrying out all direct advertising of Craft Brewing Company products to the consumers in our local market. Advertising will be conducted through the local print media. Throughout the year we will run weekly, Friday and Saturday ads in XX newspaper, the paper with the largest circulation in our local market. When XX College is in session, we will also run weekly adds in the college's XX Journal. We believe that this advertising strategy will provide the greatest exposure for our products, in the most cost effective manner. However, we will regularly survey our customers to determine whether or not they learned of our products through these printed ads. Depending on the results of these surveys, certain changes in our advertising strategy may be considered.

In regard to surveying our customers and the general beer drinking public, the following method will be employed. The president and vice president will design a survey sheet to determine the public's response to our products and our advertising campaign. These survey sheets will be distributed and collected by president and vice president in the establishments of our licensed retail customers. In addition, both president and vice president will conduct regular visits to these establishments to maintain contact with our licensed retail customers, their employees, and their customers. These fact-finding visits will be most frequent in the first year of operation, particularly in the first months when product evaluation and recipe adjustments will take place. It is our determination to never lose touch with the needs of our customers and the tastes of the beer drinking public.

Finally, in regard to the issue of public relations, we at the Craft Brewing Company believe that an ounce of prevention is worth a pound of cure. What this means in a practical sense, is that the vice president will actively pursue a strategy of meeting with local groups which are concerned about issues related to excessive drinking. It is our intention to develop an open dialogue and positive relationship with local citizen groups which advocate responsible drinking. Likewise, we will take the initiative to foster a cooperative relationship with local law-enforcement agencies, to show them that we are as concerned about alcohol misuse as they are. At the Craft Brewing Company we advocate the enjoyment of quality beer in moderation, not the consumption of alcohol in large quantities. In order to avoid any potentially harmful publicity in the future, which may stem from the misuse of our products, we will make certain that the relevant interest groups understand that we take the issue of alcohol misuse as seriously as they do.

COMPANY STRUCTURE

Management Team: The following is a list of the key management roles and the individuals who will be responsible for them.

President. XX has overall responsibility for the start-up and daily operation of the Craft Brewing Company. In the start-up phase, the president will choose and supervise all utility subcontractors; the president will approve, supervise, and assist in all construction; the president will approve the design and purchase of all brewing equipment; and the president will supervise and assist the installation of all brewing equipment.

Head brewer. In the daily operations phase of the project, XX will be responsible for all tasks related to the production of beer. The president will supervise the design of all product recipes and any necessary adjustments to those recipes. The head brewer will perform the regular brewing routine and all tasks associated with preparing Craft Brewing Company products for the market.

Sales and distribution manager. As previously indicated, the president will be responsible for acquiring and servicing accounts in our local market. Likewise, the president will be responsible for distributing full kegs and picking up empty kegs from clients. The president will be assisted in sales calls by the vice president and in distribution by corporate employees.

Vice president. XX will act as vice president which involves providing assistance to the president at every level of the brewery start-up and daily operations. Should the president be temporarily unable to perform his roles as president and head brewer, the vice president will be sufficiently familiar with all aspects of the business that the vice president will be able to train and supervise any employees needed to assist her in the full operation of the business.

General manager. XX will be responsible for all tasks associated with purchasing, inventory control, accounts receivable, accounts payable, record keeping, and the preparation of all production and sales reports required by the relevant licensing agencies. In these tasks, the general manager will be assisted by the president who will provide information on sales, beer inventory, and the status of raw materials' stocks. In addition, XX of XX will review our books regularly in preparation for the quarterly tax filing which is required. As general manager, XX will also be responsible for managing the operations of our retail outlet, XX. The general manager will be responsible for maintaining the retail inventory and tracking sales. The general manager will also be responsible for overseeing the employee hired to run the bar. When time permits, the general manager and president will take over at the bar, and the employee can be assigned to other tasks, such as brew-house sanitation and deliveries.

XX's final area of responsibility as general manager is that of promotions, advertising, and public relations for Craft Brewing Company. The general manager will supervise the design and creation of all corporate and product logos. The general manager will manage the advertising account and evaluate the influence of our advertising strategy on sales. The general manager will act as public relations officer to the community in order to enhance our image as a community entity concerned with the welfare of our community. The general manger will also assist the president in working with our customers to promote sales and maintain open lines of communication.

The president and vice president believe it is important to be personally involved with every facet of the company's operation. No task will be assigned to an employee before we have repeatedly performed that task ourselves and can then instruct and oversee the employee properly. This same philosophy extends to the management of our corporate accounting, which we intend to be directly involved in.

The president and vice president feel confident that with the assistance of the employees discussed below, they can perform the tasks outlined above. They have a long-standing relation of eleven years and a well demonstrated record of working together to solve problems. In addition, the management team will be assisted in many areas by the specially contracted professionals discussed below. For further information on the credentials and experience of the management team, see their attached resumes.

Management Compensation: For his responsibilities as head brewer, XX will draw an initial monthly salary of $XX. For her responsibilities as general manager, XX will draw an initial monthly salary of $XX. These salaries are the minimum income which XX and XX require to pay for their living expenses. At this time the management team is receiving no compensation or payments from the company. Wage payments will begin at the end of the first month of production and sales of 28 barrels or more, which is projected to be July 20XX. All future wage increases or bonuses will be granted to the president and general manager/vice president as a reward for significant production and sales increases, but only after due consideration by the Board of Directors.

Board of Directors: The Craft Brewing Company has been established by its founders and management team, XX and XX, as a corporation under the laws of XX State. The Board of Directors meets monthly to conduct any such business as may come before it. The activities and affairs of the corporation are managed by the Board of Directors. The Board of Directors has delegated responsibility for management of the day to day operation of the business to the management team, XX and XX. Members of the Board of Directors receive no compensation for their services and all directors hold office until the next annual meeting of the shareholders or until their successors have been elected and qualified. Executive officers are appointed by the Board of Directors and serve at the pleasure of the Board of Directors.

The management team has decided to provide themselves with the most reliable professional support and counseling available, in order to acquire the breadth of experience which is necessary to ensure the success of the Craft Brewing Company. Toward this end, the following individual has accepted our invitation to join the Board of Directors so that she can lend her experience to and question the decisions of the management team.

XX has accepted the management team's invitation to join the Board of Directors as a financial advisor, director, and executive secretary. Among her many responsibilities at this position, XX, has been involved in working with small businesses in the areas of finance and the preparation of commercial loan packages. XX is also currently a board member of the XX, a nonprofit corporation of XX State. XX is a community development loan fund, which pools investment dollars from individuals and organizations in order to provide loans for small businesses and nonprofit organizations that benefit the region.

XX's primary responsibilities involve providing the management team with financial advice and recommendations during Board meetings. In addition, XX will perform the role of executive secretary, preparing the company's annual reports and maintaining regular communications with shareholders. XX will not receive a salary for her efforts, but the Board of Directors may vote her a bonus for exceptional performance.

XX has demonstrated her commitment to the Craft Brewing Company by purchasing 5,000 shares of Company's stock for $XX. As an incentive to join our board and perform the responsibilities of executive secretary, XX has been awarded 5,000 matching shares in addition to the 5,000 shares the executive secretary purchased.

Executive Officers: The directors, executive officers, and significant personnel of the Company are as follows:

XX Chairman of the Board
President
Brewery Manager
Director

XX Executive Treasurer
Vice President
General Manager
Director

XX Executive Secretary
Director

Employees: The Craft Brewing Company is scheduled and budgeted to hire employees at regular intervals. The first full-time employee will be hired in July so as to have sufficient time to properly train that employee before full brewing and sales operations commence.

The first employee will be hired primarily as a beverage server and retail sales person in the tap room. However, this individual must be flexible and prepared to perform a variety of additional tasks, including cleaning, brewing assistance, and deliveries. The management is already talking with individuals they believe can be trusted to fill this position and who would be an asset to the Company as well.

In the twelfth month of operations an additional employee will be hired. Once again this person must be flexible and prepared to perform a variety of assignments on the production floor and in the tap room. However, it is anticipated that the primary responsibility of this second employee will be as a brewing and delivery assistant.

At the beginning of the nineteenth month of operation and again in the twenty-eighth month, additional employees will be hired and trained to perform a variety of tasks associated with beer production and deliveries. The need to hire these additional employees at regular intervals is anticipated because of the work load associated with projected increases in brewing capacity and sales in our local market. This brings our total number of full-time employees to help with retail sales and beer production at near full-production capacity to a total of four employees by the end of year three of operations. It is not anticipated that any additional employees will be required beyond this number.

It is the management teams philosophy that employees are an asset to the company, not a drain on resources. We intend to train our employees thoroughly, treat them well, and provide them with responsibility when they earn it. All full-time employees will be given a starting salary of $XX a month or approximately $XX per hour. Employees who perform well and demonstrate an interest in long term employment with Craft Brewing Company will be compensated for their efforts in year-end bonuses to be decided by the management team and Board of Directors. Eventually we hope to develop a profit-sharing program to properly reward all those employees of the Craft Brewing Company who make a significant contribution toward the Company's success.

Supporting Professional Services: The following individuals will be contracted by the Craft Brewing Company to provide services during the start-up and operational phases of this project. See Attachments for their resumes and references.

Technical advisor. XX will draw up the plans for formal approval by the city and will assist the president in directing the building improvements to be carried out by the Craft Brewing Company. The technical advisor will also help to choose utility subcontractors and coordinate their activities with the overall construction project.

Accounting. XX has assisted the Craft Brewing Company in identifying our tax responsibilities. During the operational phase, the accountant will also help the management team to implement their own accounting software program and periodically review tax reports.

Legal representation. XX will act as attorney for the Craft Brewing Company. XX will review our lease; prepare the initial articles of incorporation, bylaws, and subscription agreement; and provide legal council whenever necessary.

Business consultant. XX, director and business development specialist with the Small Business Development Center in XX, XX, has worked closely with the management team since the initiation of this project. XX has personally reviewed and critiqued our business plan and pro formas. XX is personally as well as professionally interested in this project, and the business consultant has offered to continue to provide business and financial counseling at no cost, whenever requested.

Master brewer. XX will act as a local resource to the president in the early stages of brewery operation. The master brewer has worked closely with our brewing consultant at XX as head brewer and manager. XX will be involved in the initial recipe formulation, and since the master brewer lives in XX, the master brewer will be available to troubleshoot any problems or assist the president whenever his services may be required.

Brewing consultant. XX will act as consultant in all matters related to designing, purchasing, and installing the brewing plant. The brewery consultant will assist the president in designing the brewery layout, choosing equipment, ordering equipment, and arranging for its delivery. The brewery consultant will supervise the installation of the brewing plant and work with utility subcontractors to connect equipment to all necessary utilities. The brewery consultant will also help design the product recipes and supervise the initial production runs.

Banker. XX is a vice president and commercial loan officer for XX, XX, XX. Primary area of expertise is small-business loans and SBA guarantees.

The management team comes to this project with a variety of important skills and experiences which will benefit the Company. In those areas where they lack experience, the management team has wisely decided to contract on a temporary or part-time basis with qualified professionals. In this way the Craft Brewing Company will be provided with all the necessary professional support, and costly mistakes will be avoided.

BUILDING AND CONSTRUCTION PLAN

Leased Facilities: The facilities being leased by the Craft Brewing Company are comprised of the following three distinct sections: (refer to the attached building and site drawings)

1. The Production Floor, 1,800 square feet (60 by 30) of open-floor warehouse, with a 19-foot high ceiling, containing the brewing plant, a cool room for fermentation and keg storage, and a loading dock for shipping and receiving
2. The Pub, 570 square feet (19 by 30) of ground floor retail sales space, adjacent to the Production Floor
3. The Corporate Office, 285 square feet (19 by 15) of second story loft above the retail sales space, including a space for grain storage and milling

These spaces have been acquired in accordance with the conditions specified in the enclosed lease.

Building Improvements: In accordance with the attached lease agreement, the following building improvements will be carried out in order to prepare the leased space for brewery operations. Likewise, the cost of these building improvements will be born in accordance with the terms of the attached Letter of Intent to Lease:

1. Removal of all extraneous hardware from the leased space
2. Power washing the interior of the leased space
3. Painting the interior of the leased space
4. Building of a demising wall between the leased space and the remainder of the building
5. Framing and finishing the loft and ground-floor retail space
6. Installing two handicap accessible bathrooms
7. Moving the stairs from the northwest to northeast loft
8. Cutting an access door in the northeast wall of the warehouse
9. Improving the sliding doors on the north end of the building
10. Installing drains at certain points on the production floor
11. Installing an insulated cool fermentation room
12. Painting the exterior of the warehouse
13. Preparing the public alley on the north end of the building to be paved by the city

The above list represents the primary building improvements which must be completed to prepare the leased space for operation. These improvements must be completed before the brewing plant can be installed and connected to the necessary utilities. The president will be assisted by the technical adviser in the planning, coordination, and execution of these building improvements. The estimated costs of these improvements are included in the financial plan cost schedule.

Subcontracting: In addition to the building improvements listed above, the following utility upgrades will be carried out by licensed professionals:

1. Plumbing: Installation of drainage system, connecting of all sinks and bathroom facilities to the drainage system, all welding necessary to prepare the brewing plant for operation, installation of separate utility meter.
2. Electrical: All wiring necessary to install appropriate lighting, all wiring necessary to prepare the brewing plant for operation, all wiring necessary to bring newly constructed walls and rooms up to code, installation of separate utility meter.
3. Gas: Installation of forced air gas heater, connecting of burners to the brewing kettle and hot liquor tank, installation of separate utility meter.
4. Refrigeration. Installation of cool room refrigeration unit and primary fermenter glycol system.
5. Telephone. Installation of business phone lines.

The subcontractors listed above will be chosen by the president through a competitive bidding process. The president will be assisted in this choice and in the overseeing of the work of these professionals by the technical adviser.

THE LEASE AGREEMENT

The management team has negotiated and executed a Letter of Intent to lease a piece of commercial real estate at XX. The Letter of Intent was signed by all parties in March 20XX. This letter is the foundation from which the final lease will be drafted, and therefore, it represents the main points of agreement between the landlords and the tenants. See the attached Letter of Intent for full details of the lease agreement.

The total area being leased is 2,365 square feet of floor space and 285 square feet of loft space. In addition, the Letter of Intent guarantees the Craft Brewing Company "first right of refusal" on any additional space which may become available in the future.

The lease is to commence on May 1, 20XX, with the rent commencement date set for July 1, 20XX. A provision delaying our full responsibility for the lease has been included, which states that should financing not be acquired by the Craft Brewing Company by December 31, 20XX, then the lease will be invalid. This clause is intended to protect the Company should the necessary start-up capital not be raised.

The lease is for five years, with a one-time option to renew the lease at the same terms and conditions for an additional five years. Rent is $XX a month, plus the triple nets (NNN) which represent our pro-rata share of the landlords taxes, insurance, and maintenance costs on the building.

OVERALL SCHEDULE

The following is an outline of the specific tasks which must be performed or milestones which must be achieved during the start-up phase of operation. This outline represents our projections of the time required to perform these tasks. These tasks have been ordered both chronologically and by priority.

MILESTONES

Period — March 15 to 31:
- Mail Out Business Proposal and Share Offering
- Begin to Raise Investor Equity Capital
- Prepare for Building Permit Plan Review
- Seek Bids on Fabricating Brewing Vessels
- Complete Bidding Process on Building Improvements
- Complete Final Licensing Applications
- Clean and Prepare Building Interior
- Approve Graphic Designs for Logos
- Finalize and Sign Lease Agreement

Period — April 1 to 15:
- Raise Investor Equity Capital
- Meet with Potential Investors to Promote Share Sales
- Choose Fabricator for Brewing Vessels
- Receive Building Permit
- Seek Bids on Utility Subcontracting

Period — April 16 to 30:
- Raise Investor Equity Capital
- Achieve Minimum Investment Level
- Notify Investors of Minimum Level
- Transfer Investor Capital to General Funds Account
- Begin Building Improvements
- Have Interior Washed and Painted
- Cut Cement Floors for Drains and Plumbing
- Disassemble Existing Stairs and Loft
- Begin to Design the Interior of the Tap Room

Period — May 1 to 15:
- Order and Make Down Payment on Brewing Vessels
- Continue to Raise Investor Equity Capital
- Building Improvements
- Rough In Plumbing
- Inspect Hook-up to Sewer System
- Grade and Pave Alley
- Pour New Cement Floor Slab
- Cut Exterior Door Openings
- Begin to Frame in Demising Wall Exterior Doors

Period — May 16 to 31:
- Continue to Raise Investor Equity Capital
- Building Improvements
- Continue Framing in New Walls
- Frame In Bathrooms
- Build New Loft Floor and Ceiling
- Schedule Framing and Wiring Inspections

Period — June 1 to 15:
- Continue to Raise Investor Equity Capital
- Purchase Miscellaneous Brewing Equipment
- Continue Building Improvements
- Complete Framing of New Walls, Doors, Etc.
- Install Heating Systems
- Framing and Wiring Inspections

Period — June, 16 to 30:
- Continue to Raise Investor Equity Capital
- Continue to Purchase Miscellaneous Brewing Equipment
- Install Cold Room and Refrigeration
- Receive Delivery of Brewing Plant
- Install and Hook-up Brewing Plant
- Complete Building Improvements
- Have Exterior of Building Painted

Period — July 1 to 15:
- Sell Final Shares for Equity Capital
- Final Occupancy and Health Inspection
- Receive Final Permits and Licenses to Operate
- Complete Brewery Installation and Hook-up
- Make Final Equipment Purchases
- Begin Installing Fixtures and Furnishings for Tap Room
- Install Tap Room Bar and Sink
- Final Utility Inspections
- Purchase Brewing Ingredients
- Begin Test Recipe Brewing
- Begin Advertising in Local Printed Media
- Meet with Local Licensed Retailers to Discuss First Sales

Period — July 16 to 31:
- Complete Tap Room Preparations
- Paint Corporate Logo on North Frontage
- Plant Sidewalk Trees
- Keg First Brew Runs
- Begin to Market Products

We believe these tasks can be completed within the scheduled time periods above. However, one serious potential delay would be in achieving the minimum level of investors equity capital which is necessary for us to begin ordering brewing equipment and scheduling building improvements. Further delays might arise in acquiring a building permit and in coordinating the work of the subcontractor with the overall project and with city inspectors which review many stages of the building improvement process. Any such delays would influence the timing of the entire project and could potentially delay start-up by as much as several months. A delay in our start-up of beer production would entail certain additional expenses until sales of beer began. Nevertheless, we are confident that even should certain reasonable delays occur, the overall success of this project would not be jeopardized.

THE FINANCIAL PLAN

Assumptions: The following information has been provided in order to fully identify the assumptions which the management team has made in projecting the growth in sales, expenses, revenue, and profit of the Craft Brewing Company for the first three years of operation.

Revenue: The Revenue section is broken down into several categories: wholesale through distributor, wholesale self-distributed, retail keg sales, and retail pint sales. All beer sales are based on barrel volumes where one barrel equals 31 gallons or two 15.5-gallon kegs. There is also a separate revenue line for food and merchandise sales. First year production and sales levels are based on our research of the local market and are considered to be relatively conservative projections of local demand. In following years, wholesale self-distributed sales are projected to increase by 1.5 percent each month, wholesale through a distributor sales are projected to increase by 6 percent each month, and retail keg sales are projected to flatten out at approximately 14 kegs each month on average. Retail pint sales are projected to flatten out at 28 kegs each month since they will be limited by the size of our tap room. See the sections on projected local, regional, and total beer sales in the business proposal.

Cost of Goods Sold: This figure includes the ingredients, energy, water, excise and business taxes required to produce beer. The numbers for brewing ingredients are based on actual costs from suppliers and correspond with the given production levels and historical production cost averages. Utility costs are based on estimates of local energy and water rates for a given level of production. Tax rates are based on current rates of $XX per barrel federal excise tax, approximately $XX per barrel state excise tax, and a nominal local business and occupation tax. These excise taxes could be subject to increases in the near future. Costs of food and merchandise sold in our retail outlet are taken to be 50 percent of the retail sales price. Costs of brewing ingredients, water, energy, and supplies are projected to remain relatively constant over time as a proportion of the costs of producing a given volume of beer (approximately $17.50 per barrel). We anticipate that rising prices for these ingredients will be offset by the savings realized through larger volume purchases.

Gross Profit: When the Total Cost of Goods Sold is subtracted from Gross Sales, the resulting figure represents our Gross Profit. Our Gross Profit percentage from year to year will decrease slightly as the ratio of beer sales through a distributor (which have the smallest profit margin) increase, while our ratio of retail beer sales (which have the largest profit margin) remain relatively stable.

Operating Expenses — General and Administrative Expenses: Refer to the Pro Forma General and Administrative Expense Schedule-First Year Supplement. These numbers are based on cost estimates from suppliers and service providers. In some cases, irregularly billed payments are spread out over the twelve months of the year as average monthly payments. The different expenses on the General and Administrative Schedule are projected to increase by 1 percent each month. The exceptions are rent and parking which remain constant, and salaries and payroll taxes which will be increased in accordance with the discussions in the sections of this proposal on employees and management compensation. The costs of all employees hired after the first year and their corresponding payroll taxes appear on separate lines in the Second and Third Years Income Statement.

The final expense which is factored into the Company's Operating Expenses is the depreciation rate on certain assets. The assets being depreciated include: start-up leasehold improvements (building construction costs), brewery equipment, handling equipment (the delivery van, keg dolly, etc.), cooperage (kegs), fixtures and furnishings (taproom furnishings, office equipment, lighting, etc.), and other capital assets purchased during the operational phase to expand production capacity. Depreciation is based on a straight line method over a period of seven years.

EBIT (Earnings Before Income Taxes): When Operating Expenses are subtracted from the Gross Profit, the resulting figure represents the Company's Earnings before corporate income taxes. Interest Income from cash in the Company's general account at Centennial Bank is then added to the EBIT line, with the resulting sum being the Company's Profit before corporate income taxes. Corporate Income Taxes are calculated at current rates and when subtracted from the Profit before taxes, result in the Company's Net Income or Loss.

Net Earnings: This line represents the Company's earnings once paid out dividends, any loan principle, and any new equipment purchases have been subtracted from the Company's Net Income/Loss.

Author Bios

ABOUT THE EDITOR

Ray Daniels is a craft beer industry veteran who brings detailed knowledge of both business and brewing to the task of editing this guide for aspiring brewers. On the brewing side he is a faculty member at the Siebel Institute of Technology and the author of *Designing Great Beers* and other books on brewing. From the business perspective he combines a Harvard Business School education with more than 20 years of practical marketing, sales and public relations experience—much of it in the brewing industry. In the past he has combined these skills while serving as editor of *The New Brewer* and *Zymurgy* magazines and he does so again here in order to shape a cohesive text that will illuminate any aspiring brewer's efforts to succeed.

CONTRIBUTORS

Mark Admire is owner of Rockhouse Development, a consulting firm to the hospitality and brewing industry. He brings more than 20 years of experience to brewery and brewpub projects.

Lew Bryson has been writing about beer and spirits full-time since 1995. He lives near Philadelphia.

Sam Calagione is the founder and president of Dogfish Head Craft Brewery and the author of books entitled *Brewing Up a Business and Extreme Brewing*.

Peter Egelston has been involved in a number of brewery startups and was a partner in the 1994 startup of Smuttynose Brewing Company in Portsmouth, NH.

Kevin Finn is an Operating Partner at Iron Hill Brewery & Restaurant which was recently named by Inc. magazine as one of the top 100 fastest growing privately held companies in America.

John Hickenlooper founded the Wynkoop Brewing Co in Denver in 1988 and was involved in a number of other successful brewpub ventures around the country before shifting his focus to the political arena. Today, Hickenlooper is the highest ranking elected official from the craft brewing industry.

Stan Hieronymus knows both sides of the bar well. He co-authored *The Beer Lovers Guide to the USA* and is a frequent contributor to publications catering to the beer industry.

Pete Johnson serves as Programs Manager for the Brewers Association, with his primary responsibilities in the area of government affairs. Prior to coming to the small brewing industry in 2001, he worked for 14 years with both state and federal elected officials.

Will Kemper was trained as a chemical engineer and has been involved in the start-up and operation of more than a dozen craft breweries.

Greg Kitsock has reported on the brewing industry for more than 15 years and currently serves as editor of *American Brewer* and *Mid-Atlantic Brewing News*.

Marcy Larson is a general managing partner of the Alaskan Brewing Company which she cofounded in 1988 with her husband Geoff.

John Mallett is the production manager for Bell's Brewery in Kalamazoo MI. He has extensive experience in brewing and brewery engineering and serves on the faculty of the Siebel Institute.

Tom McCormick has been involved in the sales, marketing and distribution of craft beer for over 20 years. He is currently the Executive Director of the California Small Brewers Association and manages ProBrewer.com, a resource site for the small brewing industry.

James McDaniel is the Principal of McDaniel Econometrics Group.

Pat Meyer has experience both as a beer wholesaler and as sales manager for Boulder Brewing Company. He has extensive experience in planning and managing sales strategies for craft beers.

Alan Moen, the editor of Northwest Brewing News, has been writing about the beer, wine and spirits industries for more than 15 years for many regional, national, and international publications.

Ralph Olson is the General Manager and Owner of HopUnion LLC, a leading supplier of hops to craft brewers based in Yakima, Washington. He has nearly 30 years of experience in all aspects of the hop business.

Jim Parker is the founder and owner of Oaks Bottom Pub in Portland, OR. He is a veteran of the craft brewing scene with many years spent both reporting on the industry and participating as a brewer, bar owner and Brewers Association staffer.

Michael J. Pronold is a veteran wastewater specialist, having served in the Bureau of Environmental Services for Portland, OR at the time that many small breweries were starting in that area.

John P. Robinson Ph. D. is a professor of sociology at the University of Maryland where he founded the Survey Research Center and directs the Internet Scholars Program. Beer is a favorite topic of research during both his work and leisure time.

Chuck Skypeck is a founding partner and director of brewing for the Boscos brewpubs in Nashville, Memphis and Little Rock.

Scott Smith is the founder and president of CooperSmith's Brewing Company in Fort Collins, Colorado and has been involved in a number of other brewery startups during nearly 20 years of involvement in the craft brewing industry.

Jack Streich is a Boston-based brewer who has consulted on start-up and operation of breweries throughout New England and New York. He is a 1991 graduate of the Siebel Institute.

Eric Warner is president of Flying Dog Brewing Company of Denver and was a founder of Tabernash Brewing Company in 1993. He is a Diplom-Braumeister from the Technical University of Munich at Weihenstephan.

Rick Wehner is an avid homebrewer and a founding member of Brewery Finance Corp, a company that specializes in finding financing for craft brewers. Brewery Finance is an allied trade member of the Brewers Association.

Peter Whalen is the owner of Whalen Insurance and developed the first insurance program tailored to breweries in the 1980s.

Glossary

adjunct. Any unmalted grain or other fermentable ingredient added to the mash.

aeration. The action of introducing air to the wort at various stages of the brewing process. Proper aeration before primary fermentation is vital to a vigorous ferment.

alcohol by volume (v/v). The percentage of volume of alcohol per volume of beer. To calculate the approximate volumetric alcohol content, subtract the final gravity from the original gravity and divide the result by 0.0075. For example: 1.050 – 1.012 = 0.038 ÷ 0.0075 = 5% v/v.

alcohol by weight (w/v). The percentage weight of alcohol per volume of beer. To calculate the approximate alcohol content by weight, subtract the final gravity from the original gravity and divide by 0.0095. For example: 1.050 – 1.012 = 0.038 ÷ 0.0095 = 4% w/v.

ale. 1. Historically, an unhopped malt beverage. 2. Now, a generic term for beers produced by top fermentation, as opposed to lagers, which are produced by bottom fermentation.

all-malt beer. A beer made with only barley malt with no adjuncts nor refined sugars.

alpha acid. A soft resin in hop cones. When boiled, alpha acids are converted to iso-alpha-acids, which provide bitterness in beer.

attenuation. The reduction in the wort's specific gravity caused by the transformation of sugars into alcohol and carbon dioxide.

autolysis. A process in which yeast feed on each other, producing a rubbery odor. To avoid this, rack beer to remove excess yeast as soon after fermentation as possible.

blending. The mixing together of different batches of beer to form a final composite intended for bottling

Bitterness Units (BU). Same as International Bittering Units.

bottle-conditioned. A beer where carbonation is the result of the fermentation of sugar by yeast in the bottle.

calcium carbonate ($CaCO_3$). Also known as chalk. Added during brewing to increase calcium and carbonate content.

calcium sulfate ($CaSO_4$). Also known as gypsum. Added during brewing to increase calcium and sulfate content.

capital. The total money invested in a business from all sources.

carbohydrates. A group of organic compounds including sugars and starches, many suitable as food for yeast and bacteria.

carbonation. The process of introducing carbon dioxide into a liquid by: (1) injecting the finished beer with carbon dioxide; (2) adding young fermenting beer to finished beer for a renewed fermentation (kraeusening); (3) priming (adding sugar to) fermented wort prior to bottling, creating a secondary fermentation in the bottle.

cash flow. Money coming into and out of the business on a routine basis. When the amount going out exceeds the amount coming in, you have a "cash flow problem."

catalyst. A substance, such as an enzyme, which promotes a chemical reaction.

chill haze. Haziness caused by protein and tannin during the secondary fermentation.

cold break. The flocculation of proteins and tannins during wort cooling.

collateral. Assets pledged to the bank (or other source of funds) through a *lien* to protect their investment. If you fail to pay off the loan, they own the collateral and can sell it to recoup their loss.

debt. Any form of financing structured as a loan and obligating the business to repay the money in the future. Often secured by a *lien* on some asset that acts as *collateral*.

decoction. A method of mashing that raises the temperature of the wash by removing a portion, boiling it, and returning it to the mash tun.

diacetyl. A potent aromatic and flavor compound in beer that adds a butterlike flavor.

dimethyl sulfide (DMS). A major sulfur compound of lagers. DMS is released during boiling as a gas that dissipates into the atmosphere.

dry-hopping. The addition of hops to the primary fermenter, the secondary fermenter, or to casked beer to add aroma and hop character to the finished beer without adding significant bitterness.

equity. Business financing that participates in the ownership and risk of the venture. When the business succeeds, equity gets a share of the profits; when it fails, equity holders usually have the last claim to the business assets.

esters. A group of compounds in beer which impart fruity flavors.

ethanol. Ethyl alcohol: the colorless, odorless, alcohol of beer, wine and spirits.

extract. The amount of dissolved materials in the wort after mashing and lautering malted barley and/or malt adjuncts such as corn and rice.

European Brewery Convention (EBC). See Standard Reference Method.

filter. To extract solids, generally yeast and protein, from beer to aid in making it clear and stable.

final gravity. The specific gravity of a beer when fermentation is complete.

fining. The process of adding clarifying agents to beer during secondary fermentation to precipitate suspended matter.

flocculent yeast. Yeast cells that form large colonies and tend to come out of suspension before the end of fermentation.

flocculation. The behavior of yeast cells joining into masses and settling out toward the end of fermentation.

fusel alcohol. High molecular weight alcohol, which results from excessively high fermentation temperatures. Fusel alcohol can impart harsh bitter flavors to beer as well as contribute to hangovers.

glucose ($C_6H_{12}O_6$). An easily fermentable sugar used in brewing, sometimes contributing a cidery character in higher quantities.

grist. The milled malt and adjuncts prior to mashing.

hop pellets. A processed form of hops made by

hammering the hops into a fine powder and then extruding them through an opening the approximate diameter of a pencil. The resulting pellets require less space for shipping and storage compared to whole hops.

hydrometer. A glass instrument used to measure the specific gravity of liquids as compared to water, consisting of a graduated stem resting on a weighed float.

infection. Growth of microorganisms in wort or beer detrimental to flavor or aroma.

infusion mash. The process of achieving target mashing temperatures by the addition of heated water at specific temperatures.

IBU (International Bitterness Units). The measurement of bittering substances in beer. Analytically assessed as milligrams of isomerized-alpha-acid per liter of beer. Procedures for this assessment are published by both the American Society of Brewing Chemists and the European Brewing Convention.

Irish moss. Modified seaweed particles or powder that help to precipitate proteins in the kettle.

isinglass. A gelatinous substance made from the swim bladder of certain fish and sometimes added to beer to help clarify and stabilize the finished product.

kraeusen. 1. The rocky head of foam which appears on the surface of the wort during fermentation. v.. 2. To add fermenting wort to fermented beer to induce carbonation through a secondary fermentation.

lager. 1. A generic term for any bottom-fermented beer. v. 2. To store beer at near-zero temperatures in order to precipitate yeast cells and proteins and improve taste.

lauter tun. A vessel in which the mash settles and the grains are removed from the sweet wort through a straining process. It has a false slotted bottom and spigot.

lien. The legal claim of a bank or other loan provider the property (*collateral*) of a business or individual to secure the payment of a debt.

Lovibond (°L). A scale used to measure color in grains and sometimes beer. See also Standard Reference Method.

malt. Barley that has been steeped in water, germinated, then dried in kilns. This process prepares the grain for use in brewing.

malt extract. A thick syrup or dry powder prepared from malt and sometimes used in brewing.

mashing. Mixing crushed malt with hot water to extract the fermentables, degrade haze-forming proteins, and convert grain starches to fermentable sugars and nonfermentable carbohydrates.

modification. 1. The physical and chemical changes in barley as a result of malting. 2. The degree to which these changes have occurred, as determined by the growth of the acrospire.

oasthouse. A farm-based facility where hops are dried and baled after picking.

original gravity. The specific gravity of wort previous to fermentation. A measure of the total amount of dissolved solids in wort.

pH. A measure of acidity or alkalinity of a solution, usually on a log scale ranging from 1 to 14 where 7 is neutral and 1 is the most acidic.

phenolic. Compounds that give a clove or cinnamon character to beer, as in the hefeweizen style.

pitching. The process of adding yeast to the cooled wort.

Plato. A measure of liquid density similar to specific gravity. This systems expresses density according to the percentage of extract by weight in the liquid being measured with common values in brewing ranging from 1 to 20.

primary fermentation. The first stage of fermentation during which most fermentable sugars are converted to ethyl alcohol and carbon dioxide.

priming sugar. A small amount of corn, malt, or cane sugar added to bulk beer prior to racking or at bottling to induce a new fermentation and create carbonation.

racking. The process of transferring beer from one container to another, especially into the final package (bottles, kegs).

recirculation. Clarifying the wort before it moves from the lauter tun into the kettle by recirculating it through the mash bed.

saccharification. The conversion of malt starch into fermentable sugars, primarily maltose.

saccharometer. An instrument that determines the sugar concentration of a solution by measuring the specific gravity. (See also hydrometer.)

Saccharomyces. The genus of single-celled yeasts which ferment sugar and are used in the making of alcoholic beverages and bread. Yeasts of the species *Saccharomyces cerevisiae* are the most common used in brewing.

secondary fermentation. 1. The second slower stage of fermentation, lasting from a few days to many months depending on the type of beer. 2. A fermentation occurring in bottles or casks and initiated by priming or by adding yeast.

sparging. Spraying the spent grains in the mash with hot water to retrieve the remaining malt sugar.

specific gravity. A measure of a liquid density sometimes used to assess the amount of extract contained in wort prior to fermentation. The weight of a specified volume of liquid is divided by the weight of an identical volume of water giving a value that generally begins with 1 and is reported to three decimal points. Common values in brewing range from 1.001 to 1.100. Specific gravity has no units because it is expressed as a ratio. Also see: Plato.

Standard Reference Method (SRM) and European Brewery Convention (EBC). Two different analytical methods of describing color developed by comparing color samples. Degrees SRM, approximately equivalent to degrees Lovibond, are used by the American Society of Brewing Chemists (ASBC) while degrees EBC are European units. The conversion factor between the two is EBC = 1.97 x SRM.

starter. A small batch of beer made for the purpose of increasing the number of yeast cells used to initiate fermentation.

step infusion. A method of mashing whereby the temperature of the mash is raised by adding very hot water, and then stirring and stabilizing the mash at the target step temperature.

strike temperature. The initial temperature of the water when the malted barley is added to it to create the mash.

torrefied wheat. Wheat which has been heated quickly at high temperature, causing it to puff up, which renders it easily mashed.

trub. Wort particles resulting from the precipitation of proteins, hop oils, and tannins during boiling and cooling stages of brewing.

tun. Any open tank or vessel.

ullage. The empty space between a liquid and the top of its container. Also called airspace or headspace.

v/v. See alcohol by volume.

vorlauf. To recirculate the wort from one mash tun through the grain bed to clarify.

w/v. See alcohol by weight.

water hardness. A measure of the quantity of minerals dissolved in water.

whirlpool. A method of bringing hot break material to the center of the kettle by stirring the wort until a vortex is formed.

working capital. Defined as the business's current or short-term assets (cash, inventory, accounts receivable, etc.) minus current or short-term liabilities (short-term debt, accounts payable, etc.). As a business grows, the amount of money tied up in working capital grows.

wort. The mixture that results from mashing the malt and boiling the hops, before it is fermented into beer.

OPENING A BREWERY?

THE BREWERS ASSOCIATION WANTS TO HEAR ABOUT IT!

Email: info@BrewersAssociation.org

Please complete this form and send it to the Brewers Association or submit an update to our brewery locator on www.BrewersAssociation.org to make sure we know about your new brewery.

(PLEASE PRINT)

Company Name ______________________________

(dba) ______________________________

Mailing Address ______________________________

Street Address (if different) ______________________________

City ____________ State/Province ____________ Zip/Postal Code ____________

Country ______________________________

Primary Telephone ______________________________

FAX ____________ E-mail ____________ Website ____________

Owner(s)/President/CEO (name/email) ______________________________

____

Marketing Director (name/email) ______________________________

____

Head Brewer (name/email) ______________________________

Primary Contact (name/email) ______________________________

Names and styles of the beers you intend to produce ______________________________

____

____

Date of first commercial sales (projected if not open yet) ______________________________

____

Check One Only ❏ Packaging Brewery (75% or more sold off premises) ❏ Brewery Restaurant ❏ Contract Brewing Co.

Annual production capacity (check one) _____❏ U.S. Barrels _____❏ Hectoliters

Total square footage (including storage, offices) ______________________________ square feet

---

Copy this form and send with any press releases, photographs suitable for printing or newspaper clippings concerning your brewery to: Brewers Association, PO Box 1679, Boulder, CO 80306-1679, USA or FAX (303) 447-2825, email: info@BrewersAssociation.org, www.BrewersAssociation.org.